BUILDING INFORMATION MODELING

BUILDING INFORMATION MODELING

– Authors –

Kuwarjeet Bava

Bipasha Sinh

Wordpen Academics

Publishing Science That Matter

ISBN: 9789389183825 (Hardback)

Published by : **WORDPEN ACADEMICS**
4736/23, Ansari Road, Darya Ganj,
New Delhi – 110 002
Phone: +91-011-35004336
E-mail: info@wordpenacademics.com

Printed at **:** **Replika Press Pvt. Ltd.**

Exclusive Distributor: ***Bio-Green Books, New Delhi***

Preface

Building Information Modeling (BIM) is a digital tool that has revolutionized the way architects, engineers, and construction professionals design and construct buildings. BIM has changed the way we think about building design and construction by providing a more efficient and effective way of collaborating and sharing information. This book is designed to provide a comprehensive overview of BIM and how it can be used in the architecture, engineering, construction, and operations (AECO) industry.

This book provides a comprehensive overview of the principles and practices of BIM, a digital modelling process used in the Architecture, Engineering, Construction, and Operations (AECO) industry. Begins with an introduction to the concept of BIM and its evolution over the years. Covers the basics of digital information and its importance in the AECO industry. It also discusses the process of digitization and its role in improving efficiency and accuracy in the industry. Provides the different types of representation used in the AECO industry, including symbolic and analogue representations. It also covers the specific representation techniques used in BIM. Focuses on data and information management in BIM and explores the basics of data and information and their importance in decision-making processes. Covers the various decision-making processes in the AECO industry and the role of information in these processes. It also covers process and information diagrams used in BIM to improve project management. It is an essential guide for professionals and students in the AECO industry who want to learn about the principles and practices of BIM. The book provides a comprehensive overview of the concepts and techniques used in BIM, making it a valuable resource for anyone looking to improve efficiency and accuracy in their projects.

We are grateful to all those persons as well as various books, manuals, periodicals, magazines, journals etc. that helped in the preparation of this book. In spite of the best efforts, it is possible that some errors may have occurred into the compilation and editing of the book. Further queries, constructive suggestions and criticisms for the improvement of the book are always welcomed and shall be thankfully acknowledged.

Kuwarjeet Bava
Bipasha Sinh

Preface

Contents

Introduction

This is the second, improved edition of a book about the foundations and principles of building information, its representation and management. In contrast to other books on the same subjects, it is not a how-to guide. It does not tell you which software or policies to choose for representing buildings and managing the resulting information. Instead, the book argues that one should not start with these practical steps before fully understanding the reasoning behind any such choice. This includes the structure of information and of the representations that contain it, the purposes of managing information in these representations and the situations in which the representations are used. In a nutshell: how information relates to the cognitive and social processes of a specific domain. Without adequate reasoning that covers all syntactic, semantic and pragmatic aspects, adopting this software or that and implementing this policy or that simply subjugate information processing to some prescriptive or proscriptive framework that may be unproductive or inappropriate for the domain and its professionals.

To explain these foundations and principles, the book brings together knowledge from various areas, including philosophy and computer science. Its perspective, nevertheless, remains bounded by the application domain: external knowledge is not imposed on domain practices but used to elucidate domain knowledge. Building information has its own peculiarities, drawn more from convention than necessity, and digitization has yet to address such matters, let alone resolve them. General knowledge about information and representation is essential for developing approaches fit for the digital era. The approach advocated in this book is above all parsimonious: in a world inundated with digital information (Part I), one should not resort to brute force and store or process everything. On the contrary, one should organize information intelligently, so that everything remains accessible but with less and more focused effort.

The first part of the book focuses on digitization as the opportunity and reason for paying even more attention to information than in previous eras, when many of the tools and approaches we still use today were formulated. This part was produced by splitting a single chapter in the first edition into two: Chapter 1 deals with digital information in general, while Chapter 2 focuses on digitization in AECO. The split hopefully makes clearer what has been happening in the domain of buildings while the digital revolution took place and why AECO needs to do more than just use available computing resources.

The second part explains representation. Many of the problems surrounding information and its management are caused when we ignore that most information, certainly regarding buildings, comes organized into representations. Knowing the structure of these representations provides connections to meaning and use, as well as insights into how information is produced and processed. Chapter 3 explains symbolic representations and analyses familiar spatial representations from a symbolic perspective. The analogue representations that still dominate building information are the subject of Chapter 4. Digitization is primarily considered with respect to BIM, as the first generation of truly symbolic, digital building representations (Chapter 5).

Information theory and management are the subjects of the third part of the book. Particular emphasis is on the meaning of information (semantics) as a foundation for utility and relevance. For this reason, this part starts by introducing a semantic theory of information that complements symbolic representation (Chapter 6). Next, Chapter 7 explains information management and how it applies to building information and BIM. It concludes with the principles that should guide building information management.

The fourth part of the book contains the most important changes from the first edition. Chapter 8 is completely new. It provides a summary of the influential dual-process theory of the mind, which has particular significance for decision making and the use of information in it. The next two chapters were produced by splitting a chapter of the first edition because some things I had originally considered a simple preliminary to developing information diagrams turned out to be a main learning objective for my students. Chapter 9 now deals more extensively with process diagrams, their structure and purpose, including in relation to cognitive biases and limitations. Chapter 10 covers the move from process to information diagrams, the validation of process designs, meaningful information management and support for Type 2 thinking.

Having explained the foundations and principles of representation and information management, the book rounds the subject off with a few larger exercises, which can be used as individual or group assignments (Part V). Through these exercises, learners can test their understanding of the approach advocated in this book and hone their skills for its application in research or practice.

Also new are the appendices. The first collects the necessary knowledge on graph theory in a compact overview and the second explains what parameterization actually does. Both are helpful for understanding critical parts of the book.

Learning objectives

1. Factual: understand the relations between information and digitization (Chapter 1)
2. Factual: use this understanding to explain the low digital uptake in AECO (Chapter 2)
3. Conceptual: comprehend the structure of symbolic representations and their relevance to digitization (Chapter 3)
4. Conceptual: recognize the differences between symbolic and analogue representations (Chapter 4)
5. Conceptual: recognize the relations between implementation mechanisms, symbols and the denoted real things or concepts (Chapter 3 & 4)
6. Procedural: learn how graphs can be used to describe symbolic representations (Chapter 3)
7. Conceptual: analyse BIM as a symbolic representation (Chapter 5)
8. Metacognitive: recognize legacy elements from analogue practices in BIM and question their effects (Chapter 5)
9. Procedural: learn how models in BIM can be analysed as graphs of symbols and relations (Chapter 5)
10. Conceptual: understand differences between syntactic, semantic and pragmatic levels (Chapter 6)
11. Conceptual: recognize semantic data types (Chapter 6)
12. Conceptual: explain the relations between data and information (Chapter 6)
13. Procedural: contrast semantic data types in analogue representations with semantic data types in BIM (Chapter 6)
14. Procedural: differentiate between semantic data types in isolated symbols and in symbols in a representation (Chapter 6)
15. Conceptual: understand the differences between structured, semi-structured and unstructured data (Chapter 7)
16. Procedural: learn how to regulate information flows (Chapter 7, 8 & 9)
17. Procedural: learn how to safeguard information quality (Chapter 7, 8 & 9)
18. Conceptual: understand dual-process theory and its relevance to AECO (Chapter 8)
19. Conceptual: identify the social and information sides of management (Chapter 8)

20. Procedural: learn how to apply graphs to describing and evaluating process designs (Chapter 9)
21. Metacognitive: investigate unwanted Type 1 thinking in process designs and stimulate Type 2 reflective thinking (Chapter 9 & 10)
22. Procedural: learn how to apply graphs to developing information management plans that operationalize and validate process designs (Chapter 10)
23. Metacognitive: apply information management to stimulate and support Type 2 processes (Chapter 10)

List of terms and abbreviations

A

AECO: architecture, engineering, construction and operation of buildings

AI: Artificial Intelligence

Arc (graphs): directed edges

B

B: byte

BIM: building information modelling

BIM checker: computer program in which one primarily views and analyses a model

BIM editor: computer program in which one primarily develops and modifies a model

Bridge (graphs): an edge that divides a graph into two unconnected parts

C

CAAD (computer-aided architectural design): the discipline covering all aspects of computerization in AECO

CAD (computer-aided design): a category of software primarily aimed at the computerization of design representations, including engineering drawings (2D) and models (3D)

Center (graphs): the vertices with an eccentricity equal to the radius of the graph

Closeness of a vertex (graphs): its inverse mean distance to all other vertices in the graph

Connected graph: a graph in which each vertex connects to every other vertex by some sequence of edges and vertices

Co-termination: the condition of two entities (e.g. walls) having a common endpoint

D

Degree of a vertex (graphs): the number of edges incident to it

Degree sequence (graphs): sequence obtained by listing the degrees of vertices in a graph

DM: design management

Diameter (graphs): the greatest eccentricity of any vertex in a graph

Directed graph (or digraph): a graph in which edges have a direction (arcs)

Distance (graphs): the number of edges in the shortest path between two vertices

E

Eccentricity (graphs): the greatest distance between a vertex and any other vertex in a graph

Edge (graphs): usually a relation between two things (represented as vertices)

Even vertex (graphs): a vertex with an even degree

Exabyte (EB): 1,000 PB

G

Gigabyte (GB): 1,000 MB

Graphs: mathematical structures that describe pairwise relations between things

I

IFC (Industry Foundation Classes): a standard underlying BIM

IM: information management

In-degree (graphs): the number of arcs incoming to a node

IoT: Internet of things

K

Kilobyte (kB): 1,000 B

L

Leaf (graphs): a vertex with a degree of 1

LoD: level of development (or detail) in BIM

M

Megabyte (MB): 1,000 KB

MEP: mechanical, electrical and plumbing

Moore's "law": the number of transistors on a chip doubles every year while the costs are halved

MTC: mathematical theory of communication, formulated by Claude Shannon

N

Node (graph): synonym of vertex, used exclusively for digraphs in this book

O

Odd vertex (graphs): a vertex with an odd degree

Order (graphs): the number of vertices in a graph

Out-degree (graphs): the number of arcs outgoing from a node

P

Path (graphs): a sequence of edges and vertices in which no vertex occurs more than once

Periphery (graphs): the vertices with an eccentricity equal to the diameter of the graph

Petabyte (PB): 1,000 TB

PDF: portable document format

R

Radius (graphs): the smallest eccentricity of any vertex in a graph

S

Sink (graphs): synonym of terminal

Size (graphs): the number of edges in a graph

Source (graphs): a node with an in-degree of 0

T

Terabyte (TB): 1,000 GB

Terminal (graphs): a node with an out-degree of 0

V

Vertex (graphs): usually the representation of a thing

W

Walk (graphs): a sequence of edges and vertices

Y

Yottabyte (YB): 1,000 ZB

Z

Zettabyte (ZB): 1,000 EB

PART I

DIGITIZATION

Information has always been important to us. There are even theories in ecological psychology that propose that information relevant to our interaction with an environment is perceived directly, without first interpreting sensory input into a description of the environment. Still, we are right in calling the current period the information age because of the impact of digital information technologies. Therefore, the starting point in our exploration of building information and information management is the reciprocal relation between information and digitization. This grand theme of our times takes a peculiar form in AECO — a form that in several respects conflicts with general tendencies.

CHAPTER 1

Digital information

The book starts with some key characteristics of the information age: how the digital revolution changed not only the amount of stored information but also attitudes toward information. Global, ubiquitous infrastructures allow for unprecedented access to information and processing power. This promotes new standards of behaviour and performance in societies and economies that are increasingly information-based.

INFORMATION EXPLOSION

We are all familiar with how significant storage capacity is: we routinely buy smartphones with gigabytes of memory and hard drives with capacities of a couple of terabytes. The availability and affordability of such devices, and even the familiarity with these data units are a far cry from not so long ago. In the last decades of the previous century, personal computers were a new phenomenon, digital photography was in its infancy and today's social media did not even exist yet. In 1983, the Apple Lisa, the commercially failed precursor to the Macintosh, had a five megabyte hard disk and cost almost US $ 10,0000 (the equivalent of over US $ 25,000 today). In 1988, a FUJIX DS-1P, the first fully digital camera, had a two megabyte memory card that could hold five to ten photographs. Our need for data storage and communication has changed a lot since those heady times.

The obvious reason for this change is the explosive increase in information production that characterizes the digital era. In a process of steady growth through the centuries, human societies had previously accumulated an estimated 12 exabytes of information. By 1944 libraries were doubling in size every 16 years, provided there was physical space for expansion. Space limitations were removed by the rise of home computers and the invention of the Internet. These allowed annual information growth rates of 30% that raised the total to 180 exabytes by 2006 and to over 1.8 zettabytes by 2011. More recently, the total more than doubled every two years, reaching 18 zettabytes in 2018 and 44 zettabytes in 2020, and expected to become 175 zettabytes by 2025.

The Internet is full of such astounding calculations and dramatic projections,[1] which never fail to warn that the total may become even higher, as the population of information users and producers keeps increasing, as well as expanding to cover devices generating and sharing data on the IoT. But even if we ever reach a plateau, as with Moore's "law" with respect to computing capacity,[2] we already have an enormous problem in our hands: a huge amount of data to manage. 1.2 exabytes are stored only by the big four (Google, Microsoft, Amazon and Facebook), while other big providers like Dropbox, Barracuda and SugarSync, and less accessible servers in industry and academia probably hold similar amounts.[3]

What makes these numbers even more important is that information is not just stored but, above all, intensively and extensively processed. Already in 2008, Google processed 20 petabytes a day.[4] In many respects, it is less interesting how much data we produce on a daily or annual basis than what we do with these data. Not surprisingly, social media and mobile phones dominate in any account of digital data processing: in 2018, people sent 473,400 tweets, shared 2 million photos on Snapchat and posted 49,380 pictures on Instagram. Google handled 3.5 billion searches a day, while 1.5 billion people (one-fifth of the world's population) were active on Facebook every day.

In 2020, the picture slightly changed as a result of the COVID-19 pandemic: we produced 1.7 MB of data per person per second, with a large share again going into social media, while communication platforms like Zoom and Microsoft Teams, as well online shopping and food ordering, attracted significantly more activity.[5] Anything good or bad happening in the world only increases our dependence on the information and communication possibilities of the Internet, especially now that so many of us can afford utilizing them anytime and anyplace on their smartphones. Consequently, safeguarding information quality, veracity, accessibility and flow already forms a major challenge for both producers and consumers of data.

The situation is further complicated by changing attitudes toward information. Not so long ago, most people were afraid of information overload.[6] Nowadays we have moved to a diametrically different point of view and are quite excited about the potential of big data and related AI approaches. From being a worry, the plethora of information we produce and consume has become an opportunity. At the same time, we are increasingly concerned with data protection and privacy, as amply illustrated by the extent and severity of laws like the General Data Protection Regulation (GDPR) of the European Union (https://gdpr.eu). Attitudes may change further, moreover in unpredictable ways, as suggested by reactions to the Facebook–Cambridge Analytica data breach in 2018 and worries about data collection in relation to COVID-19.

INFORMATION AND DIGITIZATION

It is not accidental that we talk about our era as both the information age and the digital revolution — two characterizations that (not coincidentally) appeared in quick succession. The rapid growth of information production and dissemination, the changes in human behaviours and societal standards or the shift from industrial production to information-based economies would not have been possible without digital technologies. Before the digital revolution, there were technologies for recording and transmitting information but they were not capable of processing information or available to practically all. The information age demands digital technologies, which are consequently present in almost every aspect of daily life, making information processing synonymous with digital devices, from wearables to the cloud. This also means that there is increasingly less that we do with alternative means (e.g. order food by phone rather than through an app), especially since a lot of information is no longer available on analogue media. For example, most encyclopaedias and reference works that used to adorn the bookshelves of homes in the second half of the twentieth century are either no longer available on paper or cannot compete with online sources for actuality, detail and multimedia content. Online video, audio and image sharing platforms have similarly resulted in unprecedented collections that include many digitized analogue media. Despite the frequently low resolution and overall quality of transcribed media, there is no practical alternative to the wealth and accessibility of these platforms.

Related to the dominance of these platforms is that most data transactions take place within specific channels and apps. Nobody publishes on social media in general but specifically on Facebook, Twitter, Instagram, Snapchat, TikTok or whatever happens to be popular with the intended audience at the time. Even though overarching search engines can access most of these data, production, storage and communication are restricted by the often proprietary structure of the hosting environments. As a result, digital information tends to be more fragmented than many assume. Leaving aside the thorny issues of data ownership, protection, rights and privacy, the technical and organizational problems resulting from such restrictions and fragmentation may be beyond the capacities of an individual or even a small firm. Being so dependent on specific digital means for our information needs makes us vulnerable in more respects than we probably imagine and adds to the complexity of information management. It also suggests that privacy is totally lost, as data about user actions and communications are collected by tech companies, whose digital products and services we keep on using because of some huge generic advantages, such as the immense extent and power of crowdsourcing on the Internet.

Regardless of such problems, however, it is inevitable that the means of information production, dissemination and management will remain primarily digital, with growing amounts of information available to us and often necessary for our endeavours. Digitization creates new opportunities for our information needs but, on the other hand, also adds to the problems that must be resolved and their complexity. Digitization is so widely diffuse and pervasive that we are already in a hybrid reality, where the Internet and other digital technologies form permanent layers that mediate even in mundane, everyday activities, such as answering a doorbell. In a growing number of areas, the digital layers are becoming dominant: social media are a primary area for politics, while health and activity are increasingly dependent on self-tracking data and economies are to a large extent about intangible data. Consequently, safety and security in cyberspace are at least as important as in reality. Moreover, they call for dynamic, adaptable solutions that match the fluidity and extent of a digital information infrastructure. It follows that, rather than putting our faith in currently dominant techniques, we need to understand the principles on which solution should be based and devise better approaches for the further development of information infrastructures.

Interestingly, these infrastructures are not always about us. One aspect of the digital complexity that should not be ignored is that a lot of machine-produced data (and hence a lot of computational power) goes into machine-to-machine communication and human-computer interaction, e.g. between different systems in a car (from anti-lock braking systems and touch-activated locks to entertainment and navigation systems) or in the interpretation of user actions on a tablet (distinguishing between pushing a button, selecting a virtual brush, drawing a line with the brush or translating finger pressure into stroke width). Such data, even though essential for the operations of information processing, are largely invisible to the end user and hence easy to ignore if one focuses primarily on the products rather than the whole chain of technologies involved in a task. On the other hand, these chains and the data they produce and consume are a major part of any innovation in digital technologies and their applications: we have already moved on from information-related development to development dependent on digitization.

EFFECTS OF DIGITAL INFORMATION

The practical effects of digital information technologies are widely known, frequently experienced and eagerly publicized. Digitization is present in all aspects of daily life, improving access and efficiency but also causing worries for lost skills, invasion of privacy and effects on the environment. With apps replacing even shopping lists, handwriting is practiced less and less, and handwritten text is becoming more and more illegible. Communication with friends, colleagues, banks, authorities etc. is predominantly Internet-based but cannot fully replace physical proximity and contact, as we have seen in the COVID-19 pandemic. Electricity demand keeps rising, both at home or work and for the necessary infrastructure, such as data centres.

Other, equally significant effects, are less frequently discussed, arguably because they go much deeper and affect us so fundamentally that we fail to recognize the changes. For example, with the easy availability and wide accessibility of information, it is becoming increasingly difficult to claim ignorance of anything — much harder than it has been since the newspaper and news agency boom in the second half of the nineteenth century, and the radio and television broadcasting that followed. More and more facts, events and opinions are becoming common knowledge, from what happens today all over the world to new interpretations of the past, including absurd complot theories. As patients, citizens, students, tourists or hobbyists we can no longer afford to miss anything that seems relevant to our situations or activities.

Another cardinal effect is that we are no longer the centre of the information world, the sole or ultimate possessor and processor of information. Our environment has been transformed and enriched with machine-based capacities that rival and sometimes surpass our own, so changing our relation to our environment, too. Interestingly, our reactions to this loss of exclusivity are variable and even ambivalent. On one hand, we worry about the influence of hidden algorithms and AI, and on the other, we are jubilant about the possibilities of human-machine collaboration. Dystopian and utopian scenarios abound, while we become more and more dependent on information-processing machines. One of the key messages of this book is that, regardless of hopes and fears, there are principles on which we can base our symbiosis with these machines: tasks we can safely delegate to computers and support we can expect from them in order to improve our own information processing and decision making.

Finally, the most profound and arguably lasting effect of digitization is that it invites us to interpret and even experience the world as information, understanding practically everything in terms of entities, properties, relations and processes. Our metaphors for the world were always influenced by the structure of our artefacts: the things we had designed and therefore knew intimately. Projecting their functioning and principles to other things we have been trying to comprehend, like the cosmos, made sense and enabled us to develop new knowledge and technologies. Current conceptual models of reality are heavily influenced by digital information and the machines that store and process it. Human memory processes are explained analogically to hard drive operations and our visual perception is understood by reference to digital image capture and recognition. Such conceptual models are a mixed blessing. As explanations of the mind or social patterns they can be reductionist and mechanistic but at the same time they can be useful as bridges to processing related information with computers.

INFORMATION MANAGEMENT

All the above makes information management (IM) a task that is not exclusive to managers and computer specialists. It involves everyone who disseminates, receives or stores information. Very few people are concerned with IM just for the sake of it. Most approach information and its management in the framework of their own activities, for which information is an essential commodity. This makes IM not an alien, externally imposed obligation but a key aspect of everyone's activities, a fundamental element in communication and collaboration, and a joint responsibility for all — a necessity for anyone who relies on information for their functioning or livelihood.

Given the complexity of our hybrid reality and the lack of transparency in many of our approaches to it, this book bypasses technical solutions and focuses on the conceptual and operational structure of IM: the principles for developing clear and effective approaches. These approaches can lead to better information performance, including through reliable criteria for selecting and evaluating means used for their implementation. In other words, we need a clear understanding of what we have to do and why before deciding on how (which techniques are fitting for our goals and constraints).

The proposed principles include definitions of information and representation, and operational structures for connecting process management to IM. IM therefore becomes a matter not of brute force (by computers or humans) but of organization and relevance. One can store all documents and hope for the best but stored information is not necessarily accessible or usable. As we know from searches on the Internet, search machines can be very clever in retrieving what there is out there but this does not necessarily mean that they return the answers we need. If one asks for the specific causes of a fault in a building, it is not enough to receive all documents on the building to browse and interpret. Identifying all information that refers precisely to the relevant parts or aspects of the building depends on how archives and documents have been organized and maintained. To achieve that, we cannot rely on exhaustive, labour-intensive interpretation, indexing and cross-referencing of each part of each document. Instead, we should try to understand the nature and structure of the information these documents contain and then build better representations and management strategies, which not only improve IM but also connect it better to our processes and the tasks they comprise.

RECOMMENDED FURTHER READING

- Blair, A. et al. (eds.), 2021, *Information: a historical companion.* Princeton: Princeton University Press.
- Graham, M., & Dutton, W.H. (eds.), 2019, *Society and the Internet.* Oxford: Oxford University Press.
- Floridi, L., 2014. *The fourth revolution.* Oxford: Oxford University Press.

Key Takeaways

- *Digitization has added substantial possibilities to our information-processing capabilities and promoted the accumulation of huge, rapidly growing amounts of information*
- *Digital information and its processing are already integrated in our everyday activities, rendering them largely hybrid*
- *We are no longer the exclusive possessor or even the centre of information and its processing: machines play an increasingly important role, including for machine-to-machine and human-to-machine interactions*
- *Information management is critical for the utilization of digital information; instead of relying on*

brute-force solutions, we should consider the fundamental principles on which it should be based

Exercises

1. Calculate how much data you produce per week, categorized in:
    1. Personal emails
    2. Social media (including instant messaging)
    3. Digital photographs, video and audio for personal use
    4. Study-related emails
    5. Study-related photographs, video and audio
    6. Study-related alphanumeric documents (texts, spreadsheets etc.)
    7. Study-related drawings and diagrams (CAD, BIM, renderings etc.)
    8. Other (please specify)
2. Specify how much of the above data is stored or shared on the Internet and how much remains only on personal storage devices (hard drives, SSD, memory cards etc.)
3. How do the above (data production and storage) compare to worldwide tendencies?

Notes

1. Calculations and projections of information accumulated by human societies can be found in: Rider, F., 1944, *The Scholar and the Future of the Research Library*. New York: Hadham Press; Lyman, P. & Varian, H.P. 2003, "How much information 2003?" http://groups.ischool.berkeley.edu/archive/how-much-info/; Gantz, J. & Reinsel, D., 2011, "Extracting value from chaos." https://www.emc.com/collateral/analyst-reports/idc-extracting-value-from-chaos-ar.pdf;Turner, V., Reinsel D., Gantz J. F., & Minton S., 2014. "The Digital Universe of Opportunities" https://www.emc.com/leadership/digital-universe/2014iview/digital-universe-of-opportunities-vernon-turner.htm; "Rethink data" Seagate Technology Report, https://www.seagate.com/nl/nl/our-story/rethink-data/
2. Intel co-founder Gordon Moore observed in 1965 that every year twice as many components could fit onto an integrated circuit. In 1975 the pace was adjusted to a doubling every two years. By 2017, however, Moore's "law" no longer applies, as explained in: Simonite, T., 2016. "Moore's law Is dead. Now what?" *Technology Review* https://www.technologyreview.com/s/601441/moores-law-is-dead-now-what/
3. Source: https://www.sciencefocus.com/future-technology/how-much-data-is-on-the-internet/
4. The claim was made in a scientific journal paper: Dean, J., & Ghemawat, J., 2008. "MapReduce: simplified data processing on large clusters" *Commun. ACM* **51**, 1 (January 2008), 107–113, https://doi.org/10.1145/1327452.1327492. Regrettably, Google and other tech companies are not in the habit of regularly publishing such calculations.
5. There are several insightful overviews of what happens every minute on the Internet, such as: https://www.visualcapitalist.com/?s=internet+minute; https://www.domo.com/learn/infographic/data-never-sleeps-8; https://www.domo.com/learn/infographic/data-never-sleeps-6

6. The notion of information overload was popularized in: Toffler, A., 1970. *Future shock.* New York: Random House.

CHAPTER 2

Digitization in AECO

This chapter presents the background of AECO digitization, starting with general tendencies and moving on to particular developments in AECO, including BIM. It explains these developments from a historical perspective and outlines the limitations they cause to further digitization and decision making in AECO.

PRIVATE VERSUS BUSINESS

While in our private lives we are quite digitally minded and data savvy, there is little to suggest that digitization similarly dominates professional activities in AECO. Despite the enthusiastic reception of technological developments, such as 3D printing, digitization has yet to reach a substantial depth or breadth in AECO. We use computer programs like BIM and CAD to draw or spreadsheets to calculate but reality in AECO remains analogue, dominated by information carriers like drawings and other conventional documents on paper: remnants of an era when we did not have the same information processing capacities as today. This is unlike e.g. the music industry, where vinyl, CD and other carriers are just a matter of nostalgia, while the content has become fully digital, or online on-demand services like Netflix or Spotify, which have moreover changed digital attitudes in spectacular ways, practically eliminating music and video piracy.

The probable reason is that AECO generally remains attached to analogue, largely pre-industrial processes that require little if any mediation from digital technologies — much like fishing and hunting, two other industries with a low investment in digitization. These processes cause legacy information solutions, such as paper-based documents, to persist, severely limiting the potential and nature of digitization. Resisting or even ejecting digitization is, of course, justified if there is no reason for it. Regrettably, this is not the case with AECO, given its far from satisfactory performance. It follows that the high contrast with other industries or even private life calls for a closer investigation of the particular circumstances of AECO, towards a clearer identification of underlying causes and resulting problems.

DIGITAL UPTAKE

There is broad consensus that AECO is one of the least digitized sectors.[1] Everyone seems to be in agreement: on the Internet, in professional and academic publications, in software advertisements. A critical note is that the claim is based on few data, chiefly proxies, and a lot of opinions of people in AECO or digitization, i.e. with vested interests in the deployment of new technologies. Still, the slow digital uptake in AECO seems so plausible that it is widely used as justification for various digital solutions: manifestos by policy makers, standards by professional bodies, new approaches by academic researchers, new software by commercial developers. So, from a vague problem, we jump directly to specific solutions, such as BIM, digital twins, Industry 4.0 etc.: panaceas for all the ills of AECO. The promise of the solutions is invariably deemed so high that the resulting changes in AECO do not just solve the problem; they make it disappear completely.

This poses an interesting conundrum: if the solutions are so readily available and so powerful, there must be at least a significant minority in AECO that adopts them and benefits from observable and convincing improvements in performance. In turn, this should stimulate wider adoption of the solutions in AECO and general advances. In short, things should develop rapidly and smoothly, changing practices and behaviours, as we can see with most digital technologies, from email to satellite navigation. This, however, does not seem to be the case with digitization in AECO. Even CAD and BIM have always been considered primarily with respect to costs and obstacles. This suggests that most of these solutions have little overall effect on the problems of AECO or that they fail to fully utilize the potential of digitization.

The viewpoint advocated in this book is that most solutions do hold some promise for solving real problems in AECO. However, instead of jumping ahead and imposing any solution willy-nilly, we need first to understand the relation between problems and solutions: describe and explain it, so that we can judge if a solution is suitable and feasible. This calls for a closer, more detailed inspection of digitization in AECO and its background, which reveals that more than from slow uptake, digitization in AECO suffers from having a secondary role. Even if investment is low in comparison to other sectors, digitization is clearly present in AECO: drawings are already made with CAD or, increasingly, BIM, while office automation is complete and there are enough crossovers between the two, such as invoicing software that draws data from CAD or BIM. In fact, between 1997 and 2015 investment in digitization among German AECO enterprises more than doubled.

Presence, however, is not enough because digitization remains too far in the background of AECO decision and production processes. Digital technologies are mostly found at the office, where they used to produce conventional analogue documents, for use in outdated decision processes and arguably more significantly in largely manual production processes: building construction still relies more on cheap labour than on digital means, such as productive robotization. AECO appears to have limited investment to basic digitization, such as CAD and electronic invoicing. More advanced and domain-specific technologies, from 3D scanning to robotics, are rare, despite their acknowledged potential for competitiveness, innovation and productivity. The reason for that may be that there is little incentive in advanced technologies that are unrelated or conflicting with current practices: why invest in 3D-scanning precision if the tolerances in building construction remain high? This affects even basic digitization, such as CAD and BIM: why invest in well-structured, precise models if the sole purpose of the software is to produce drawings on paper? It is enough that these drawings look correct.

INFORMATION EXPLOSION IN AECO

Despite the slow, limited uptake of digital technologies, there is ample evidence of the explosive growth of digital information in AECO. On one end of the spectrum, we have new information sources that produce big data, such as smartphones and sensors. These tell us a lot about users and conditions in the built environment, and so promise a huge potential for the analysis and improvement of building performance, but also require substantial investment in technologies and organization. Predictably, there is limited interest for this end, despite the appeal of subjects like prop-tech and smart buildings.

At the other end of the spectrum, we encounter general-purpose technologies (basic digitization) that have already become commonplace and ubiquitous, hence also in AECO. Office automation has taken over the production and dissemination of memos, reports, calculations and presentations. Email, for instance, dominates communication and information exchange by offering a digital equivalent to analogue practices like letter writing. A main characteristic of these technologies is the replication of fragmented analogue practices , to the detriment of integrated, domain-specific technologies. For example, communicating on issues in a BIM-based project via email and reports produced with text processors and spreadsheets is redundant because most BIM software includes facilities for reporting issues and making calculations in direct connection with the model.

Domain-specific technologies, which attempt to structure AECO processes and knowledge, exist in the diffuse zone between the two ends of the spectrum. These try to offer more relevant alternatives to general-purpose technologies, as well as connections to the abundance of digital data. Currently paramount among them is BIM, an integrated approach that is usually justified with respect to performance.[2] Performance improvement through BIM requires intensive and extensive collaboration, which adds to both the importance and the burden of information. Integration in BIM and return on investment also require coverage of most aspects of a project and put emphasis on larger projects. Both comprehensive digitization and larger projects, however, come against interoperability, capacity and coordination problems, making BIM deployment even harder and often haphazard.

The end result is that AECO still resides in the mentality of information overload. In a 2015 survey,[3] 70% of AECO professionals claim that project information deluge actually impedes effective collaboration, while 42% feel unable to integrate new digital tools in their organizations. We have no reason to assume that the problems have been alleviated since then. As information needs in AECO have changed little since the 1980s, when digitization was in its infancy, this suggests that the problem lies primarily not with the unchanged quantities of information but with the way information is accessed through the new, digital means. Therefore, the resulting dissatisfaction with digitization cannot be dismissed as a teething issue. If digitization approaches in AECO were successful, any such issue would have been resolved long ago. Its persistence suggests fundamental misunderstandings that impede the deployment of real solutions to AECO information needs. AECO consequently appears to share many of the problems of the digital information explosion without enjoying adequate benefits from the information-processing opportunities of the digital era.

ORIGINS AND OUTCOMES

To identify and explain these misunderstandings, we have to go back in history and look at the origins of AECO digitization. AECO has always been an intensive producer and consumer of information. In fact, most of its disciplines produce information on buildings rather than buildings, primarily documents that specify what should be constructed and how. Especially drawings have been a major commodity in AECO, both as a widely accessible isomorphic representation of buildings and as a basis for conceptualizing designs through geometry. Throughout the history of AECO, drawings have been ubiquitous in all forms of specification and communication, as well as quite effective in supporting all kinds of decision making.

The history of digitization in AECO starts quite early, already in the 1960s, but with disparate ambitions. Some researchers were interested in automating design (even to the extent of replacing human designers with computers), while others were keen to computerize drawing. In the end, the two ambitions coexisted in the scientific area of CAAD, where design automation was generally treated as the real goal. 3D modelling was acceptable, especially if directly linked to design processes, while computerized drawing was largely left to software companies. With the popularization of computers in the 1990s, however, it was computerized drawing (CAD) that dominated AECO digitization in practice.

As with other software, the original use of CAD was the production of analogue documents: conventional drawings like floor plans and bills of materials on paper. For many years, the advantages of computerized drawing were presented in terms of efficiency improvement over drawing by hand on paper: faster production of drawings, easier modification and compact storage. Even after the popularization of the Internet, the emphasis on conventional documents remained. The only difference was that, rather than working with paper-based documents only, one could also produce and exchange digital files like PDFs.

In this manner, AECO information remained firmly entrenched in conventional, document-based practices. While analogue documents like telephone directories were being replaced by online information systems and people adapted to having their day planners and address lists on mobile phones or using navigation apps instead of maps, AECO stubbornly stuck to analogue practices and documents, prolonging their life into the digital era. This is evident even in BIM, which has stronger relations to design automation than drawing computerization but still retains drawings not only as the main output but also as the primary interface with the information contained in a model.

A further consequence is that the digital AECO information comes in huge amounts, with many and often large files that are poorly connected to each other. The content of these files is accessible through separate, usually proprietary software (as opposed to e.g. browsers that can access all information on the Internet) and involves human interaction and interpretation. The user remains the centre as well as the main actor in information processing, which further increases the number of documents, as users tend to summarize and combine sources. This reveals the biggest problems of this file-inundated information landscape: more than the amounts of information, file sizes and inefficient software, they are redundancy (multiple files covering the same subjects with considerable overlaps), lack of coherence (poor conceptual and operational connections between these files) and low consistency (different descriptions of the same aspects in various files and different descriptions of related aspects).

BIM: RADICAL INTENTIONS

The latest big chapter in the history of AECO digitization concerns BIM. Drawing from product modelling, BIM emerged as a radical improvement of computerized drawing that could provide a closer relation to design. The difference with earlier attempts at design automation was that it did not offer prescriptive means for generating a design but descriptive support to designing: structured representation of buildings, collaboration between AECO disciplines, integration of aspects and smooth transition between phases. By doing so, it shifted attention from drawings to the information they contained. At least, this is the popular perception of BIM. Behind it, lies something more fundamental that forms a recurring theme in this book: meaningful symbolic representation.

The wide acceptance of BIM is unprecedented in AECO computerization. Earlier attempts were often met with reluctance, not in the least for the cost of hardware, software and training they required. By contrast, the reception of BIM was much more positive, even though BIM is more demanding than its predecessors in terms of cost (an issue that nevertheless resurfaced after the initial euphoria). Arguably more than its attention to information or collaboration, it was its apparent simplicity (a Lego-like assembly of a building) that made BIM appealing, especially to non-technical stakeholders. The arcane conventions and practices of analogue drawing no longer seemed necessary or relevant.

Still, BIM remained rooted in these conventions. It may have moved from the graphic to the symbolic but it did so through interfaces laden with graphic conventions. For example, entering a wall in BIM is normally done in a floor plan projection, in a fashion that largely replicates analogue drawing: the user selects the wall type and then draws a line to indicate its axis. As soon as the axis is drawn, the wall symbol appears fully detailed according to the wall type that has been chosen: lines, hatches and other graphic elements indicating the wall materials. The axis is not among the normally visible graphic elements. Such attachment to convention impedes users from understanding that they are actually entering a symbol in the model rather than generating a drawing.

More on such matters follows later in the book. For the moment, it suffices to note that BIM signifies a step forward in AECO digitization but remains a transitional technology that may confuse or obscure fundamental information issues. Even so, as the currently best option for AECO, it deserves particular attention and therefore constitutes the main information environment in this book: representation and IM are discussed in the framework of BIM. Future technologies are expected to follow the symbolic character of BIM, so any strategies developed with respect to BIM will probably remain applicable. It is telling that current proposals on digital twins (representations that capture not only the form and structure of buildings but also their behaviour, as reported in real time by sensors in the real thing) generally depart from BIM-like models.

LIMITATIONS AND NECESSITIES

The current digitization tendencies in AECO are dangerously confusing. While digitization invites us to interpret and even experience the world as information, AECO is still entrenched in analogue practices that keep information implicit. This means that we miss the opportunity to develop new conceptual models of reality, which are a prerequisite to digitization and information processing by machines. Instead, we use the old and arguably outdated analogue practices as the domain of discourse (the stuff that should be digitized).

Equally limiting is that digitization in AECO still calls for human interpretation, which runs contrary to the general tendency to remove ourselves from the centre of the information world. As a result, the explosively increasing amounts of digital information become a burden rather than an opportunity: we still focus on the availability of information for human consumption instead of on the information-processing capacities of machines that can support us in reliable, meaningful ways.

Even worse, the very availability of information may be underplayed. While digitization in general makes increasingly difficult to claim ignorance of anything, in AECO a project can be an isolated microworld that fails to acknowledge what exists beyond its scope. Learning and generalizing from precedents remains unsupported by AECO information technologies but even within a project many silos persist. The brief and budget, for example, are practically never integrated in the setup of a model in BIM, thereby leaving powerful options for design guidance and automation severely underutilized.

Such limitations do not merely affect IM; they also undermine decision making. As we shall see in the chapter on decisions and information, there is strong evidence that human thinking comprises two kinds of processes. The first kind (Type 1) is fast, automatic, effortless and nonconscious, while the second (Type 2) is slow, effortful, conscious and controlled. Type 1 thinking dominates daily life and allows us to be quite efficient in many common tasks but it also regularly leads to errors, especially in complex tasks. Regrettably, we tend to rely too much on the economical Type 1 processes and accept their products, even in situations that clearly call for Type 2 thinking. For example, we tend to make judgements on the basis of the limited information available in our memory at a given moment (e.g. news stories of the past few weeks), instead of taking the trouble to collect all relevant data and analyse them properly before reaching a decision.

This type of thinking occurs only too frequently with respect to the built environment: we become concerned about fire safety only after a publicized disaster and then go into a frenzy of activity that nevertheless soon subsides, especially if there is no similar disaster to rekindle our interest or if a disaster of a different kind occurs, even though the probability and risks of building fires remain the same. Moreover, we do not exhibit the same concern about stair safety, despite the fact that annually there are more victims of stair falls than of building fires, probably because each stair fall usually involves only one person, while a single building fire can have tens of victims.

That such problems are not restricted to AECO is not a consolation but a further danger: studies of human decision making reveal that people take decisions intuitively, on the basis of readily available rather than necessary, well-structured information, even in sensitive, high-risk and high-gain areas like finance. Share trading, for instance, is usually presented as a highly skilled business but performance is not consistent: it seems more a game of luck than one of skill. It is therefore important to take such failures into account also when we try to learn from other areas, especially with respect to management.

In addition to acknowledging and controlling our biases, so as to use Type 2 processes more frequently and purposely, we must take care that we always have access to the right information for these processes. This information, structured in transparent and operational descriptions of a task and its context, is the real goal for digitization in any AECO project: it returns human-computer partnerships, where machines support human decision making through extensive data collection, analysis and representation. Note that this does not imply a lessening role for humans in decision making. On the contrary, it adds to the capacities of humans by facilitating Type 2 thinking through explicit information, as well as by freeing resources for Type 2 processes.

The general conclusion is that AECO digitization is in urgent need of substantial improvement but this improvement is not merely a matter of importing new technologies as panaceas. The prerequisite to any change is a thorough understanding of building information and how it relates to our cognitive and social processes. As we shall see in the following chapters, once this is achieved, all goals, including IM and decision support, become clear and fundamentally feasible.

Key Takeaways

- *AECO digitization is characterized by slow, limited uptake, bounded by analogue conventions and confused by its dual origins: automation of design and computerization of drawing*
- *The persistence of analogue practices makes digital AECO information not only inefficient but also redundant, incoherent and inconsistent*
- *BIM is a transitional technology, still bounded by analogue practices, but, as a symbolic representation, also an indication of things to come*
- *Digitization is critical not only for information management but also for decision making*

Exercises

1. Calculate how much data a design project may produce and explain your calculations analytically, keeping in mind that there may be several design alternatives and versions. Use the following categories:
    1. CAD or BIM files
    2. PDFs and images produced from CAD & BIM or other software
    3. Alphanumeric files (texts, spreadsheets, databases etc.)
    4. Other (please specify)
2. Calculate how much of the above data is produced by different stakeholders, explaining your calculations analytically:
    1. Architects
    2. Structural engineers
    3. MEP engineers
    4. Clients
    5. Manager

Notes

1. Two examples of studies of digitization in AECO are: (a) a typically opinion-based view of digitization in AECO: https://www.mckinsey.com/business-functions/operations/our-insights/imagining-constructions-digital-future#, and (b) a more detailed account, using relevant data and meaningful proxies: https://www.zew.de/en/publications/zukunft-bau-beitrag-der-digitalisierung-zur-produktivitaet-in-der-baubranche-1.
2. Performance and in particular the avoidance of failures and related costs are among the primary reasons

for adopting BIM, as argued in: Eastman, C., Teicholz, P.M., Sacks, R., & Lee, G., 2018. BIM handbook (3rd ed.). Hoboken NJ: Wiley.

3. Research conducted in 2015 in the UK: https://www.newforma.com/news-resources/press-releases/70-aec-firms-say-information-explosion-impacted-collaboration/

PART II

REPRESENTATION

In the previous part we have considered how digitization affects our treatment of information and our attitudes concerning information. We have seen that there are marked differences between general tendencies and what is happening in AECO. Many of the differences are due to the way information is represented. Digitization relies heavily on symbolic representations that allow efficient and reliable processing of information contained in the symbols and their relations. This lessens the importance of isomorphic representations like drawings, which retain much of the visual appearance of the real things. In this part, we look at the fundamental structure of symbolic representations, differences with analogue representations and how the two come together in BIM, in a way that exemplifies the transitional character of current AECO digitization.

CHAPTER 3

Symbolic representation

This chapter introduces symbolic representations: how they are structured and how they describe things, including spatial ones. It introduces graphs for the description of spatial symbolic representations (which presupposes knowledge of the content of Appendix I) and presents some of the advantages of such mathematical foundations. The chapter concludes with the paradigmatic and syntagmatic dimensions of representations, and their relevance for interpretation and management.

SYMBOLIC REPRESENTATIONS

Many of the misunderstandings concerning information occur when people do not appreciate what representations are and how they convey information. Representations are so central to our thinking that even if the sender of some information fails to structure it in a representation, the receiver does so automatically. A representation can be succinctly defined as a system for describing a particular class of entities. The result of applying a representation to an entity is a *description*. Representations of the symbolic kind, which proliferate human societies, consist of two main components:

- A set of symbols, usually finite
- Some rules for linking these symbols to the entities they describe

The decimal numeral system is such a symbolic representation. Its symbols are the familiar Hindu-Arabic numerals:

$$S_D = \{0,1,2,3,4,5,6,7,8,9\}$$

The rules by which these symbols are linked to the quantities they describe can be summarized as follows:

$$n_n \cdot 10^n + n_{n-1} \cdot 10^{n-1} + \ldots + n_1 \cdot 10^1 + n_0 \cdot 10^0$$

These rules underlie positional notation, i.e. the description of a quantity as:

$$n_n n_{n-1} \ldots . n_1 n_0$$

For example, the description of seventeen becomes:

$$1 \cdot 10^1 + 7 \cdot 10^0 \Rightarrow 17$$

The binary numeral system is essentially similar. Its symbol set consists of only two numerals and its rules employ two as base instead of ten:

$$S_B = \{0,1\}$$

$$n_n \cdot 2^n + n_{n-1} \cdot 2^{n-1} .+ ... + n_1 \cdot 2^1 + n_0 \cdot 2^0$$

This means that seventeen becomes:

$$1 \cdot 2^4 + 0 \cdot 2^3 + 0 \cdot 2^2 + 0 \cdot 2^1 + 1 \cdot 2^0 \Rightarrow 10001$$

There are often alternative representations for the same class of entities. Quantities, for example, can be represented by (from left to right) Roman, decimal and binary numerals, as well as one of many tally mark systems:

XVII = 17 = 10001 = IIII IIII IIII II

A representation makes explicit only certain aspects of the described entities. The above numerical representations concern quantity. They tell us, for example, that there are seventeen persons in a room. The length, weight, age and other features of these persons are not described. For these, one needs different representations.

Each representation has its advantages. Decimal numerals, for example, are considered appropriate for humans because we have ten fingers that can be used as an aid to calculation. Being built out of components with two states (on and off), computers are better suited to binary numerals. However, when it comes to counting ongoing quantities, like people boarding a ship, tally marks are better suited to the task. Some representations may be not particularly good at anything: it has been suggested that despite their brilliance at geometry, ancient Greeks and Romans failed to develop other branches of mathematics to a similar level because they lacked helpful numeral representations.

We should also appreciate that representation are heavily constrained by their *implementation mechanisms:* the things physically used to make them. Cuneiform characters, for example, are strongly related to they styli used for imprinting them on clay tablets: the strokes one could make with these styli on clay. Interestingly, such strokes remained the basis of subsequent writing systems. This suggests that some elements of a representation are transferred from one technology to another, despite the changes in implementation. At the same time, such transitions form a clear progress towards minimizing effort and increasing speed in writing, regardless of script or language.

From an IM viewpoint, symbolic representations are the culmination of a long process of trying to order information into discrete parcels and networks that link them. In this process, we encounter many technologies for organizing large quantities of information, for example card-filing systems, indices, dictionaries and encyclopaedias. In an illustration of the significance of information for management, the structure such technologies provide connects to attempts to order the world and organize our interactions with it. This is something many states and businesses discovered in the nineteenth century, when many of these technologies took off. For example, classifications of professions, races, genders etc. were reduced to what the technologies afforded, sometimes with deleterious effects. Symbolic representations concluded the process and allowed use of the computer as an information and communication device by supporting the parsing of the content of any document into symbols and relations that can be easily digitized.

SYMBOLS AND THINGS

The correspondence between symbols in a representation and the entities they denote may be less than perfect. This applies even to the Latin alphabet, one of the most successful symbolic representations and a cornerstone of computerization. The letters (phonograms) that describe sounds (phonemes) in a language are a very compact set of symbols that afford a more economical way of describing words than syllabaries or logographies (graphemes corresponding to syllables or things and ideas). Using the Latin alphabet as the symbol set turns a computerized text into a string of ASCII characters that combine to form all possible words and sentences. Imagine how different text processing in the computer would be if its symbols were not alphabetic characters but pixels or lines like the strokes we make to form the characters in handwriting.

At the same time, the correspondence between letters in the Latin alphabet and phonemes in the languages that employ them is not straightforward. In English, for example, the letter 'A' may denote different phonemes:

- **ɑ**: (as in 'car')
- æ (as in 'cat')
- **ɒ** (as in 'call')
- **ə** (as in 'alive')
- **ɔ**: (as in 'talk')

The digraph TH can be either:

- θ (as in 'think') or
- ð (as in 'this')

Conversely, the phoneme e**ɪ** can be written either as:

- AY (as in 'say')
- EI (as in 'eight')

The lesson we learn from these examples is that abstraction and context are important in representation. Abstraction allows for less strict yet reasonably clear relations between symbols and things: the letter 'A' represents only vowels, moreover of a similar kind. A one-to-many correspondence like that is trickier than a simple one-to-one relation but is usually clarified thanks to the context, in our case proximal alphabetic symbols: 'car' and 'cat' are very similar strings but most English learners soon learn that they are pronounced differently and associate the right phoneme rather than the letter with the word. Similarly, in the floor plan of a building one soon learns to distinguish between two closely spaced lines denoting a wall and two very similar lines representing a step (Figure 1).

Figure 1. Walls and step in a floor plan: both entities are represented by two closely spaced parallel lines

SPATIAL SYMBOLIC REPRESENTATIONS

Symbolic representations are also used for spatial entities. Familiar examples are metro and similar public transport maps. A common characteristic of many such maps is that they started life as lines drawn on a city map to indicate the route of each metro line and the position of the stations (Figure 2). As the size and complexity of the transport networks increased, the metro lines and stations were liberated from the city maps and became separate, diagrammatic maps: spatial symbolic representations, comprising symbols for stations and connections between stations (Figure 3).

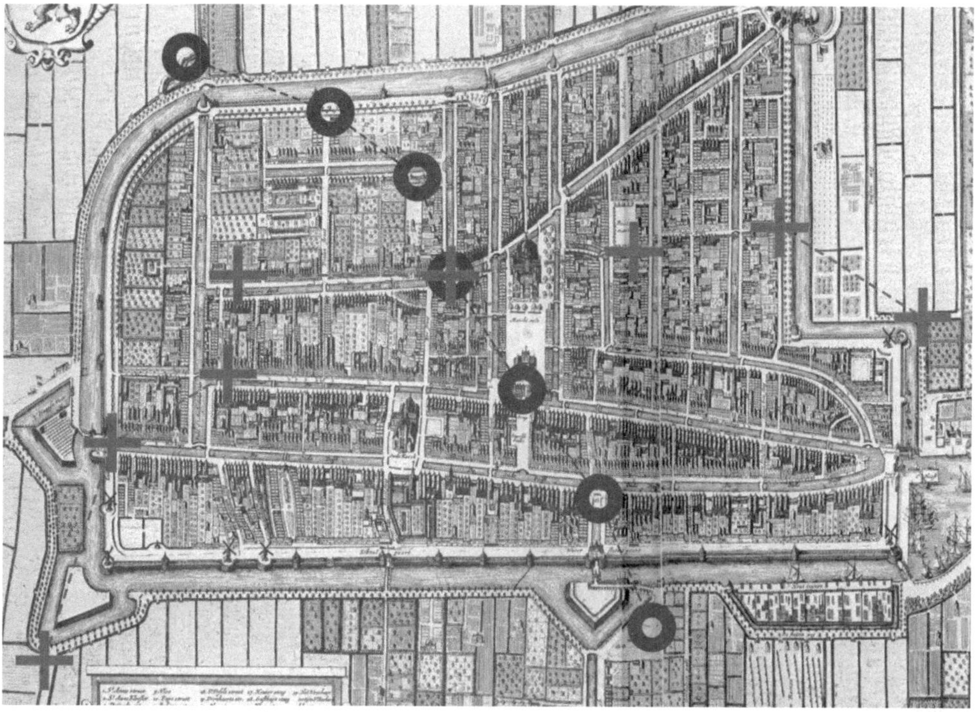

Figure 2. Metro lines and stations on a city map

In these maps, the symbols are similar for each line but can be differentiated by means of shape or colour, so that one can distinguish between lines. The symbol set for a metro network comprising two lines (the red O line and the blue Plus line) would therefore consist of the station symbol for the red line, the station symbol for the blue line, the connection symbol for the red line and the connection symbol for the blue line:

$$S_M = \{\text{o}, +, |_{\text{o}}, |_{+}\}$$

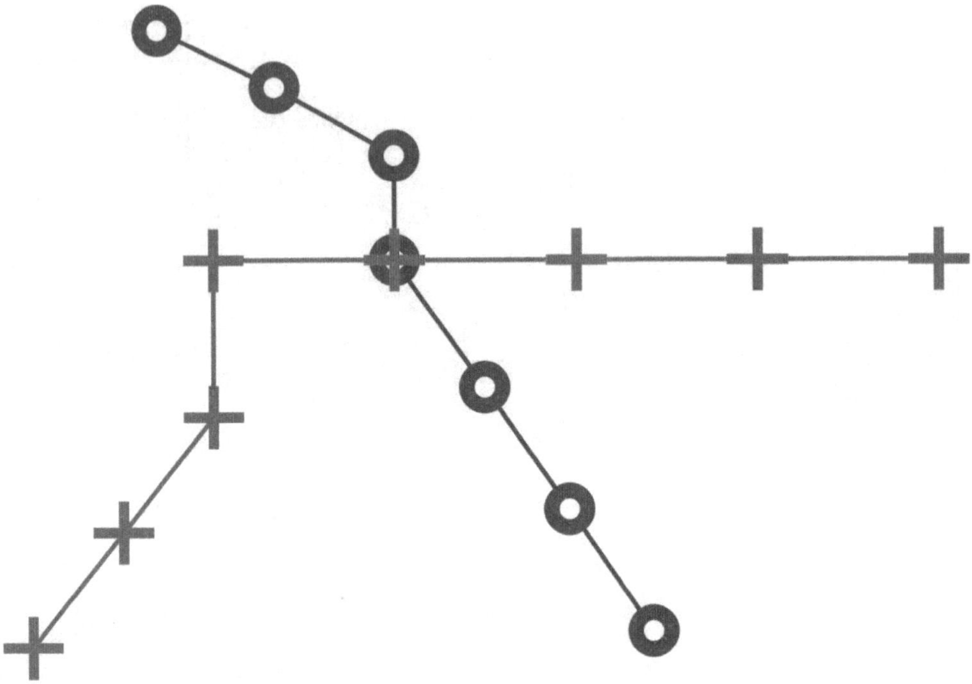

Figure 3. Metro map

The rules that connect these symbols to real-world entities can be summarized as follows:

- Each station on a metro line (regardless of the complexity of the building that accommodates it) is represented by a station symbol of that line
- Each part of the rail network that connects two stations of the same line is represented by a line symbol of that line

These common-sense, practical principles underlie many intuitive attempts at spatial representation and, as discussed later on, even a branch of mathematics that provides quite useful and powerful means for formalizing and analysing symbolic spatial representations.

Our familiarity with metro maps is to a large degree due to their legibility and usability, which make them excellent illustrations of the strengths of a good representation. As descriptions of an urban transport system, they allow for easy and clear travel planning, facilitate recognition of interchanges and connections, and generally provide clear overview and support easy understanding. To manage all that, metro maps tend to be abstract and diagrammatic (as in Figure 3), in particular by simplifying the geometry of the metro lines (usually turning them into straight lines) and normalizing distances between stations (often on the basis of a grid). As a consequence, metro diagrams are inappropriate for measuring geometric distances between stations. Still, as travelling times on a metro primarily depend on the number of stations to be traversed, metro maps can be used to estimate the time a trip may take. However, for finding the precise location of a station, city maps are far more useful.

A comparison of metro maps to numerals shows that the increase in dimensionality necessitates explicit representation of relations between symbols. In the one-dimensional numerals, relations are implicit yet unambiguous: positional notation establishes a strict order that makes evident which numeral stands for hundreds in a decimal number and how it relates to the numerals denoting thousands and tens. Similarly, in an alphabetic text (also a one-dimensional representation), spaces and punctuation marks are used to indicate the clustering of letters into words, sentences and paragraphs, and thus facilitate understanding of not only phonemes but also meanings in the text.

In two-dimensional representations like the metro diagrams, proximity between two station symbols does not suffice for inferring the precise relation between them. One needs an explicit indication like a line that connects the two symbols. A metro map missing such a connection (Figure 4) is puzzling and ambiguous: does the missing connection mean that a metro line is still under development or simply that the drawings is incomplete by mistake? Interestingly, such an omission in a metro diagram is quite striking and does not normally go unnoticed, triggering questions and interpretations, which will be discussed in the chapter on data and information (in relation to anti-data).

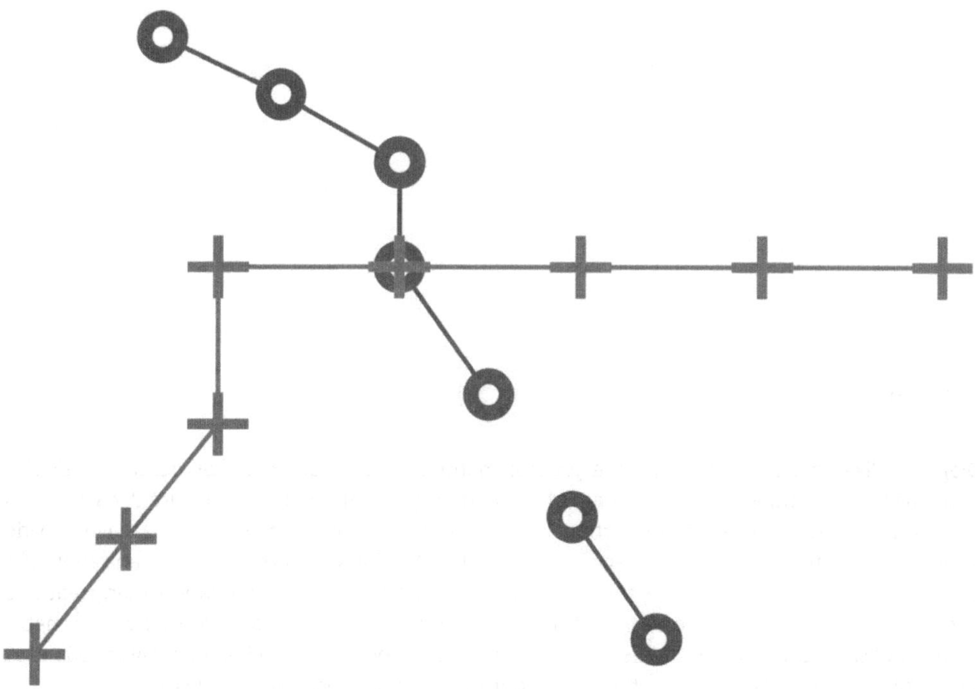

Figure 4. Metro map missing a connection between stations

Similarly puzzling is a metro map where stations of different lines are close to each other, even touching (Figure 5): does this indicate that the stations are housed in the same building, so that one can change from one line to the other, or that the stations are close by but separate, in which case one has to exit the metro and enter it again (which may involve having to buy a new ticket)? In a metro map where stations are clearly connected or coincide (Figure 3), there is no such ambiguity concerning interchange possibilities.

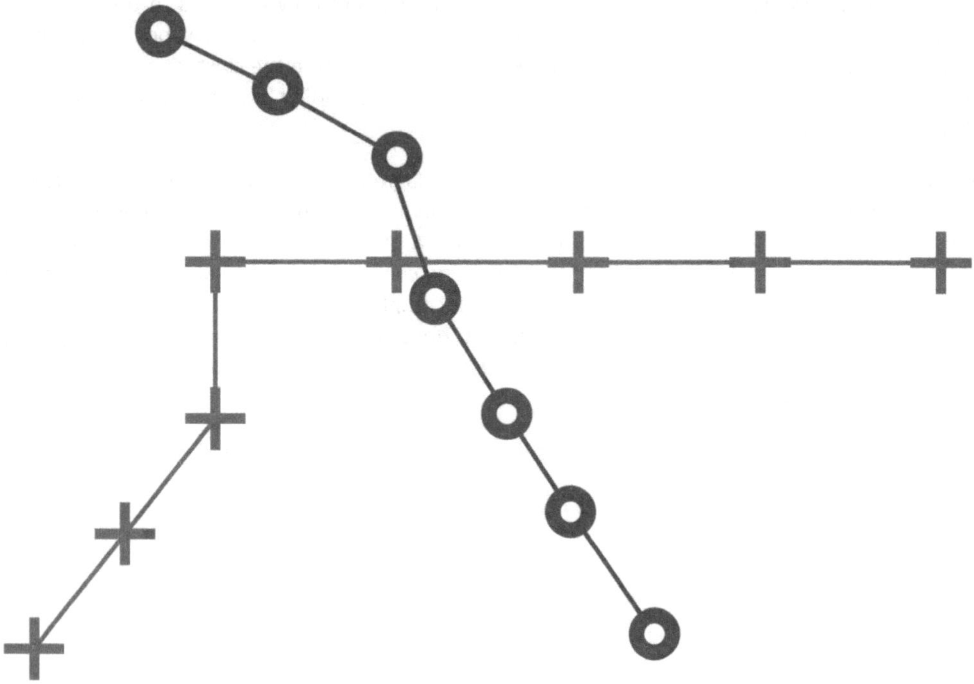

Figure 5. Metro map unclear about interchange possibilities

GRAPHS

Diagrams like these metro maps are *graphs*: mathematical structures that describe pairwise relations between things (for a summary of graph theory see Appendix I). In Figure 3, each metro station is a vertex and each connection between two stations an edge. Graphs have a wide range of applications, from computer networks and molecular structures to the organization of a company or a family tree, because the tools supplied by graph theory help quantify many features and aspects. For example, the *degree* of a vertex is a good indication of complexity. In a metro map, it indicates the number of lines that connect there. The only interchange in Figure 3 is easy to identify by its degree (4), as are the end stations of the two lines, which are *leaves*.

The *degree sequence* of a graph obviously helps with similar aspects. In a map of a metro line (i.e. the subgraph consisting of the vertices and edges belonging to the line), this sequence is a good indication of opportunities for crossing over to other lines, as well as of how busy the line and its stations may become as passengers avail themselves of these opportunities.

The *eccentricity* of a metro station relates to its remoteness or poor connectivity. The *diameter* of the graph indicates the extent of remoteness in the metro network. Together with the *radius,* they are used to detect the *center* and the *periphery* of the graph: respectively, the well-connected part where most things happen and the more quiet part where little happens.

Finally, in order to be able to travel on the metro, the graph has to be *connected:* each vertex should connect to every other vertex by some path (the graph in Figure 5 is therefore not connected). Connectivity is affected by *bridges*. In our metro example, all edges are bridges, making the metro particularly sensitive: any problem between two stations renders it partly unusable, as passengers cannot move along alternative routes.

What the above examples illustrate is that a well-structured representation can rely on mathematical tools that help formalize its structure and analyses. This is important for two reasons: firstly, formalization makes explicit what one may recognize intuitively in a representation; secondly, it supports automation, especially of analyses. Allowing computers to perform painstaking and exhaustive analyses complements, liberates and enhances the creative capacities of humans.

GRAPHS AND BUILDINGS

Graph-like representations are also used for buildings. Architects, for example, use bubble and relationship diagrams to express schematically the spatial structure of a design (Figure 3). In such diagrams, nodes usually denote spaces where some specific activities take place (e.g. "Expositions" or "Library"), while edges or overlaps indicate proximity or direct access.

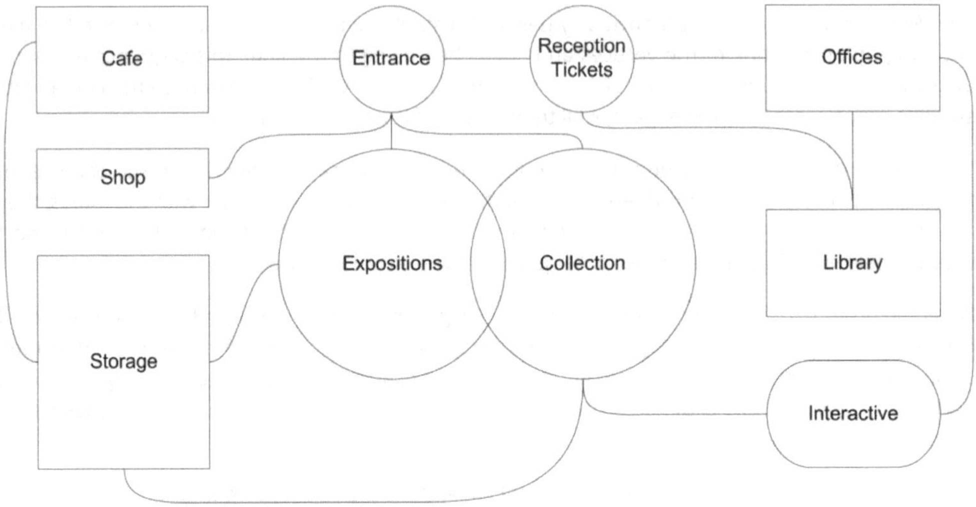

Figure 6. Relationship diagram

On the basis of graph theory, more formal versions of these diagrams have been developed, such as *access graphs*. Here nodes represent spaces and edges openings like doors, which afford direct connection between spaces. Access graphs are particularly useful for analysing circulation in a building.[1]

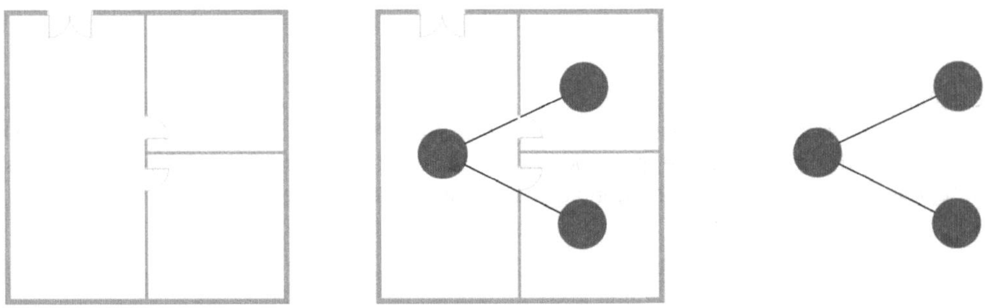

Figure 7. Floor plan and its access graph

The access graph demonstrates the significance of explicit structure: pictorially it may have few advantages over relationship diagrams, as both make explicit the entities in a representation and their relations. However, imposing the stricter principles of a mathematical structure reduces vagueness and provides access to useful mathematical tools. In a relationship diagram one may use both edges and overlaps to indicate relations, and shapes, colours and sizes to indicate properties of the nodes. In a graph, one must use only vertices and edges, and label them with the necessary attributes. This improves consistency and clarity in representation, similarly to the standardization of spelling in a language. It also facilitates application of mathematical measures which give clear indications of design performance. For example, the eccentricity of the node representing the space from where one may exit a building is a useful measure of how long it may take for people to leave the building, which is critical for e.g. fire egress. Similarly, the significance of a space for pedestrian circulation is indicated by its degree in the access graph, while edges that form bridges are doorways that cut off a part of the building when closed. This makes them potential bottlenecks in pedestrian circulation but also opportune control points, e.g. for security checks: points of singular importance, either as threats or as opportunities. For all these reasons, graphs are a representational basis to which we will returning in this book.

PARADIGMATIC AND SYNTAGMATIC DIMENSIONS

In a symbolic representation we can analyse descriptions along two dimensions: the paradigmatic and the syntagmatic.[2] The paradigmatic dimension concerns the symbols in the representation, e.g. letters in a text. The syntagmatic dimension refers to the sequence by which these symbols are entered in the description. The meaning of the description relies primarily on the paradigmatic dimension: the symbols and their arrangement in the description. Syntagmatic aspects may influence the form of these symbols and their arrangement but above all reveal much about the cognitive and social processes behind the representation and its application, as well as mechanical aspects. For instance, in a culture where left-to-right writing is dominant, one would expect people to write numerals from left to right, too. However, the Dutch language uses a ten-before-unit structure for number words between 21 and 99 (as opposed to the unit-and-ten structure in English), e.g. "vijfentwintig" (five-and-twenty). Consequently, when writing by hand, e.g. noting down a telephone number dictated by someone else, one often sees Dutch people first enter the ten numeral, leaving space for the unit, and then backtrack to that space to enter the unit numeral. With a computer keyboard such backtracking is not possible, so the writer normally pauses while listening to the ten numeral, waits for the unit numeral and then enters them in the reverse order. Matching the oral representation to the written one may involve such syntagmatic peculiarities, which are moreover constrained by the implementation means of the representation (writing by hand or typing).

In drawing by hand, one may use a variety of guidelines, including perspective, grid and frame lines, which prescribe directions, relations and boundaries. These lines are normally entered first in the drawing, either during the initial setup or when the need for guidance emerges. The graphic elements of the building representation are entered afterwards, often in direct reference to the guidelines: if a graphic element has to terminate on a guideline, one may draw it from the guideline or, if one starts from the opposite direction, slow down while approaching the guideline, so as to ensure clear termination. Similar constraining influences may also derive from already existing graphic elements in the drawing: consciously or unconsciously one might keep new graphic elements parallel or similarly sized as previously entered ones, terminate them against existing lines etc. Such mechanical and proportional dependence on existing graphic elements has led to the development of a wide range of object-snap options and alignment facilities in computerized drawing.

Any analysis of the paradigmatic dimension in a description aims at identifying symbols, e.g. relating each stroke in a handwritten text to a letter. To do that, one has to account for every stroke with respect to not only all symbols available in the representation but also various alternatives and variations, such as different styles of handwriting. Analyses of the syntagmatic dimension have to take into account not only the paradigmatic dimension (especially symbols and implementation mechanisms) but also cognitive, social, mechanical aspects that may have played a role in the temporal process of making a description, such as the tendency to draw *from* an existing graphic element to ensure clear termination. Similarly, in most BIM editors, one enters openings like doors or windows only after the walls that host them have been entered in the model and rooms are defined only after the bounding walls have been completed.

As all this relates to the organization of a design project and the relations between members of a design team, the syntagmatic dimension is of particular relevance to the management of information processes. Thankfully, there are sufficient tools for registering changes in a digital representation: adding a timestamp to the creation, modification and eventual deletion of a symbol in a computer program is easy and computationally inexpensive. Making sense of what these changes mean requires thorough analysis of the sequences registered and clear distinctions between possible reasons for doing things in a particular order.

The significance of the syntagmatic dimension increases with the dimensionality of the representation: in a one-dimensional representation like a text, the sequence by which letters are entered is quite predictable, including peculiarities like the way Dutch words for numbers between 21 and 99 are structured. In representations with two or more dimensions, one may enter symbols in a variety of ways, starting from what is important or opportune and moving iteratively through the description until it is complete (although completeness may be difficult to ascertain syntagmatically, making uncertain when the process should terminate). This clearly indicates the significance of the syntagmatic dimension for the management of 3D and 4D representations of buildings.

Key Takeaways

- *Symbolic representations employ usually finite sets of symbols and rules to relate these symbols to specific classes of entities in order to produce descriptions of these entities*
- *Familiar spatial symbolic representations like metro diagrams are graphs: mathematical structures that describe pairwise relations between things, using vertices for the things and edges for their relations*
- *Graphs are a useful representational basis for buildings because they make symbols and relations between symbols explicit and manageable*
- *Symbolic descriptions have a paradigmatic and a syntagmatic dimension, relating respectively to the symbols they contain and the sequence by which the symbols have been entered in the description*
- *Interpretation of a description relies primarily on the paradigmatic dimension, while management strongly relates to the syntagmatic dimension*

Exercises

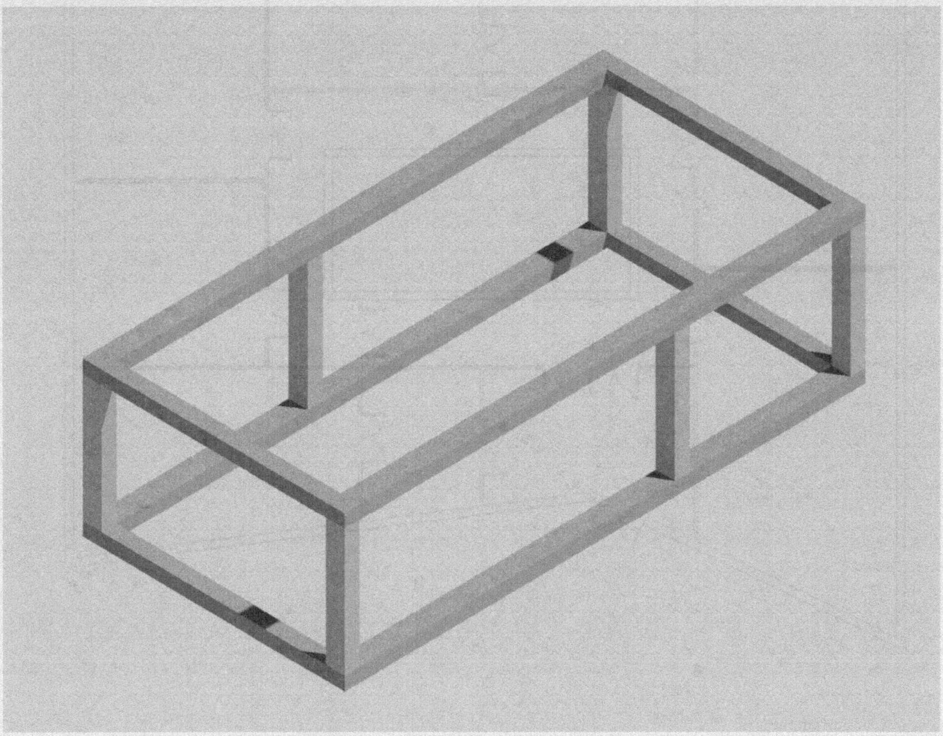

Figure 8. A post-and-beam structure

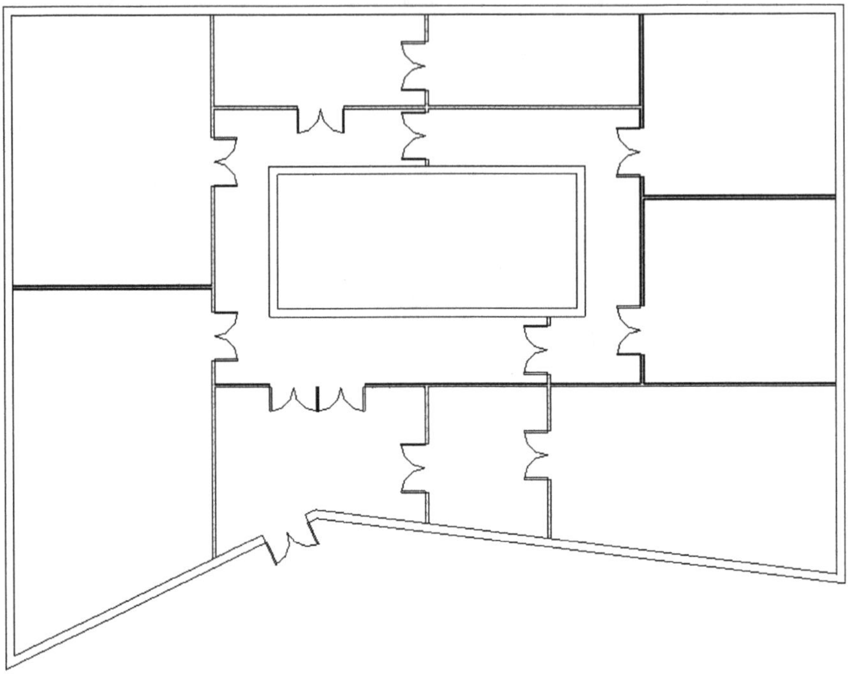

Figure 9. A floor plan

1. Add a third, circular line to the metro in Figure 3 using existing stations only:
    1. Which stations should the circular line connect?
    2. How can you justify your decisions with graph measures?
2. Draw graphs for the post-and-beam structure in Figure 8:
    1. One using vertices for the posts and beams and edges for their connections
    2. One using vertices for the junctions and edges for the posts and beams
    3. Calculate the following for both graphs:
        1. The degree and eccentricity of each vertex
        2. The diameter and radius of each graph
3. Draw an access graph for the floor plan in Figure 9. In the access graph:
    1. Calculate the degree and eccentricity of each vertex

2. Calculate the diameter and radius of the graph
3. Indicate the vertices belonging to the center and the periphery
4. Identify any bridges in the access graph

Notes

1. Graph-based applications in the representation of buildings are discussed extensively in: Steadman, P., 1983. *Architectural morphology: an introduction to the geometry of building plans.* London: Pion.
2. The discussion on the paradigmatic and syntagmatic dimensions in visual representations draws from: Van Sommers, P., 1984. *Drawing and cognition: descriptive and experimental studies of graphic production processes.* Cambridge: Cambridge University Press.

CHAPTER 4

Analogue representations

To understand many of the problems surrounding building information, we first need to examine the analogue representations that still persist in AECO. This chapter presents some of the key characteristics that have made these representations so successful but do not necessarily agree with digital environments. Effective computerization replaces the human abilities that enable analogue representations with capacities for information processing by machines.

PICTORIAL REPRESENTATIONS AND GEOMETRY

Familiar building representations tend to be drawings on paper, such as orthographic projections like floor plans and sections, and projective ones, including isometrics and axonometrics: two-dimensional depictions of three-dimensional scenes, through which one tries to describe the spatial arrangement, construction or appearance of a building. What these drawings have in common is:

- They are pictorial representations (not symbolic)
- They rely heavily on geometry

Even though drawings were used in building design already in antiquity, it was in the Renaissance that applied geometry revolutionized the way Europeans represented and conceptualized space, in many cases raising the importance of the graphic image over the written text. Geometry was not merely a handy foundation for descriptive purposes, i.e. formalizing pictorial representations of buildings, but also a means of ordering space, i.e. organizing people's experiences and thoughts to reveal some inherent order (including that of the cosmos). Consequently, building drawings evolved from schematic to precise and detailed representations that matched the perception of actual buildings, as well as most levels of decision making and communication about building design and construction.

This gave geometry a central position in building design. Many architects and engineers became engrossed in geometric explorations closely linked to some presumed essence or ambition of their profession. With geometry both an overlay and underlay to reality, a complex relation developed between building design and geometry, involving not only the shape of the building but also the shape of its drawings. In turn, this caused building drawings to become semantically and syntactically dense pictorial representations, where any pictorial element, however small, can be significant for interpretation. In comparison to more diagrammatic representations, the interpretation of building drawings involves a larger number of pictorial elements, properties and aspects, such as colour, thickness, intensity and contrast. As representations, building drawings were therefore considered a mixed and transitional case.[1]

The computerization of such complex, highly conventional analogue representations was initially superficial, aiming at faithful reproduction of their appearance. To many, the primary function of digital building representations, including not only CAD but also BIM, is the production of conventional analogue drawings either on paper (prints) or as digital facsimiles (e.g. a PDF of a floor plan). This makes computerization merely an efficiency improvement, especially concerning ease of drawing modification, compactness of storage and speed of dissemination. This is a testimony to the power and success of analogue building drawings but at the same time a major limitation to a fuller utilization of the information-processing capacities of computers. Analogue drawings work well in conjunction with human abilities for visual recognition, allowing us to develop efficient and effective means of specification and communication. For example, most people recognize the same number of spaces in a floor plan on paper; scanning the floor plan transforms it into a computer file but computers generally only recognize it as an array of pixels. Recognizing the rooms and counting them by computer requires explicit representation of spaces.

VISUAL PERCEPTION AND RECOGNITION

Building drawings are surprisingly parsimonious: they manage to achieve quite a lot with a limited repertory of graphic primitives. With just a few kinds of lines, they produce floor plans, sections, perspectives etc., as well as depict a wide variety of shapes and materials in all these projections. To a large degree this is thanks to the ingenious ways they trigger the human visual system and allow us to see things. For example, we tend to associate similar elements if they are proximal. Therefore, two closely parallel lines become one: the depiction of a wall. But if the distance between the lines increases beyond what might be plausible for a thick wall, they become just parallel lines. Seeing two lines as a wall does not necessarily mean they have to be strictly parallel or straight (Figure 1).

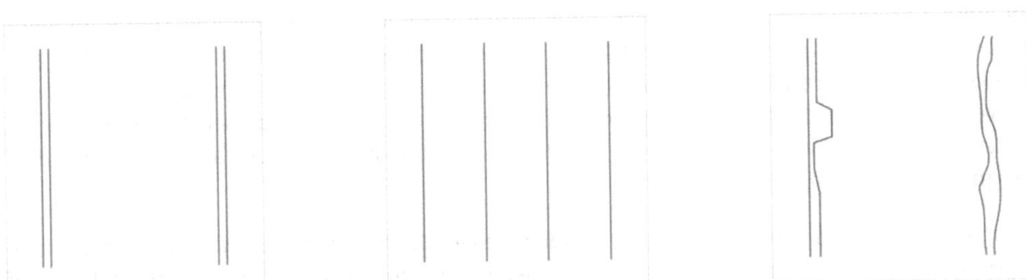

Figure 1. In a floor plan, closely spaced parallel lines are often paired into depictions of walls (left); if the distance between parallel lines increases, perceiving them as walls becomes hard or impossible (middle); perturbations or irregularities do not necessarily disqualify closely spaced, roughly parallel lines as wall depictions (right)

It is similarly easy to identify columns in a floor plan. Even more significantly, the arrangement (repetition, collinearity, proximity etc.) and similarity of columns allow us to recognize colonnades: groups of objects with a specific character (Figure 2). A colonnade may be recognizable even when the columns are not identical and their arrangement not completely regular (Figure 3). However, if the arrangement is truly irregular, proximity or similarity do not suffice for the recognition of a colonnade (Figure 4).

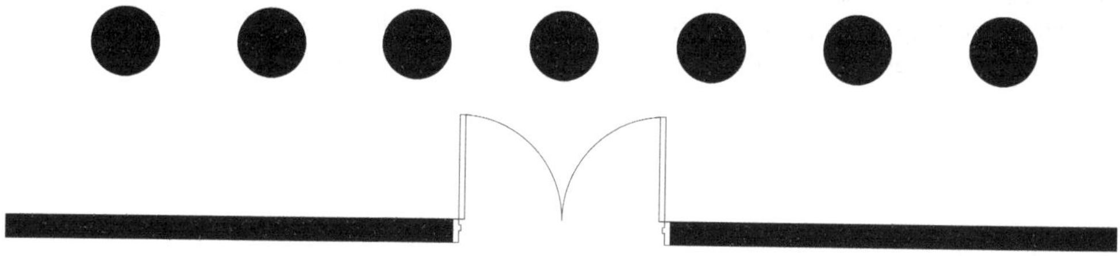

Figure 2. Colonnade in floor plan: recognition of the columns as a group is based on their arrangement and similarity

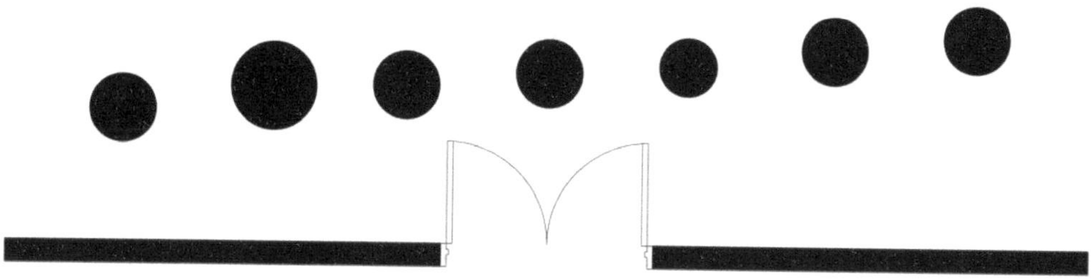

Figure 3. A colonnade may be recognized even if there are irregularities in the size and arrangement of the columns

Figure 4. Randomly placed columns do not make a colonnade

Probably the most unnoticed and yet striking part of reading a drawing concerns the recognition of spaces: in a floor plan, one enters graphic elements that develop into depictions of building elements and components, like walls, doors and windows. Spaces are what is left over on paper, essentially background coming through the drawing. Yet most people with a basic understanding of building drawings are capable of recognizing the spaces in a floor plan (inferring them from the bounding building elements) with precision, accuracy and reliability (Figure 5).

Figure 5. Floor plan of a building with three rooms: the drawing consists of just the walls but the rooms are also instantly recognizable

ABSTRACTION AND INCOMPLETENESS

Pictorial representations are characterized by a high potential for abstraction, which is evident in the different scales of building drawings: a wall at a scale like 1:20 is depicted by a large number of lines indicating various layers and materials; at 1:100 the wall may be reduced to just two parallel lines; at 1:500 it may even become a single, relatively thick line. Similarly, a door in a floor plan at 1:20 is quite detailed (Figure 6), at 1:100 it is abstracted into a depiction that primarily indicates the door type (Figure 7) and at 1:500 it becomes just a hole in a wall (Figure 8). At all three scales both the wall and the door are clearly recognizable, albeit at different scales of specificity and detail. Such abstraction is largely visual: it mimics the perception of a drawing (or, for that matter, of any object) from various distances. It also corresponds to the design priorities in different stages. In early, conceptual design, one tends to focus on general issues, zooming out of the drawing to study larger parts, while deferring details to later stages. Therefore, the precise type, function and construction of a door may be relatively insignificant, making abstraction at the scale of 1:500 suitable. However, that abstraction level is inappropriate for the final technical design, when one has to specify not just the function and construction of a door but also its interfacing with the wall. To do so, one has to zoom in and use a scale like 1:20 to view and settle all details.

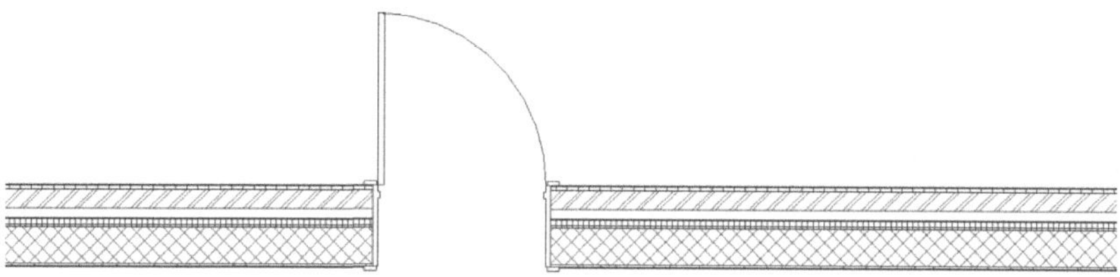

Figure 6. Wall and door at 1:20

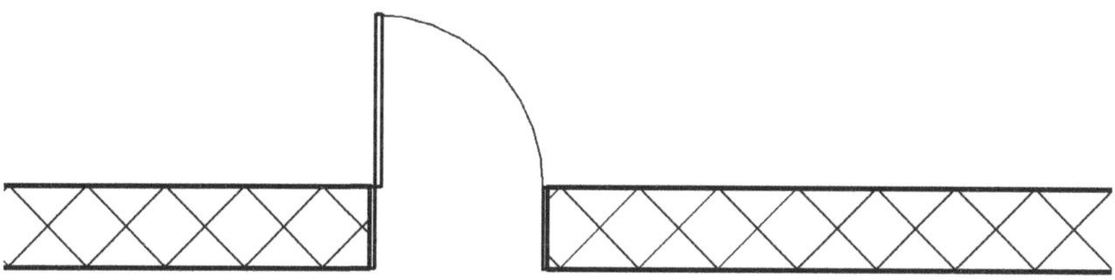

Figure 7. Wall and door at 1:100

Figure 8. Wall and door at 1:500

In addition to visual abstraction, one may also reduce common or pertinent configurations, however complex, into a single, named entity, e.g. an Ionic or Corinthian column, a colonnade (Figure 2) or "third floor" and "north wing". Such mnemonic or conceptual abstraction is constrained by visual recognition, as outlined above, but also relies on cultural convention: it is clearly not insignificant that we have a term for a colonnade. As a result, mnemonic abstraction plays a more important role in symbolic representation than purely visual abstraction.

Pictorial representations are also relatively immune to incompleteness: a hastily drawn line on paper, with bits missing, is still perceived as a line (Figure 9). A house partially occluded by an obstacle is similarly perceived as a single, complete and coherent entity (Figure 10).

Figure 9. An imperfectly drawn line may still be perceived as a line

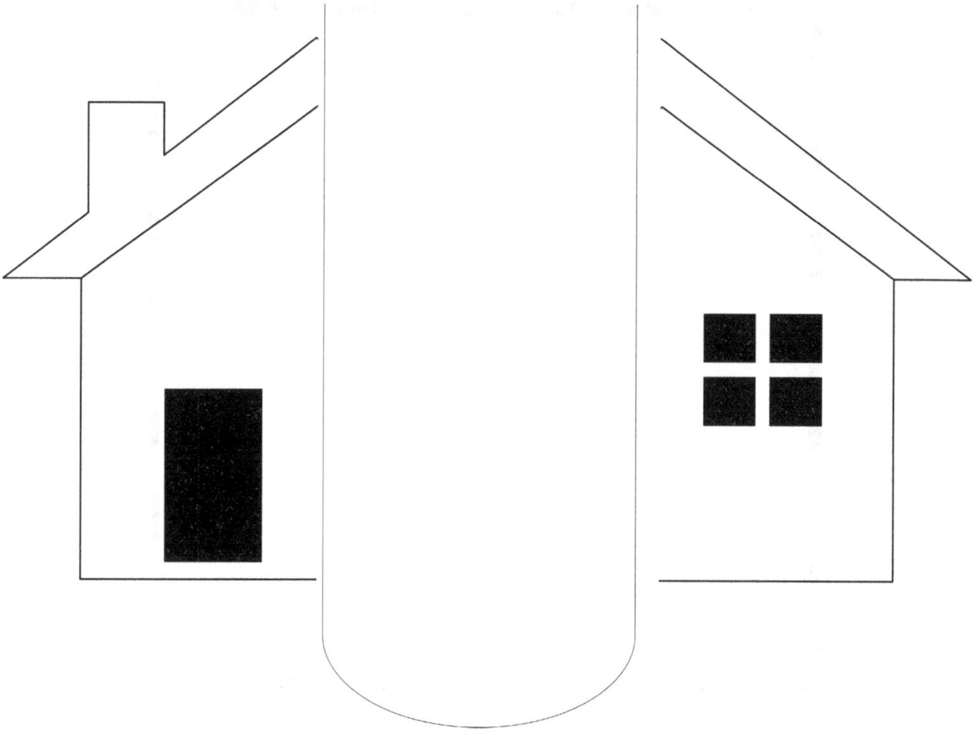

Figure 10. A house partially occluded by another object is still perceived as a single house

Dealing with incomplete descriptions is generally possible because not all parts are critical for understanding their meaning, even if they are not redundant. In English, for example, keeping only the consonants in a text may suffice for recognizing most words:

TH QCK BRWN FX JMPS VR TH LZY DG

(THE QUICK BROWN FOX JUMPS OVER THE LAZY DOG)

This practice, currently known as disenvoweling, is widely applied in digital short messages. In the past, it was used to similar effect by telegraph operators, note takers and others who wanted to economize on message length and the time and effort required for writing or transmitting a message. Identifying the missing vowels is often a matter of context: 'DG' in a farmyard setting probably means 'DOG' but in an archaeological one it may stand for 'DIG'. If a word contains many vowels, it may be hard even then: 'JMPS' is highly probably 'JUMPS' in most contexts but 'DT' as a shorthand of 'IDIOT' may be far from effective in any context.

Likewise in images, some parts are more critical than others for recognition. A basic example is dashed lines: even with half of the line missing, the human visual system invariably recognizes the complete lines and the shapes they form (Figure 11).

Figure 11. A square drawn with dashed lines

Interestingly, a shape drawn with dashed lines is more easily recognized if the line junctions are present. This relates to a general tendency of the human visual system to rely on points of maximum curvature in the outline of shapes.[2] Corners, in particular, are quite important: the presence of corners often suffices for the perception of illusory figures (Figure 12). The form of a corner gives perceivers quite specific expectations concerning the position and form of other corners connected to it, even if the geometry is curvilinear (Figure 13). The presence of compatible corners in the image leads to perception of an illusory figure occluding other forms. Perception of the illusory figure weakens if occlusion occurs at non-critical parts of the figure, such as the middle of its sides (Figure 14).

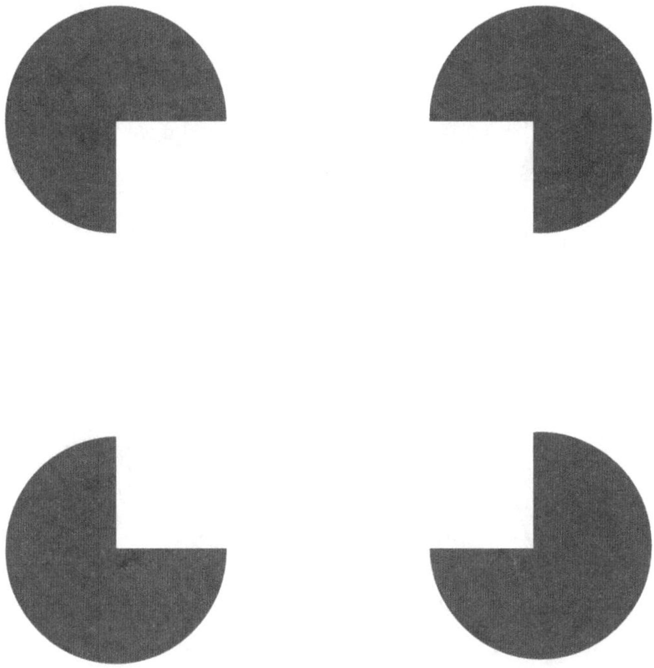

Figure 12. An illusory square

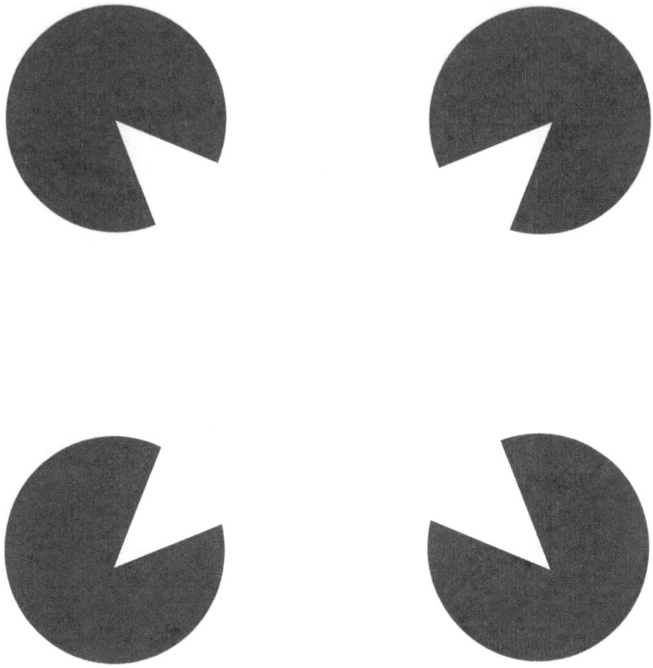

Figure 13. A curvilinear illusory figure

Figure 14. Missing corners make perception of illusory figures uncertain or vague; in this case, it is uncertain if the illusory square has rounded-off or bevelled corners

The importance of corners underlay one of the early successes in artificial intelligence. Based on a typology of edge junctions (Figure 15), expectations about the connectivity of these types and the orientation of resulting surfaces, computers were able to recognize the composition of scenes with trihedral geometric forms: faces, volumes and their relative positions (Figure 16).[3]

Figure 15. The four basic edge junction types in trihedral scenes

Figure 16. Recognition of objects in a trihedral scene can be based on the types of edge junctions in Figure 15 and their connectivity

The above examples illustrate how analogue representations can be parsimonious and simultaneously effective but only if complemented with quite advanced and expensive recognition capacities. Empowering computers with such capacities is an emerging future but for the moment at least symbolic representations that contain explicit information are clearly preferable.

IMPLEMENTATION MECHANISMS

Symbols can exist in various environments, so we use means appropriate to each environment for their implementation. A letter of the alphabet can be handwritten on paper with ink or graphite particles, depending on the writing implement (although one might claim that the strokes that comprise the letter are the real implementation mechanisms with respect to both the paradigmatic and the syntagmatic dimensions). In the computer, the same letter is implemented as an ASCII character in a text processing, spreadsheet and similar programs. In a drawing program, it may comprise pixels or vectors corresponding to the strokes (depending on the type of the program). In all cases, the symbol (the letter) is the same; what changes are the implementation mechanisms used for it.

In analogue building representations, the overemphasis on geometry results in a dominance of implementation mechanisms over symbols. As geometric primitives are the graphic implementation mechanisms in pictorial building representations (underlay) and geometry exercises significant ordering influence on building design (overlay), it has been easy to sidetrack attention to the geometric implementation mechanism of building representations, not only in the analogue but also in the digital versions. This geometric fixation meant lack of progress in CAD and many misunderstandings in BIM.

To understand the true significance of geometric implementation mechanisms for the symbols in a building representation, consider the differences between alternative depictions of the same door in a floor plan (Figure 17). Despite differences between the graphic elements and their arrangement, they all carry the same information and are therefore equivalent and interchangeable. Many people reading the floor plan are unlikely to even notice such differences in notation, even in the same drawing, especially if the doors are not placed close to each other.

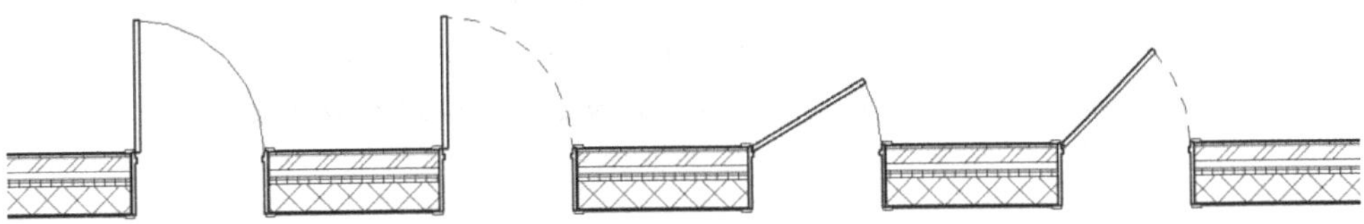

Figure 17. Alternative depictions of the same door

Using different door depictions for the same door type in the same drawing makes little sense. Differences in notation normally indicate different types of doors (Figure 18): they trigger comparisons that allow us to identify that there are different door types in the design and facilitate recognition of the precise differences between these types, so as to be able to judge the utility of each instance in the design. These differences are meaningful for understanding the depicted design, not accidental variations or stylistic preferences. In both Figure 17 and 18, we recognize doors but the differences in implementation mechanisms matter only in Figure 18, where they derive from the differences between the door types.

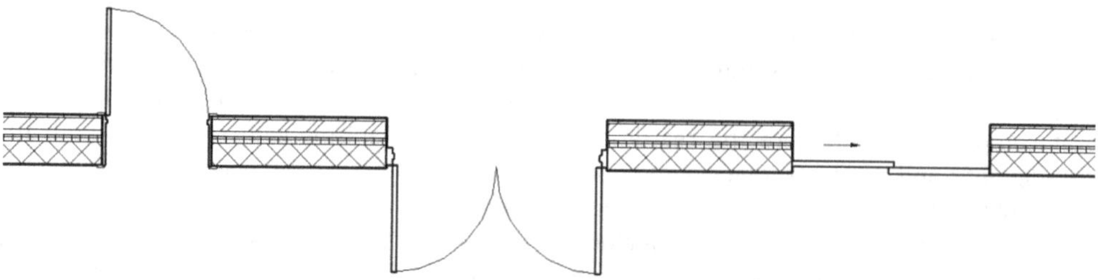

Figure 18. Alternative types of doors

In conclusion, one of the key advantages of symbolic representations is the preeminence of symbols and the attenuation of confusion between symbols and implementation mechanisms. In computerized texts, letters are not formed by handwritten strokes that produce the required appearance; the appearance of letters is added to the letter symbols through properties like font and size. Analogue building representations are similar to handwritten texts in that they may put too much emphasis on graphic elements because it is only through the interpretation of these that one can know e.g. the materials and layers that comprise a wall. In a symbolic representation, the materials and composition of the wall are explicit properties of an explicit symbol: we do not have to infer them from the graphics in a drawing. As these properties are described alphanumerically, symbolic representation removes ambiguity and makes visual displays like drawings just one of the possible views of building information.

Key Takeaways

- *Analogue building representations are pictorial and rely heavily on geometry*
- *Visual perception and recognition are essential for the success of pictorial representations*
- *The reliance of analogue building representations on geometry leads to overemphasis on implementation mechanisms like graphic elements, even in digital environments*

Exercises

1. Identify the building elements and components in Figure 6 and list the properties described graphically and geometrically in the drawing
2. List and explain the differences between the above and what appears in Figure 7 and Figure 8

Notes

1. There are many treatises on building drawings, their history, significance and relation to geometry. The summary presented here draws in particular from: Cosgrove, D., 2003. Ptolemy and Vitruvius: spatial representation in the sixteenth-century texts and commentaries. A. Picon & A. Ponte (eds) *Architecture and the sciences: exchanging metaphors.* Princeton NJ: Princeton University Press; Evans, R., 1995. *The Projective Cast: Architecture and Its Three Geometries.* Cambridge MA: MIT Press; Goodman, N., 1976. *Languages of art; an approach to a theory of symbols* (2nd ed.). Indianapolis IN: Hackett.
2. The significance of points of maximum curvature, corners and other critical parts of an image is described among others in: Attneave, F., 1959. *Applications of information theory to psychology; a summary of basic concepts, methods, and results.* New York: Holt; Kanizsa, G., 1979. *Organization in vision: essays on Gestalt perception.* New York: Praeger.
3. The algorithmically and conceptually elegant recognition of scenes with trihedral objects was finalized in: Waltz, D., 1975. Understanding line drawings of scenes with shadows. P.H. Winston (ed) *The psychology of computer vision.* New York: McGraw-Hill.

CHAPTER 5

Building representation in BIM

This chapter approaches BIM as a symbolic building representation and explains its key differences from analogue representations and their facsimiles in CAD. It analyses how a model is built out of symbols that may have an uneasy correspondence with real-world objects and how abstraction applies to these symbols. It concludes with a view of models as graphs that reveals what is still missing in BIM.

SYMBOLS AND RELATIONS IN BIM

BIM is the first generation of truly symbolic digital building representations.[1] CAD also used discrete symbols but these referred to implementation mechanisms: the geometric primitives that comprised a symbol in analogue representations. In BIM, the symbols explicitly describe discrete building elements or spaces — not their drawings. BIM symbols usually come in "libraries" of elements, i.e. predefined symbols of various types. The types can be specific, such as windows of a particular kind by a certain manufacturer or abstract, e.g. single-hung sash windows, or even just generic windows. The hierarchical relations between types enable specificity and abstraction in the representation, e.g. deferring the choice of a precise window type to a later design stage, without missing information that is essential for the present stage, as all currently relevant properties of the window, e.g. its size and position, exist in a generic window symbol.

Entering an instance of a symbol in a model normally follows the next procedure:

- The user selects the symbol type from a library menu or palette
- The user positions and dimensions the instance in a geometric view like a floor plan, usually interactively by:
    - Clicking on an insertion point for the location of the instance, e.g. on the part of a wall where a window should be
    - Clicking on other points to indicate the window width and height relative to the insertion point (this only if the window does not have a fixed size)

Modifications of the instance are performed in three complementary ways:

- Changes of essential properties such as the materials of a component amount to change of type. This is done by selecting a different symbol type from the library menu or palette and linking it to the instance.
- Changes in the geometry of an instance involve either repositioning the reference points or numerically changing the relevant values in any of the ways allowed by the program interface: in dialogue boxes that pop up by right-clicking on the instance, in properties palettes, through dimension lines or schedules.
- Changes in additional properties that do not conflict with the type, e.g. the occupancy of a space or the stage where a wall should be demolished, are entered through similar facilities in the interface, like a properties palette. Some of these properties are built in the symbols, while others can be defined by the user.

BIM symbols make all properties explicit, whether geometric or alphanumeric. The materials of a building element are not inferred from its graphic appearance but are clearly stated among its properties, indicated either specifically or abstractly, e.g. "oak" or "wood". Most properties in an instance are inherited from the type. This concerns not just materials but also any fixed dimensions: each wall type typically has a fixed cross section. This ensures consistency in the representation by keeping all similar elements and components truly similar in all critical respects. Consistency is essential for many tasks, such as cost estimation or procurement.

Many of the relations between symbols are present in BIM, even if they are not always obvious or directly accessible. Openings like doors and windows, for example, are hosted by a wall. They are normally entered in a model after the wall has been placed and in strict connection to it: moving a window out of the hosting wall is not allowed. Connected walls may also have a specific relation, e.g. co-termination: if one is moved, the others follow suit, staying connected in the same manner. Similarly, spaces know their bounding elements (which also precede them in the representation) and if any of these is modified, they automatically adapt themselves. Through such relations, many links between symbols are hidden in BIM. A door schedule, for example, (Figure 1) reveals that, in addition to its hosting wall, a door knows which two spaces it connects (or separates when closed).

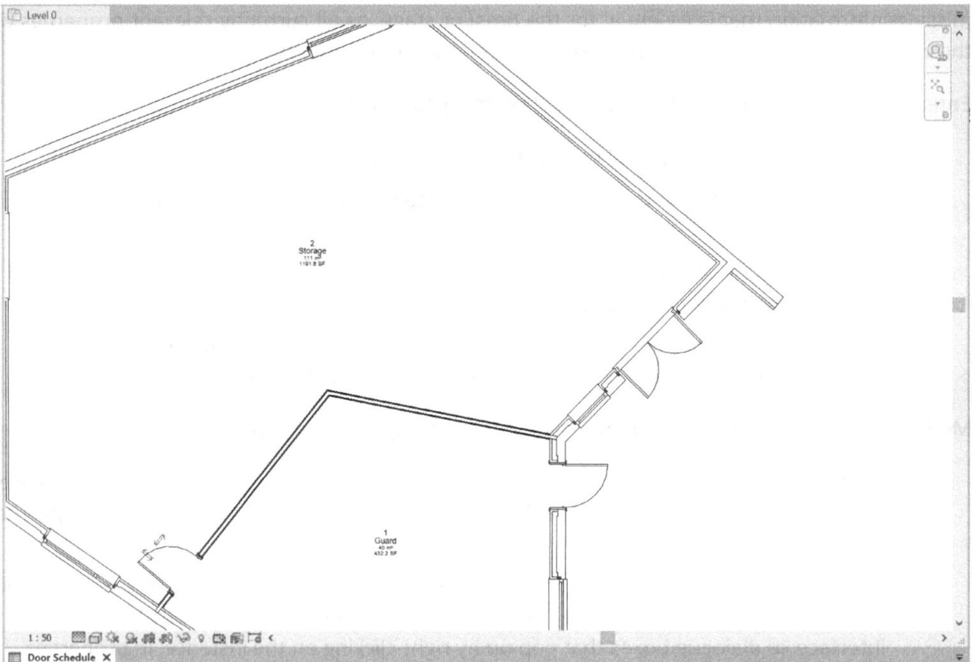

<Door Schedule>

A	B	C	D	E	F	G	H	I	J
Family	Family and Type	Operation	Level	Height	Width	From Room: Name	From Room: Area	To Room: Name	To Room: Area
Doors_ExtDbl_Flush	Doors_ExtDbl_Flush: 1810x2110mm	DoubleDoorSingleSwing	Level 0	2110	1810			Storage	111 m²
Doors_IntSgl	Doors_IntSgl: 1010x2110mm	SingleSwingRight	Level 0	2110	1010	Guard	40 m²	Storage	111 m²
Doors_IntSgl	Doors_IntSgl: 1010x2110mm	SingleSwingRight	Level 0	2110	1010	Guard	40 m²		

Figure 1. A door schedule in BIM reveals that each door is aware of the spaces it connects

Quite important is the explicit symbolic representation of both the 'solids' out of which a building is constructed (building elements like walls, floors, doors and windows) and the 'voids' of the building (the spaces bounded by the building elements). In analogue representations, the spaces are normally implicit, i.e. inferred by the reader. Having them explicit in BIM means that we can manipulate them directly and, quite significantly from the perspective of this book, attach to them information that cannot be linked to building elements. Similarly to specifying that a window is made of sustainable wood, one can specify that a space is intended for a particular use, e.g. "office" or for specific activities like "small group meeting" or "CEO's meeting room". Such characterizations relate to various requirements (usually found in the brief), such as floor area and performance specifications, e.g. acoustics or daylighting, which can also be attached to the space and used to guide and evaluate the design. Making spaces explicit in the representation therefore allows for full integration of building information in BIM and, through that, higher specificity and certainty. Spaces, after all, are the main reason and purpose of buildings, and most aspects are judged by how well spaces accommodate user activities.

BIM SYMBOLS AND THINGS

BIM has many advantages but, in common with other symbolic representations, also several ambiguities. One of the most important concerns the correspondence between symbols and real-world things. Building representations in BIM are truly symbolic, comprising discrete symbols. Unfortunately, the structure of building elements often introduces fuzziness in the definition of these symbols. In general, there are two categories of 'solids' in buildings. The first is building elements that are adequately represented by discrete symbols. Doors and windows, for example, are normally complete assemblies that are accommodated in a hole in a wall. Walls, on the other hand, are typical representatives of the second category: conceptual entities that are difficult to handle in three respects. Firstly, walls tend to consist of multiple layers of brickwork, insulation, plaster, paint and other materials. Some of these layers continue into other elements: the inner brick layer of an external wall may become the main layer of internal walls, forming a large, complex and continuous network that is locally incorporated in various walls (Figure 2).

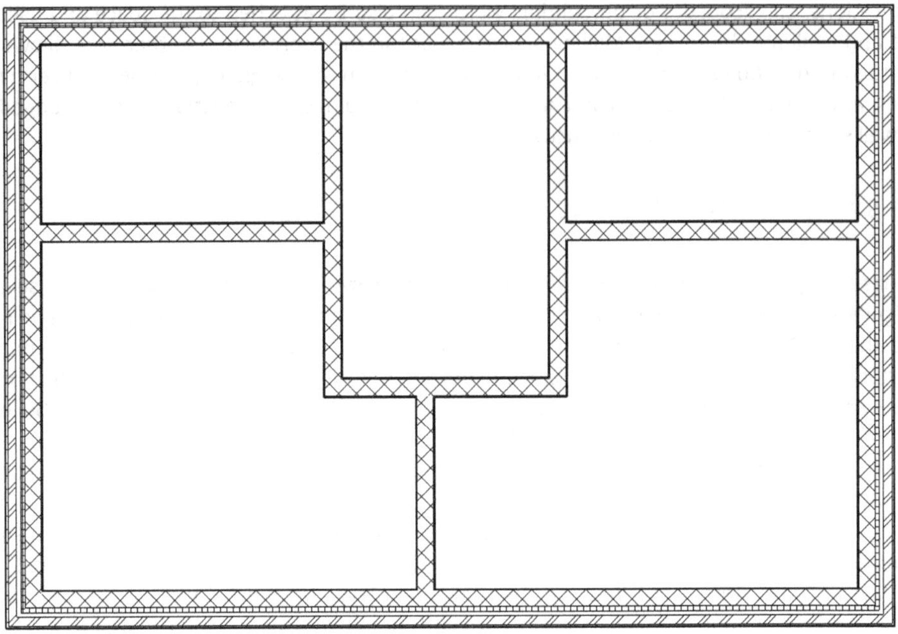

Figure 2. Continuous brick layer locally incorporated in two different kinds of wall

Secondly, BIM retains some of the geometric bias of earlier building representations, for example in the definition of elements like walls that have a fixed cross section but variable length or shape. When users have to enter the axis of a wall to describe this length or shape, they inevitably draw a geometric shape. BIM usually defines symbols on the basis of the most fundamental primitives in this shape. Even if one uses e.g. a rectangle to describe the axis, the result is four interconnected yet distinct walls, each corresponding to a side of the rectangle. Similarly, a wall with a complex shape but conceptually and practically unmistakably a single, continuous structure, may be analysed into several walls, each corresponding to a line segment of its axis (Figure 3).

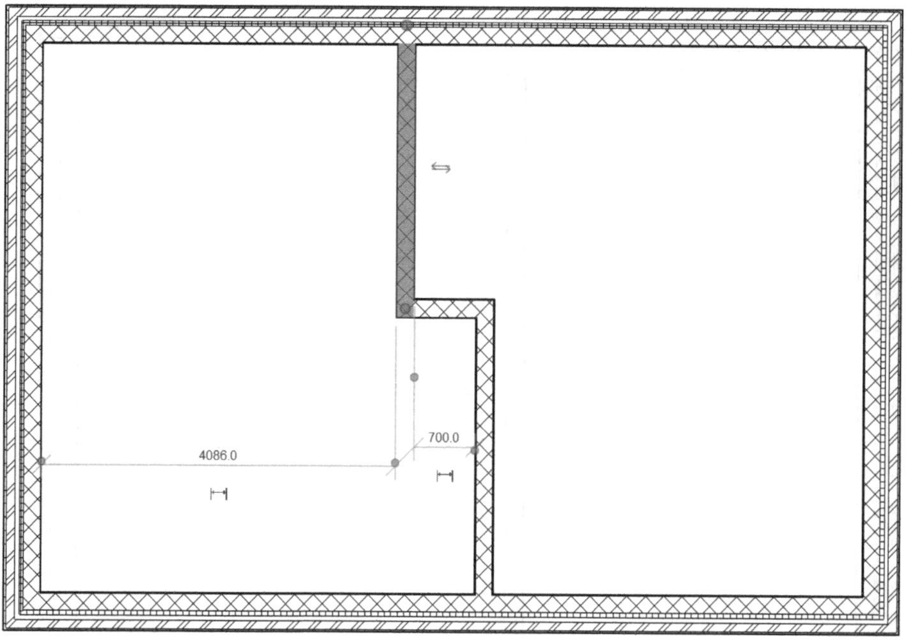

Figure 3. The internal wall is a single, continuous structure but in BIM each segment may be represented as a distinct wall

Thirdly, our own perception of elements like walls may get in the way. Standing on one side of a wall, we see only the portion of the wall that bounds the room we are in. Standing on the other side, we perceive not only a different face but possibly also a different part of the wall (Figure 4). As a result, when thinking from the perspective of either space, we refer to parts of the same entity as if they were different walls.

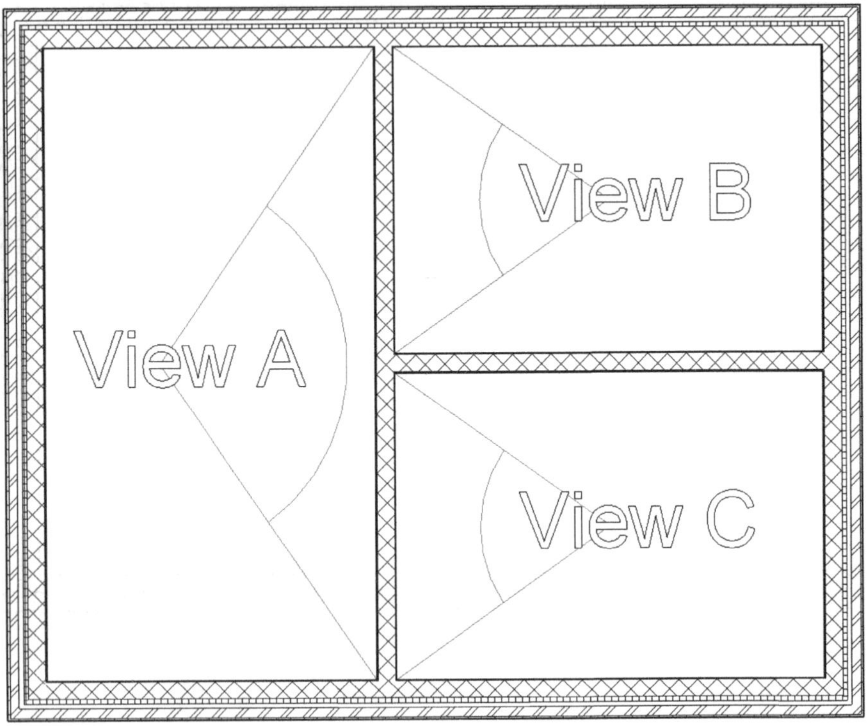

Figure 4. Three different views of the same wall

The inevitable conclusion is that some symbols in BIM may require further processing when considered with respect to particular goals. One may have to analyse a symbol into parts that are then combined with parts of other symbols, e.g. for scheduling the construction of the brick network in Figure 2. Other symbols must be grouped together by the user, for instance the internal wall in Figure 3. Such manipulations should not reduce the integrity of the symbols; it makes little sense to represent each layer of a wall separately. At the same time, one has to be both consistent and pragmatic in the geometric definition of building elements. In most cases, acceptance of the BIM preference for the simplest possible geometry is the least painful option: representing each of the two internal walls in Figure 4 as a single, separate entity is a compromise that accommodates all perspectives, including those indicated in the figure.

ABSTRACTION AND GROUPING IN BIM

BIM symbols cover a wide range of abstraction levels, from generic symbols like "internal wall" without any further specifications to highly detailed symbols, e.g. of a very specific wall type, including precise descriptions of materials from particular manufacturers. A building representation in BIM often starts with abstract symbols, which become progressively more specific, in parallel with the design or construction process. It is also possible to backtrack to a higher abstraction level rather than sidestep to a different type on the same level, e.g. when some conflict resolution leads to a dead end and one needs to reconsider their options. This typologic abstraction is one of the strong points of BIM but also something one has to treat with care because a model may contain symbols at various abstraction levels. Managing the connections between them, e.g. deciding on the interfacing between a highly specific window and an abstract wall, requires attention to detail. On the positive side, one can use such connections to guide decision making, e.g. restrict the choice of wall type to those that match the expectations from the window.

Symbolic representations have considerable capacities for bottom-up grouping on the basis of explicit relations between symbols, ranging from similarity (e.g. all vowels in a text) to proximity (all letters in a word). As is typical of digital symbolic representations, BIM allows for various groupings of symbols, e.g. the set of all instances of the same door type in a design, all spaces with a particular use on the second floor or the parts of a design that belong to the north wing. For the latter, some additional user input may be required, such as a shape that represents the outline of the north wing or the labelling of every symbol with an additional wing property. No user input is required for relations built into the behavioural constraints of a symbol, e.g. the hosting of openings in walls.

Through the combination of standard symbol features (like their properties) and ad hoc, user-defined criteria (like the outline of a wing), one can process the representation at any relevant abstraction level and from multiple perspectives, always in direct reference to specific symbols. For example, it is possible to consider a specific beam in the context of its local function and connections to other elements but simultaneously with respect to the whole load-bearing structure in a single floor or the whole building. Any decision taken locally, specifically for this beam, relates transparently to either the instance or the type and may therefore lead not only to changes in the particular beam but also reconsideration of the beam types comprising the structure, e.g. a change of type for all similar beams. Reversely, any decision concerning the general type of the structure can be directly and automatically propagated to all of its members and their arrangement.

The automatic propagation of decisions relates to parametric modelling: the interconnection of symbol properties so that any modification to one symbol causes others to adapt accordingly (see Appendix II). In addition to what is built into the relations between types and instances or in behaviours like hosting, one can explicitly link instance properties, e.g. make several walls remain parallel to each other or vertical to another wall. One can also specify that the length of several walls is the same or a multiple of an explicitly defined parameter. Changing the value of the parameter leads to automatic modification of the length of all related walls. Parametric design holds significant promise. People have envisaged building representations in which it suffices to change a few values to produce a completely new design. However, establishing and maintaining the constraint propagation networks necessary for doing so in a reliable manner remains a major challenge. For the moment, parametric modelling is a clever way of grouping symbols with explicit reference to a relation underlying the grouping, e.g. parallelism of walls. Still, even in such simple cases, the effects of parametric relations in combination with built-in behaviours can lead to unpredictable or undesirable results.

In views that replicate conventional drawings, BIM software often also incorporates visual abstraction that mimics that of scales in analogue representations. By selecting e.g. "1:20" and "fine" one can make the visual display of a floor plan more detailed than with "1:200" and "coarse" (Figure 5). Such settings are useful only for visual inspection; they alter only the appearance of symbols, not their type or structure.

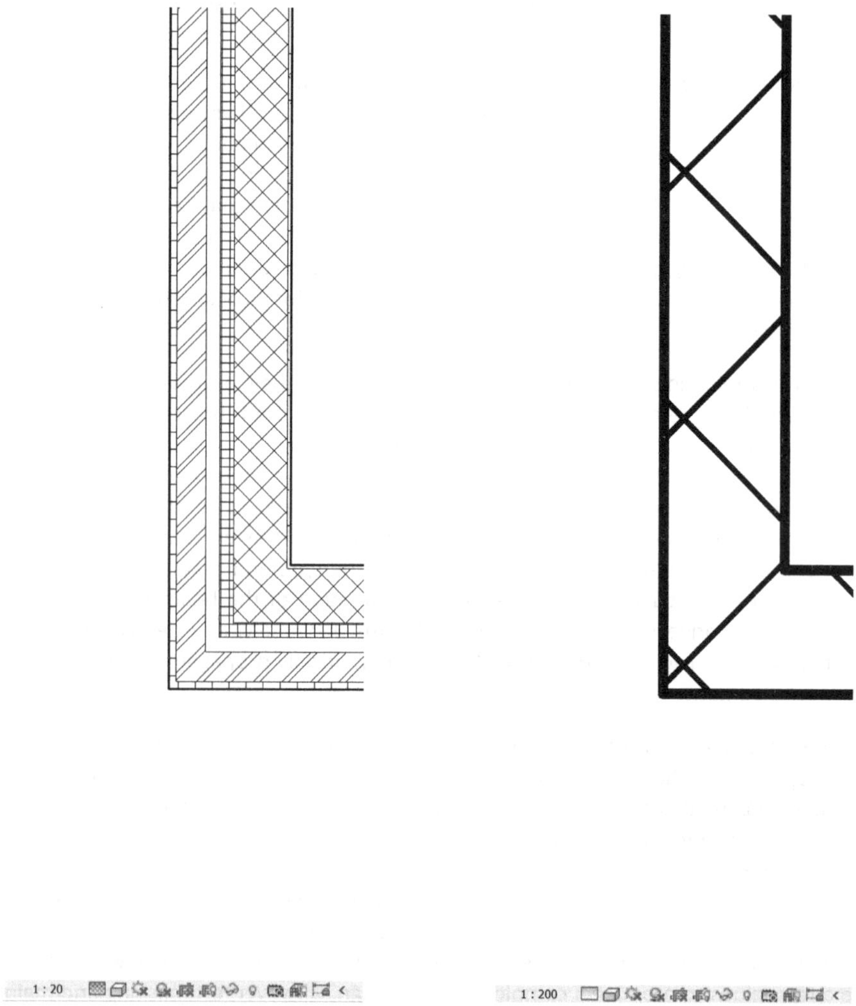

Figure 5. Display of the same wall in a BIM floor plan, under settings 1:20 and fine (left), and 1:200 and coarse (right)

The LoD (standard on the specificity of information in a model) is also related to abstraction. Adherence to LoD standards in a representation is a throwback to analogue standards regarding drawing scale and stage, which runs contrary to the integration and compression of stages advocated by BIM theory. LoD standardization often fails to appreciate that information in a model has a reason and a purpose: some people have taken decisions concerning some part or aspect of a design. The specificity of these decisions and of the resulting representations is not accidental or conventional. Rather, it reflects what is needed for that part or aspect at the particular stage of a project. The LoD of the model that accommodates this information can only be variable, as not all parts or aspects receive the same attention at any stage.

Specificity should therefore be driven by the need for information rather than by convention. If information in a representation is at a higher specificity level, one should not discard it but simply abstract in a meaningful way by focusing on relevant properties, relations or symbols. A useful analogy is with how human vision works: in your peripheral vision, you perceive vague forms and movement, e.g. something approaching you rapidly. If you turn your eyes and pay attention to these forms, you can see their details and recognize e.g. a friend rushing to meet you. As soon as you focus on these forms, other parts of what you perceive become vague and schematic. In other words, the world is as detailed as it is; your visual system is what makes some of its parts more abstract or specific, depending on your needs. By the same token, the specificity of a building representation should be as high as the available information allows. Our need for information determines the abstraction level at which we consider the representation, as well as actions by which we can increase the specificity of some of its parts.

IMPLEMENTATION MECHANISMS IN BIM

Despite its symbolic structure, BIM appears to use the same implementation mechanisms as CAD: the same geometric primitives that reproduce the graphic, isomorphic appearance of analogue representations. The key difference is that these primitives are just part of pictorial views, in which they express certain symbol properties. The type of a door, for example, is explicitly named, so that we do not have to infer its swing from the arc used to represent it in a floor plan; the width of a wall is a numerical property of its symbol, so that we do not have to measure the distance between the two lines indicating the outer faces of the wall. On the contrary, this distance is determined by the width property of the symbol. These and other properties are explicit in the model database, making the Unicode symbols in it and their bits and bytes the true implementation mechanisms of BIM. Unfortunately, as this database remains largely hidden from view, users may fail to appreciate its significance.

The above covers the paradigmatic dimension, allowing us to consider any graphic primitive in a drawing view a mere product of real symbols. As we have seen, however, implementation mechanisms used in the syntagmatic dimension still influence the structure of a building representation in other respects: a wall is still partly determined by drawing its axis and so by the geometric shape one draws, as well as by dependencies between this shape to others in the model or view. On the whole, therefore, one should consider BIM largely immune to undue influences from graphic implementation mechanisms but at the same time remain aware of persistent geometric biases both in how BIM treats building representations and in the mindset of BIM users.

MODELS AS GRAPHS

Being symbolic representations, models in BIM can be described by graphs that express their structure in terms of symbols and their relations. These graphs are similar but not the same as the building, adjacency or access graphs discussed in a previous chapter: those are graphs that describe the design rather than the representation. In the graphs that describe a BIM model, symbols are usually represented by vertices and relations between symbols by edges (Figure 6 & 7). The edges often make explicit what is implicit in the model, for example, that each window or door is hosted by a particular wall and that walls connect to each other in a specific manner, e.g. co-terminate at the ends.

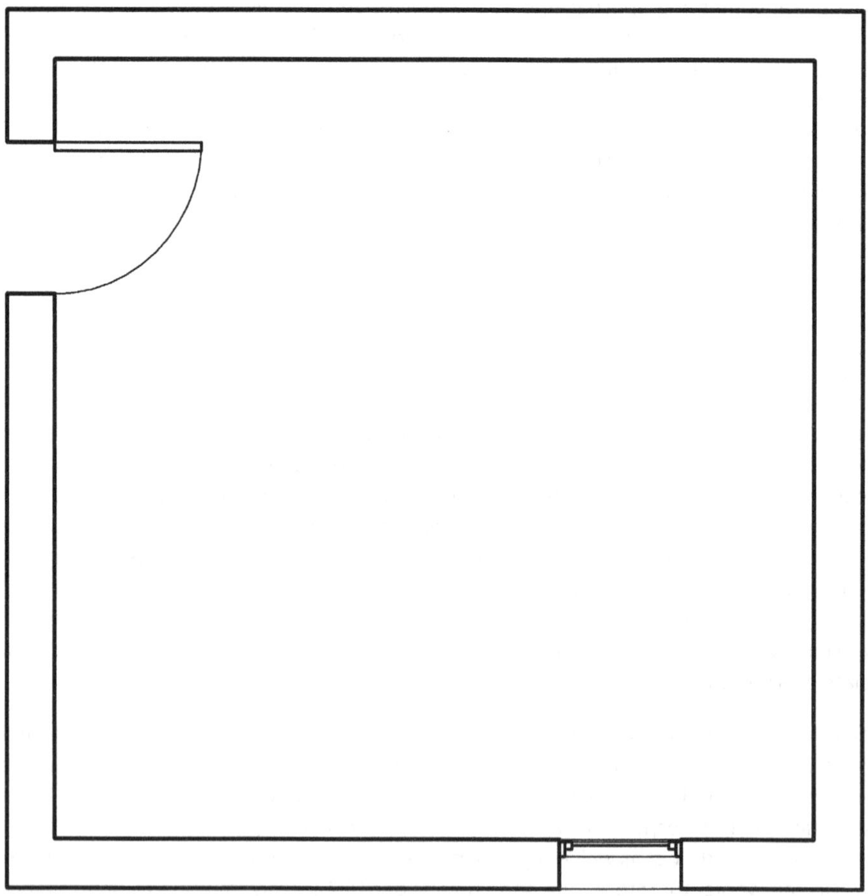

Figure 6. Floor plan of a model in BIM, comprising four walls, a door and a window

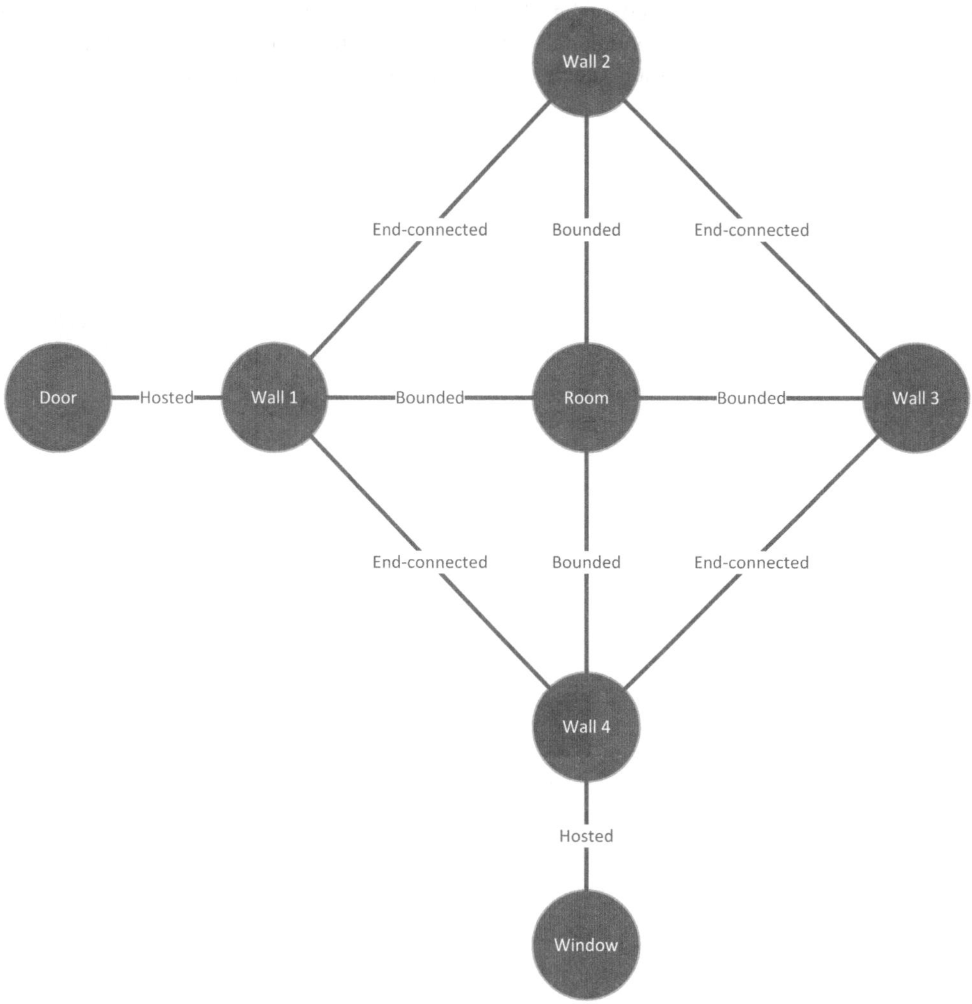

Figure 7. Graph of symbols in Figure 6

The graph summarizes the basic structure of the model: the entities it comprises and their basic relations, including dependencies, e.g. between the shape and size of the room and the configuration of walls that bound it. These relations and their constraints underlie many behaviours in BIM, for example, that doors and windows tend to stick to the hosting walls and that walls try to retain their end-connections.

From an information perspective, this becomes even more interesting if we zoom in on the properties of the symbols and see how they are affected by relations and constraints, as in the case of a window and the wall that hosts it (Figure 8). Both elements are represented by discrete symbols, each with its own set of properties. The hosting relation means that some of the properties of the wall are inherited by the window. For example, the orientation of the window is by definition the same as the orientation of the wall. This constrains the behaviour of the window symbol when the user positions it in the model or modifies either the window or the wall.

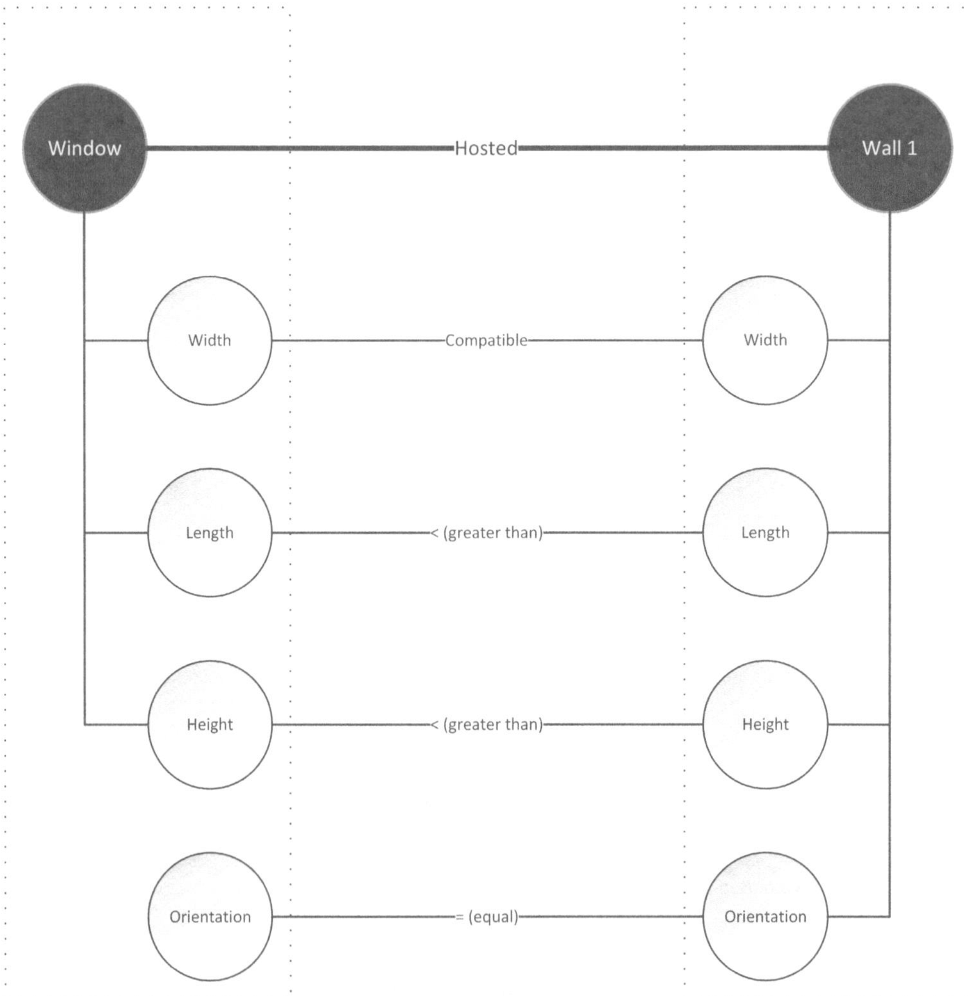

Figure 8. Graph of a window and the wall that hosts it in a model

Describing such dependencies is especially important for relations that may be missing from the orthographic views and modelling workflows of BIM software, for example between walls and floors (Figure 9). The vertical dimensions of walls are usually determined by a combination of wall symbol properties and constraints, model setup (levels) and the presence of symbols like floors to which the top or base of a wall can attach. Users have to manipulate the wall and floor dimensions and relations in multiple views, which can be summarized in this rather simple graph that affords the overview necessary for IM.

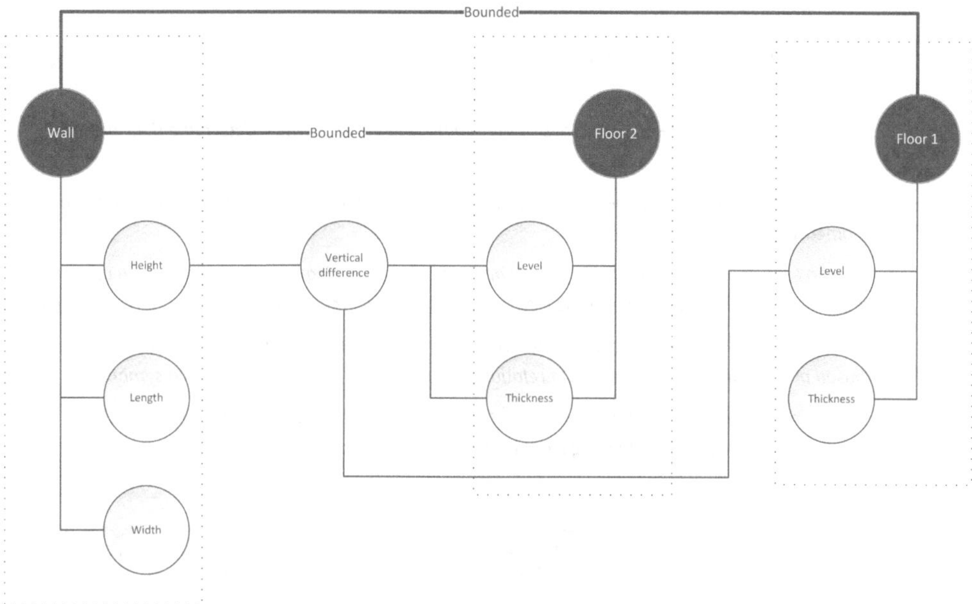

Figure 9. Graph of a wall and its relations to floors

Such graphs also reveal other relations that determine the compatibility of symbols in a relation (a type of parameterization that remains neglected). Wall and window width, for example, must be such that there is a technical solution for inserting the wall in the window: the width of a wall constraints the acceptability of window types. The same applies to length and height: assuming that the window comes in a standard size, the wall should be longer and higher (or at least equal) in order to accommodate it. The example seems trivial but dimensional incompatibilities of this kind are common in walls that combine multiple openings and different components.

Understanding the building representation in terms of symbols, relations and constraints is key to both parameterization and decision making. Therefore, it becomes a main task for IM. In addition to using graphs to describe the structure of a model, the model should be set up in a way that transparently expresses all dependencies and safeguards them effectively and consistently in all workflows. This concerns relations between symbols in the representation, as well as with external constraints, such as planning regulations, building codes and briefs. For example, modellers should make explicit the maximum height allowed by the planning regulations for a particular design and connect it to the relevant symbols and properties, e.g. the position of the roof. By doing this at the onset of a design project, they ensure that designers are aware of the constraints within which they work, e.g. that they are not allowed to place roofs or other elements higher than permitted. As will be discussed in following chapters, such *feedforward* that guides design is preferable to *feedback*, i.e. allowing designers to generate solutions that are then tested according to regulations they may have not taken into account.

Key Takeaways

- *BIM is a truly symbolic building representation that employs discrete symbols to describe building elements and spaces*
- *Symbols in BIM integrate all properties of the symbolized entities, which determine their pictorial appearance*
- *BIM symbols are largely independent of graphic implementation mechanisms and immune to most geometric biases*
- *The correspondence between BIM symbols and some building elements is problematic in certain respects due to the structure of these elements, persisting geometric biases and human perception*
- *Abstraction in BIM is both typological (as symbols are at various abstraction levels) and mnemonic (based on similarity of properties and relations like proximity and hosting between symbols)*
- *Models in BIM can be described by graphs of symbols and relations; these graphs afford the overview and transparency missing from BIM software interfaces*

Exercises

1. In a BIM editor of your choice (e.g. Revit), make an inventory of all wall types (*Families* in Revit) in the supplied library. Classify these types in terms of abstraction, clearly specifying your criteria.
2. In a BIM editor of your choice, make a simple design of a space with four walls and two floors around it. Identify properties of the building elements and space symbols that connect them (e.g. dimensions) and overlapping properties (e.g. space properties that refer to finishings of the building elements).
    1. Make schedules and graphs that illustrate your findings.
    2. Compare the schedules and graphs.
3. Expand your design with another space and a door that connects them. Make a schedule and a graph that illustrate the key relations between the spaces.
4. In the expanded design, describe step by step how a change in the size of one room is propagated to other symbols in the model.

Notes

1. A comprehensive general introduction to BIM is: Eastman, C., Teicholz, P.M., Sacks, R., & Lee, G., 2018. *BIM*

handbook (3rd ed.). Hoboken NJ: Wiley.

PART III

INFORMATION

The previous parts have presented the tandem of digitization and information, and explained the structure of representations, in particular of the symbolic ones that populate digital environments. Now we move to the content of these representations: the data and information they accommodate. The combination of structure and content is the foundation of building information management. It sounds straightforward but is plagued by inadequate definitions and outdated approaches that keep information management vague, labour-intensive and inefficient. Consequently, the main goal of this part is to separate the wheat from the chaff and establish principles for effective, operational approaches to building information.

CHAPTER 6

Data and information

What constitutes data and information is a fundamental question that attracts much interest and invites numerous definitions. This chapter introduces definitions suitable to the symbolic representations discussed in the previous part, towards a transparent basis for information management.

THEORIES AND DEFINITIONS

There is nothing more practical than a good theory: it supplies the definitions people need in order to agree what to do, how and why; it explains the world, providing new perspectives from which we can view and understand it; it establishes targets for researchers keen to improve or refute the theory and so advance science and knowledge. In our case, there is a clear need for good, transparent and operational definitions. Terms like 'information' and 'data' are used too loosely, interchangeably and variably to remove ambiguities in information processing and management. Management, computing and related disciplines abound with rather too easy, relational definitions of data, information, knowledge, strategy etc., e.g. that data interpreted become information, information understood turns into knowledge and so forth. Such definitions tend to underestimate the complexity of cognitive processes and are therefore not to be trusted. Even methodically sound studies, involving large numbers of leading scholars, can do little to elucidate the meaning and usage of these terms.[1] Arguably, asking for succinct, all-encompassing definitions abstracts the context from which the definitions derive and renders them too axiomatic or too vague.

A theory that resolves these problems cannot draw from the AECO domains only. It needs a firm foundation in general theories of information, especially those that take the potential and peculiarities of digital means into account. Thankfully, there are enough candidates for this.

SYNTACTIC, SEMANTIC AND PRAGMATIC THEORIES

When one thinks of information theory in a computing context, Shannon's MTC springs to mind.[2] The MTC is indeed foundational and preeminent among formal theories of information. It addresses what has been visualized as the innermost circle in information theory (Figure 1):[3] the syntactic core of information, dealing with the structure and basic, essential aspects of information, including matters of probability, transmission flows and capacities of communication facilities — the subjects of the technical side of information theory.

The outermost circle in the same visualization is occupied by pragmatics: real-life usage of meaningful information. IM theories (discussed in the next chapter) populate this circle, providing a general operational framework for supporting and controlling information quality and flow. To apply this framework, one requires pragmatic constraints and priorities from application areas. For example, a notary and a facility manager have different interests with regard to the same building information.

Between the syntactic and the pragmatic lies the intermediate circle of semantics, which deals with how meaning is added to the syntactical components of information before they are utilized in real life. As syntactic approaches are of limited help with the content of information and its interpretation, establishing a basis for IM requires that we turn to semantic theories of information.

Arguably the most appealing of these is by Luciano Floridi, who is credited with establishing the subject of philosophy of information. The value of his theory goes beyond his position as a modern authority on the subject. The central role of semantics in his work is an essential contribution to the development of much-needed theoretical principles in a world inundated with rapidly changing digital technologies. In our case, it promises a clear and coherent basis for understanding AECO information and establishing parsimonious structures that link different kinds of information and data. These structures simplify IM in a meaningful and relevant manner: they allow us to shift attention from *how* one should manage information (the technical and operational sides) to *which* information and *why*.

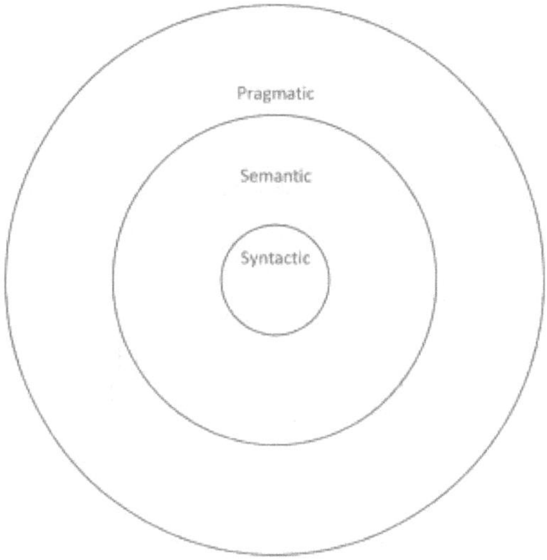

Figure 1. A classification of information theories

In this book, we focus on data, information and their relation in the operational context of digital building representations. Utilization of information and resulting benefits for individuals, enterprises, disciplines or societies are subjects that require extensive analyses well beyond the scope of the present book. Information certainly contributes to achieving these benefits; in many cases it may even be a prerequisite but seldom suffices by itself. Rather than making unfounded claims about knowledge and performance, we focus on more modest goals concerning IM: understanding building information, its quality and flows, and organizing them in ways that may help AECO take informed decisions, in the hope that informed also means better.

A SEMANTIC THEORY FOR BUILDING INFORMATION

DATA AND INFORMATION INSTANCES

A fundamental definition in Floridi's theory[4] concerns the relation between data and information: an instance of information consists of one or more data which are well-formed and meaningful. Data are defined as lacks of uniformity in what we perceive at a given moment or between different states of a percept or between two symbols in a percept. For example, if a coffee stain appears on a floor plan drawing on paper (Figure 3), this is certainly a lack of uniformity with the previous, pristine state of the drawing (Figure 2) but it is neither well-formed nor meaningful within the context of architectural representations. It tells us nothing about the representation or the represented design, except that someone has been rather careless with the drawing (the physical carrier of the representation).

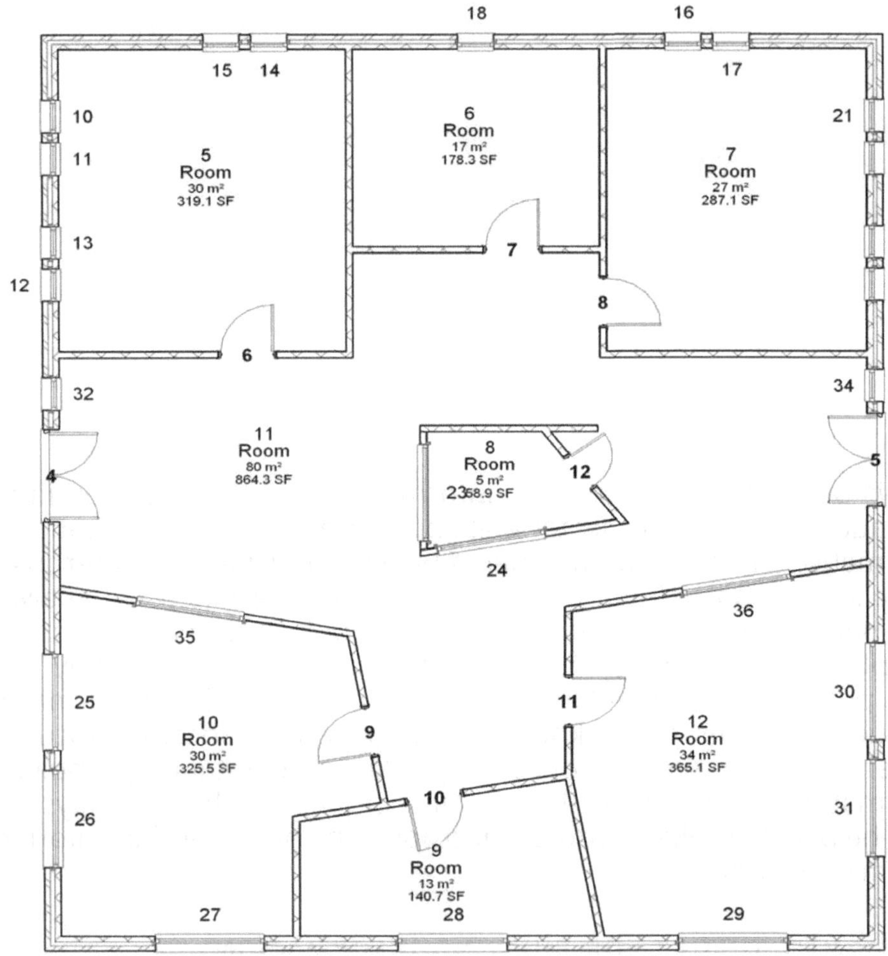

Figure 2. Floor plan

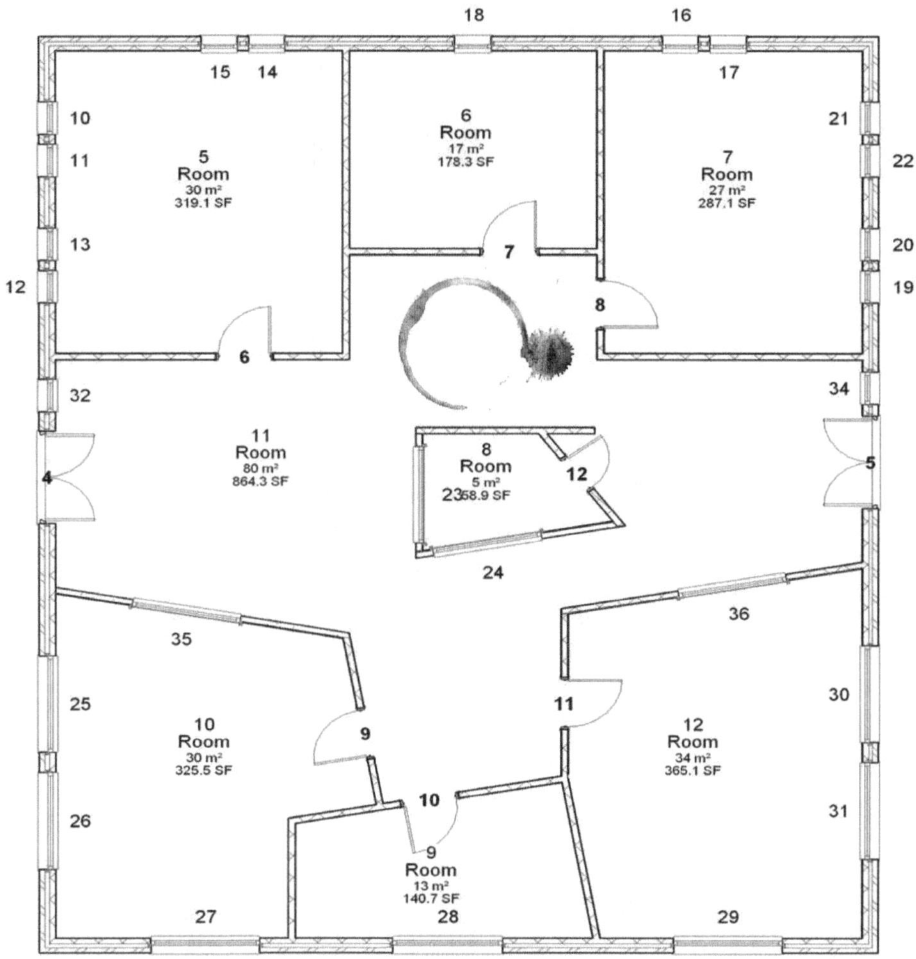

Figure 3. A new state of the floor plan: the coffee stain is neither well-formed nor meaningful in the framework of a line drawing

On the other hand, if the lack of uniformity between the two states is a new straight line segment across a room in a floor plan (Figure 4), this is both well-formed (as a line in a line drawing) and meaningful (indicating a change in the design, possibly that the room has now a split-level floor).

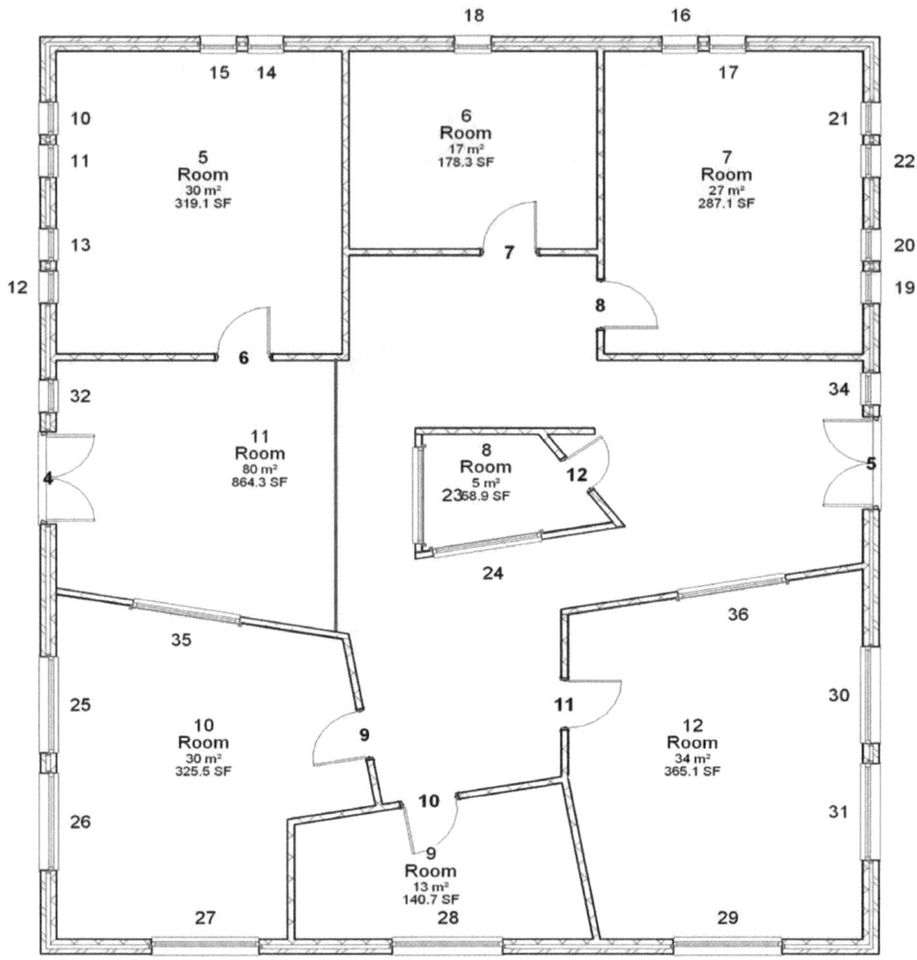

Figure 4. A different new state of the floor plan: the line segment is both well-formed and meaningful

DATA AND INFORMATION TYPES

The typology of data is a key component in Floridi's approach. Data can be:

- *Primary*, like the name and birth date of a person in a database, or the light emitted by an indicator lamp to show that a radio receiver is on.
- *Anti–data,*[5] i.e. the absence of primary data, like the failure of an indicator lamp to emit light or silence following having turned the radio on. Anti-data are informative: they tell us that e.g. the radio or the indicator lamp are defective.

- *Derivative:* data produced by other, typically primary data, which can therefore serve as indirect indications of the primary ones, such as a series of transactions with a particular credit card as an indication of the trail of its owner.
- *Operational*: data about the operations of the whole system, like a lamp that indicates whether other indicator lamps are malfunctioning.
- *Metadata*: indications about the nature of the information system, like the geographic coordinates that tell where a digital photograph has been taken.

These types also apply to information instances, depending on the type of data they contain: an information instance containing metadata is meta-information.

In the context of analogue building representations like floor plans (Figure 5), lines denoting building elements are primary data. They describe the shape of these elements, their position and the materials they comprise.

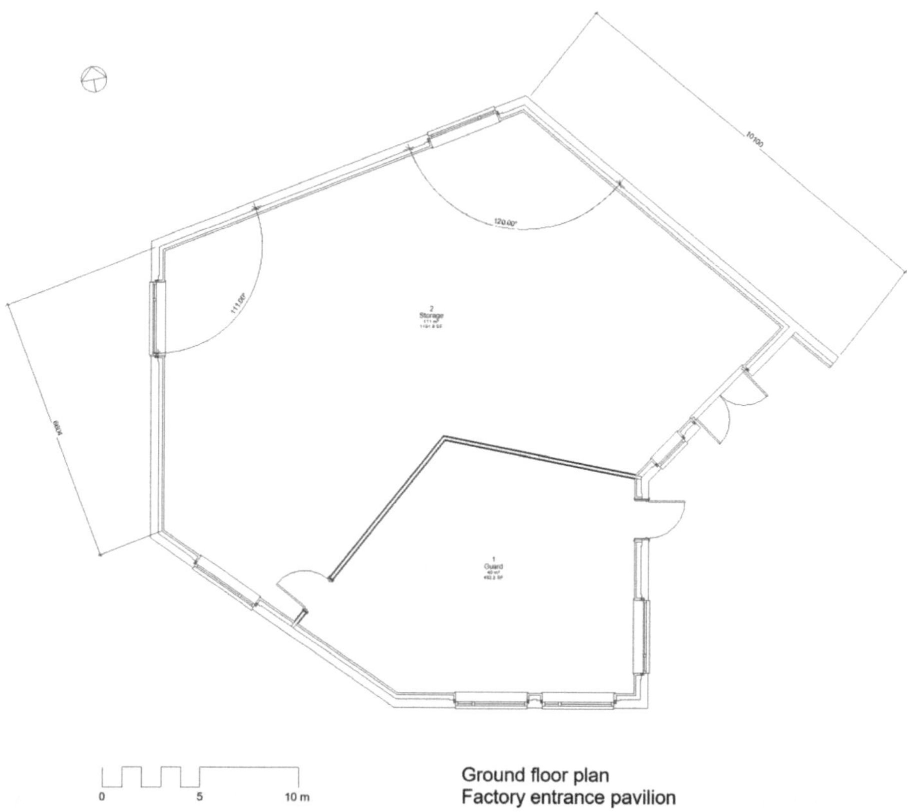

Figure 5. In an analogue floor plan, lines denoting building elements are primary data

In addition to geometric primary data, an analogue floor plan may contain alphanumeric primary data, such as labels indicating the function of a room or dimension lines (Figure 6). A basic principle in hand drawing is that such explicitly specified dimensions take precedence over measurements in the drawing because amending the dimensions is easier than having to redraw the building elements.

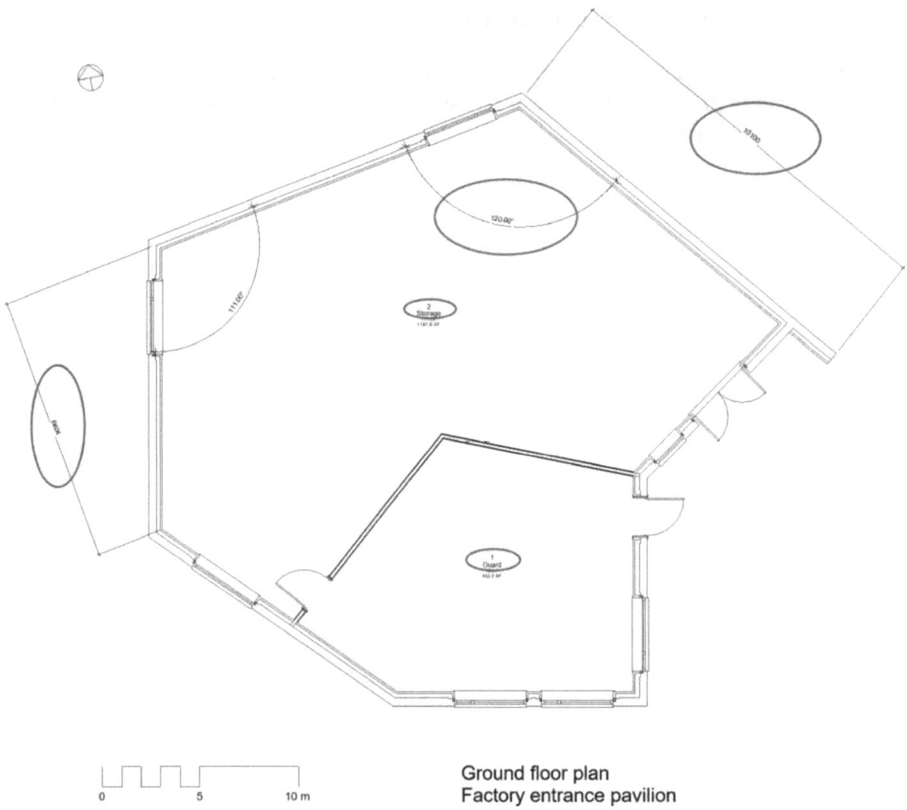

Figure 6. Alphanumeric primary data in an analogue floor plan

Anti-data are rather tricky to identify in the typically abstract and elliptical analogue building representations. Quite often it is hard to know if something is missing. One should therefore consider absence as anti-data chiefly when absence runs contrary to expectation and is therefore directly informative: a door missing from the perimeter of a room indicates either a design mistake or that the room is inaccessible (e.g. a shaft). Similarly, a missing room label indicates either that the room has no specific function or that the drawer has forgotten to include it in the floor plan (Figure 7).

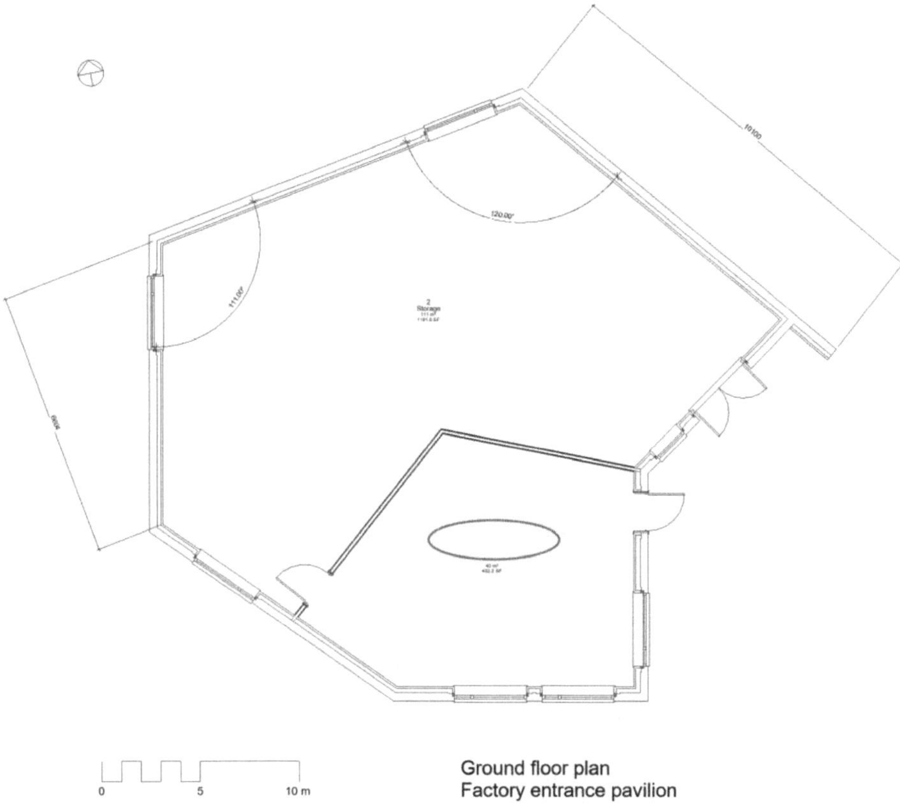

Figure 7. Anti-data in an analogue floor plan

Derivative data in building representations generally refer to the abundance of measurements, tables and other data produced from primary data in the representation, such as floor area labels in a floor plan (Figure 8). One can recognize derivative data from the fact that they can be omitted from the representation without reducing its completeness or specificity: derivative data like the area of a room can be easily reproduced when necessary from primary data (the room dimensions). An important point is that one should always keep in mind the conventions of analogue representations, like the precedence of dimension lines over measurement in the drawing, which turns the former into primary data.

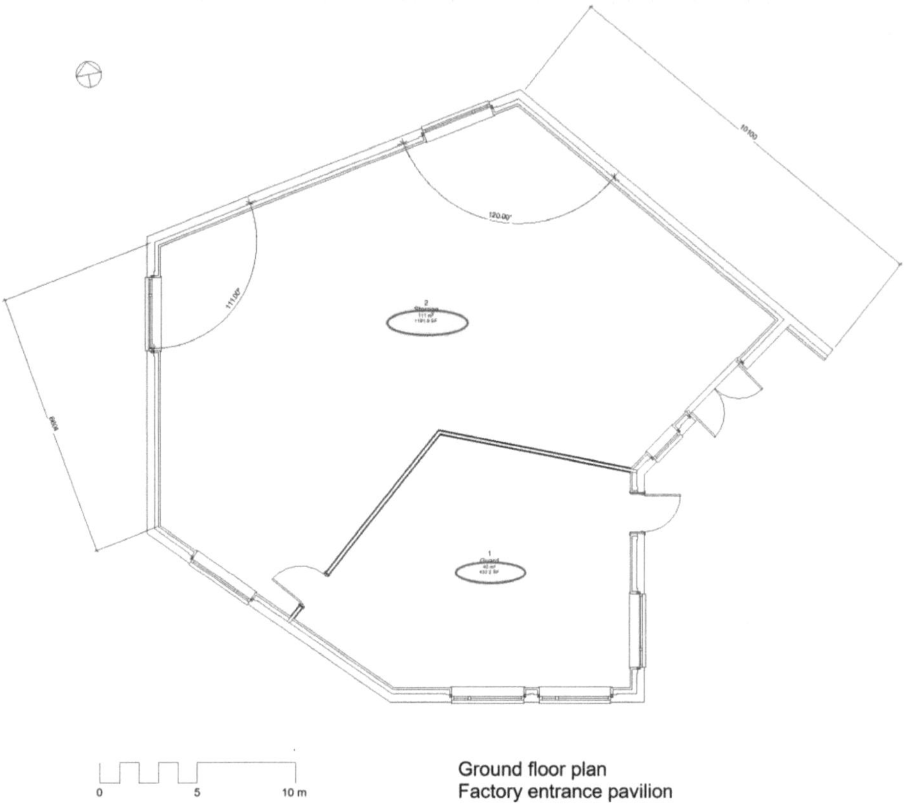

Figure 8. Derivative data in an analogue floor plan

Operational data reveal the structure of the building representation and explain how data should be interpreted. Examples include graphic scale bars and north arrows, which indicate respectively the true size of units measured in the representation and the true orientation of shapes in the design (Figure 9).

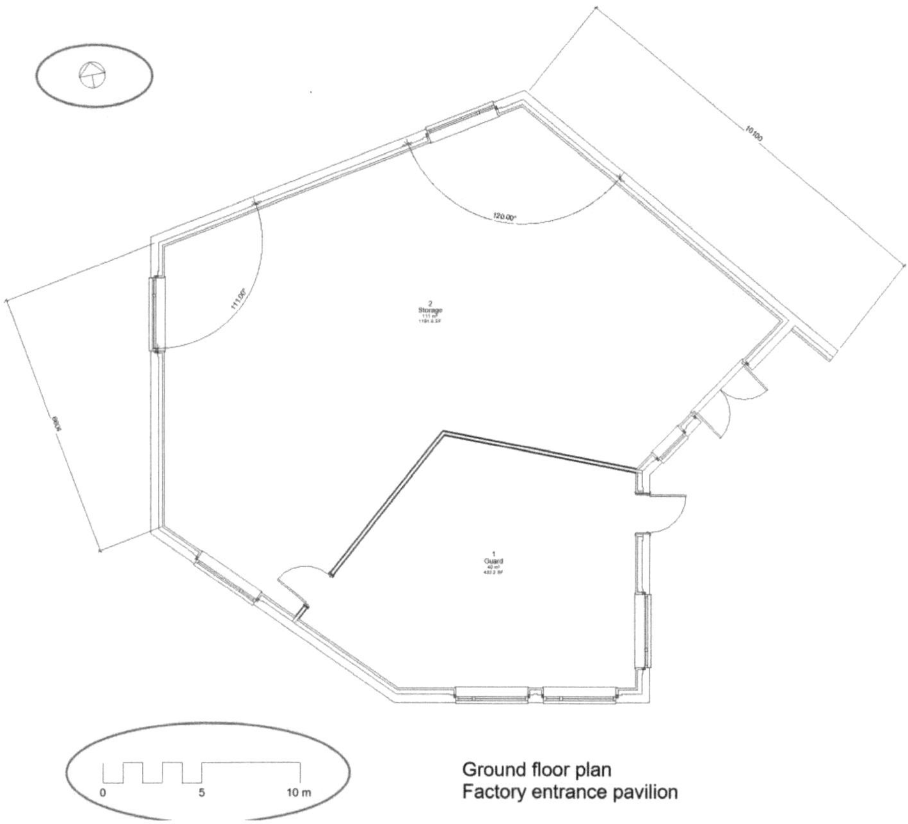

Figure 9. Operational data in an analogue floor plan

Finally, metadata describe the nature of the representation, such as the projection type and the design project or building, e.g. labels like 'floor plan' (Figure 10).

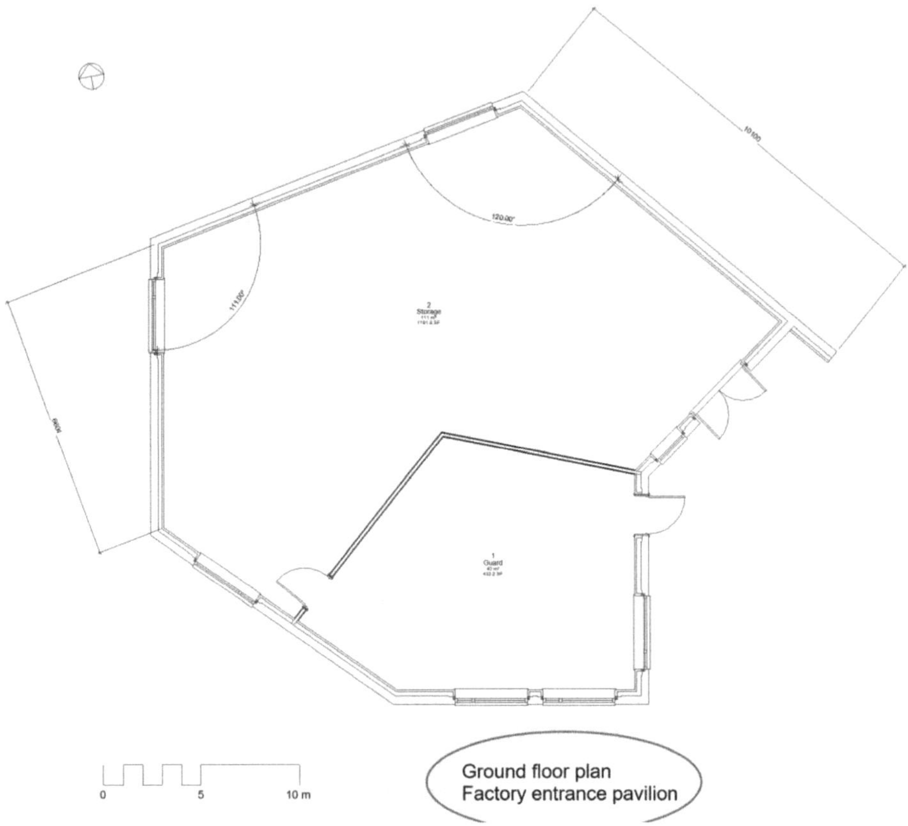

Figure 10. Metadata in an analogue floor plan

BIM, INFORMATION AND DATA

DATA TYPES IN BIM

As we have seen in previous chapters, computerization does not just reproduce analogue building representations. Digital representations may mimic their analogue counterparts in appearance but can be quite different in structure. This becomes evident when we examine the data types they contain. Looking at a BIM editor on a computer screen, one cannot help observing a striking shift in primary and derivative data (Figure 11 & 12): most graphic elements in views like floor plans are derived from properties of symbols. In contrast to analogue drawings, dimension lines and their values in BIM are derivative, pure annotations like floor area calculations in a space. This is understandable: the ease with which one can modify a digital representation renders analogue practices of refraining from applying changes to a drawing meaningless.

Less intuitive is that even the lines denoting the various materials of a building element are derivative, determined by the type of the symbol: if the type of a wall changes, then all these graphic elements change accordingly. In analogue representations the opposite applies: we infer the wall type from the graphic elements that describe it in terms of layers of materials and other components.

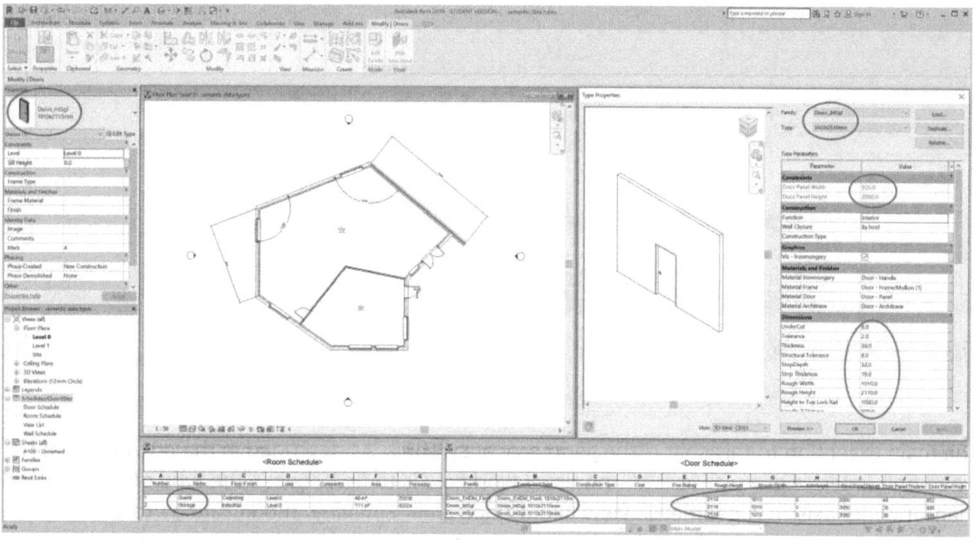

Figure 11. Primary data in BIM

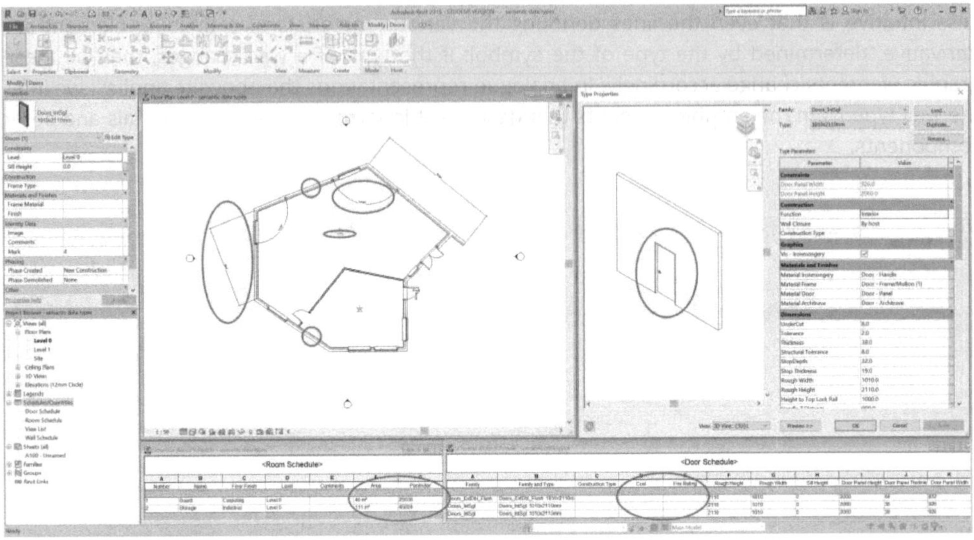

Figure 12. Derivative data in BIM

The main exception to this shift is the geometry of symbols. As described in the previous chapter, when one enters e.g. a wall in BIM, the usual workflow is to first choose the type of the wall and then draw its axis in a geometric view like a floor plan. Similarly, modifications to the location or shape of the wall are made by changing the same axis, while other properties, like layer composition and material properties of each layer, can only be changed in the definition of the wall type. One can also change the axis by typing new coordinates in some window but in most BIM editors the usual procedure is interactive modification of the drawn axis with a pointer device like a mouse. Consequently, primary data appear dispersed over a number of views and windows, including ones that chiefly contain derivative data.

One should not be confused by the possibilities offered by computer programs, especially for the modification of entities in a model. The interfaces of these programs are rich with facilities for interacting with shapes and values. It seems as if programmers have taken the trouble to allow users to utilize practically everything for this purpose. For example, one may be able to change the length of a wall by typing a new value for its dimension line, i.e. via derivative data. Such redundancy of entry points is highly prized in human-computer interaction but may be confusing for IM, as it tends to obscure the type of data and the location where each type can be found. To reduce confusion and hence the risk of mistakes and misunderstandings, one should consider the character of each view or window and how necessary it is for defining an entity in a model. A schedule, for example, is chiefly meant for displaying derivative data, such as area or volume calculations, but may also contain primary data for reasons of overview, transparency or legibility. Most schedules are not necessary for entering entities in a model, in contrast to a window containing the properties of a symbol, from where one chooses the type of the entity to be entered. In managing the primary data of a symbol one should therefore focus on the property window and its contents.

Computer interfaces also include more operational data, through which users can interact with the software. Part of this interaction concerns how other data are processed, including in terms of appearance, as with the scale and resolution settings in drawing views mentioned in the previous chapter (Figure 13).

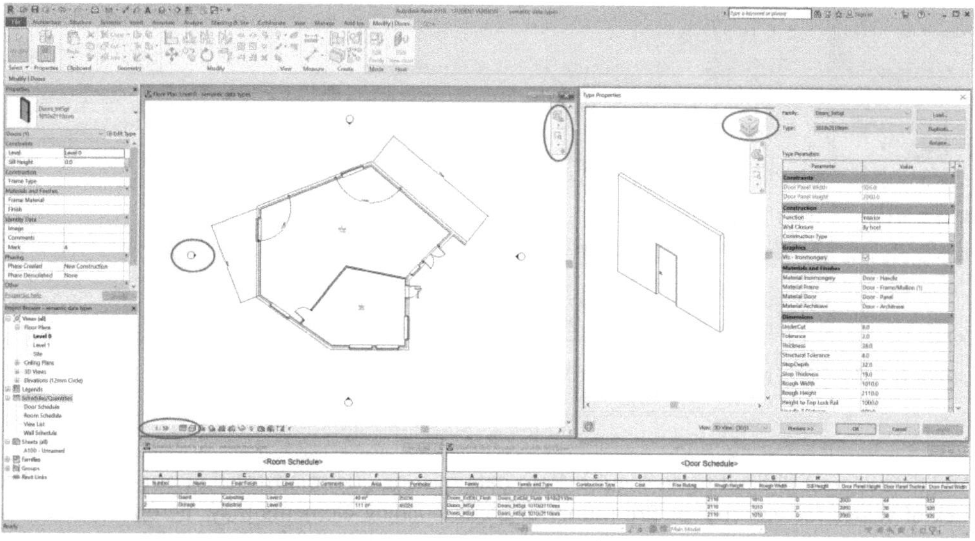

Figure 13. Operational data in BIM

The presence of multiple windows on the screen also increases the number of visible metadata, such as window headers that describe the view in each window (Figure 14).

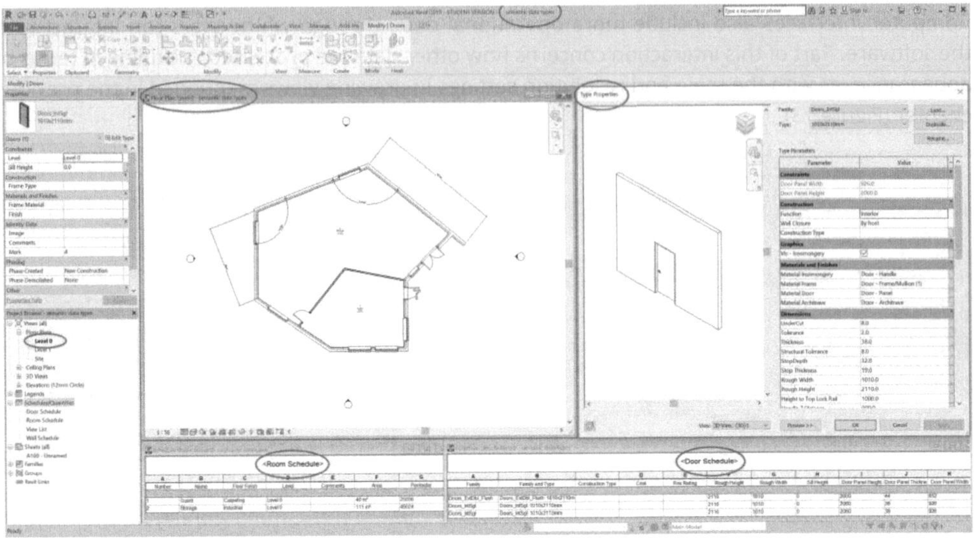

Figure 14. Metadata in BIM

Anti-data remain difficult to distinguish from data missing due to abstraction or deferment. The lack of values for e.g. cost or fire rating for some building elements may merely indicate that their calculation has yet to take place, despite the availability of the necessary primary data. After all, both are calculated on the basis of materials present in the elements: if these materials are known, cost and fire ratings are easy to derive. One should remember this inherent duality in anti-data: they do not only indicate missing primary data but the presence of anti-data is significant and meaningful by itself. For example, not knowing the materials and finishes of a window frame, although the window symbol is quite detailed, signifies that the interfacing of the window to a wall is a non-trivial problem that remains to be solved. Interfacing typically produces anti-data, especially when sub-models meet in BIM, e.g. when the MEP and architectural sub-models are integrated, and the fastenings of pipes and cables to walls are present in neither. Anti-data generally necessitate action: no value (or "none") for the demolition phase of an entity suggests that the entity has to be preserved during all demolition phases — not ignored but actively preserved with purposeful measures, which should be made explicit (Figure 15).

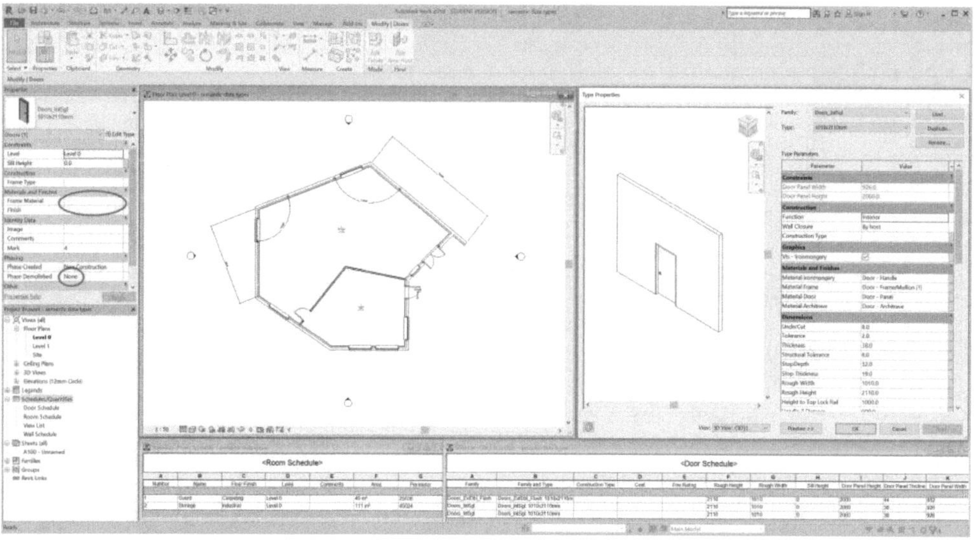

Figure 15. Anti-data in BIM

INFORMATION INSTANCES IN BIM

Knowing the type of data in BIM is a prerequisite identifying information as it emerges in a model. The next step is to recognize it in the interfaces of the software. As described in the previous section, data are to be found in the symbols: their properties and relations. In the various views and windows of BIM software, one can easily find the properties of each symbol, either of the instance (Figure 16 & 18) or of the type (Figure 17). What one sees in most views and windows is a mix of different data types, with derivative data like a volume calculation or thermal resistance next to primary data, such as the length and thickness of a wall. Moreover, no view or window contains a comprehensive collection of properties. As a result, when a property changes in one view, the change is reflected in several other parts of the interface that accommodate the same property or data derived from it.

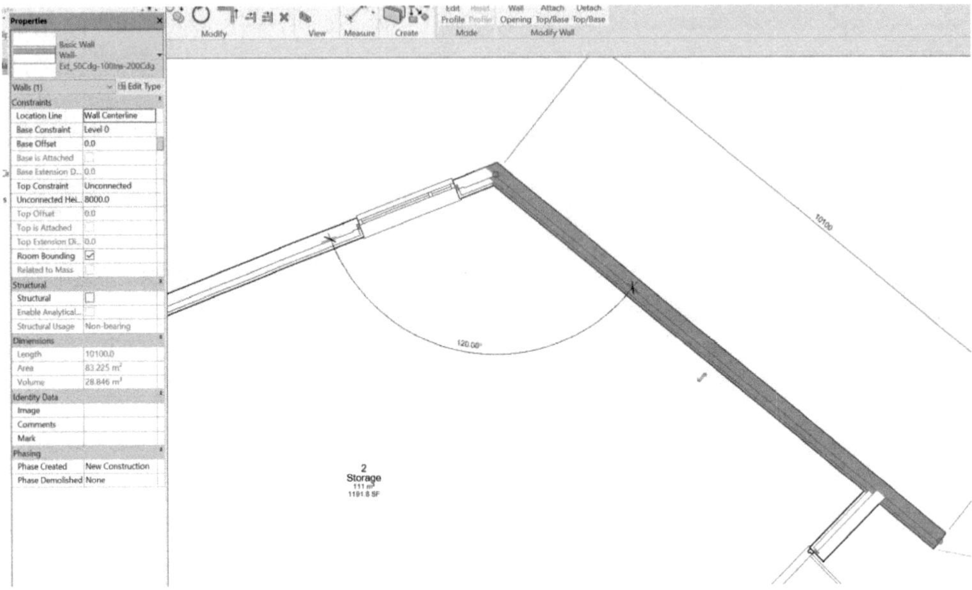

Figure 16. Instance properties palette in a BIM editor (Revit)

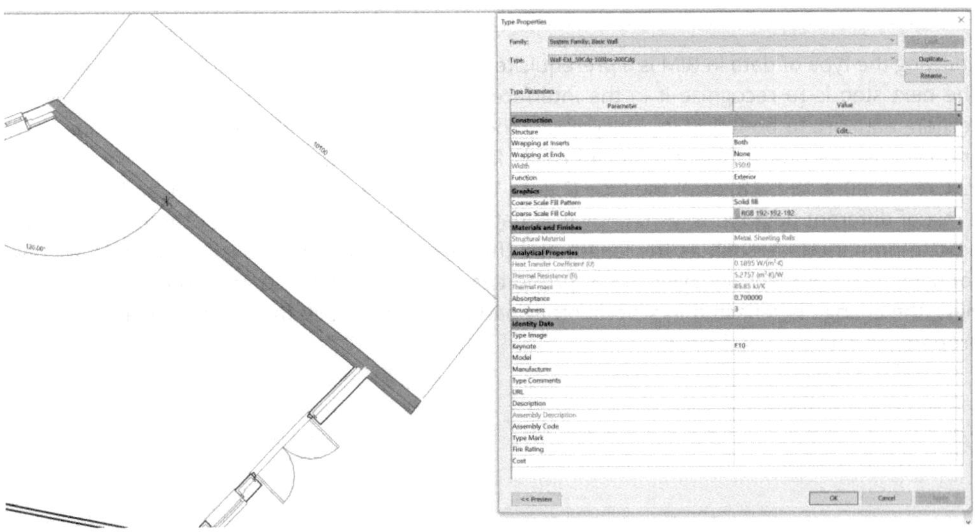

Figure 17. Type properties window in a BIM editor (Revit)

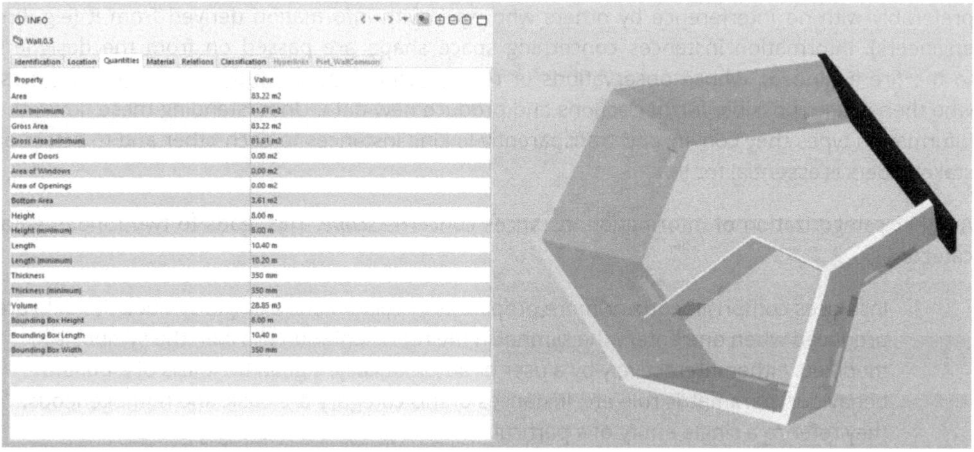

Figure 18. Properties window in a BIM checker (Solibri)

Any lack of uniformity in these properties, including the addition of new symbols to a model, qualifies as data. One can restrict the identification of data to each view separately but it makes more sense for IM to include all clones of the same property, in any view. Any derivative data that are automatically produced or modified as a result of the primary data changes count as different data instances. So, any change in the shape of a space counts as a single data instance, regardless of the view in which the user applies the change or of in how many views the change appears. The ensuing change in the space area value counts as a second instance of data; the change in the space volume as a third.

Relations between symbols are even more dispersed and often tacit. They can be found hidden in symbol behaviours (e.g. in that windows, doors or wash basins tend to stick to walls or in that walls tend to retain their co-termination), in explicit parametric rules and constraints, as well as in properties like construction time labels that determine incidental grouping. Discerning lacks of uniformity in relations is therefore often hard, especially because most derive variably from changes in the symbols. For example, modifying the length of a wall may inadvertently cause its co-termination with another wall to be removed or, if the co-termination is retained, to change the angle between the walls. Many relations can be made explicit and controllable through appropriate views like schedules. As we have seen, window and door schedules make explicit relations between openings and spaces. This extends to relations between properties of windows or doors and of the adjacent spaces, e.g. connects the fire rating of a door to whether a space on either side is part of a main fire egress route or the acoustic isolation offered by the door to the noise or privacy level of activities accommodated in either adjacent space.

Information instances can be categorized by the type of their data: primary, derivative, operational etc. Type is important for IM because it allows, firstly, to prioritize in terms of significance and, secondly, to link information to actors and stakeholders concerning authorship and custodianship. Primary information obviously carries a higher priority than derivative. Moreover, primary information (e.g. the shape of spaces) is produced or maintained by specific actors (e.g. designers), preferably with no interference by others who work with information derived from it (e.g. fire engineers). Information instances concerning space shape are passed on from the designers to the fire engineers, whose observations or recommendations are fed back to the designers, who then initiate possible further actions and produce new data. Understanding these flows, the information types they convey and transparently linking instances to each other and to actors or stakeholders is essential for IM.

Another categorization of information instances concerns *scope*. This leads to two fundamental categories:

1. Instances comprising one or more properties or relations of a single symbol: the data are produced when one enters the symbol in the representation or when the symbol is modified, either interactively by a user or automatically, e.g. on the basis of a built-in behaviour, parametric rule etc. Instances of this category are basic and homogeneous: they refer to a single entity of a particular kind, e.g. a door. The entity can be:
    1. Generic in type, like an abstract internal door
    2. Contextually specific, such as a door for a particular wall in the design, i.e. partially defined by relations in the representation
    3. Specific in type, e.g. a specific model of a particular manufacturer, fixed in all its properties
2. Instances comprising one or more properties or relations of multiple symbols, added or modified together, e.g. following a change of type for a number of internal walls, or a resizing of the building elements bounding a particular space. Consequently, instances of this category can be:
    1. Homogeneous, comprising symbols of the same type, e.g. all office spaces in a building
    2. Heterogeneous, comprising symbols of various types, usually related to each other in direct, contextual ways, e.g. the spaces and doors of a particular wing that make up a fire egress route

These categories account for all data and abstraction levels in a representation, from sub-symbols (like the modification of the geometry of a door handle in the definition of a door type) to changes in the height of a floor level that affects the location of all building elements and spaces on that floor, the size and composition of some (e.g. stairs) and potentially also relations to entities on adjacent floors. Understanding the scope of information is essential for IM: it determines the extent to which any information instance or change should be propagated to ensure consistency and coherence.

SYMBOLS AND THEIR PROPERTIES IN CONTEXT

So far we have considered the semantic data types of symbol properties in isolation, as if each symbol were a separate entity rather than incorporated in a representation. However, in the symbol graphs discussed in a previous chapter, we have seen that relations in a model profoundly affect the properties of each symbol. Parameterization adds to the number and complexity of such relations but even without parameterization there are many primary properties that become derivative in the context of a representation due to common, often implicit relations.

In the example of a window and the wall that hosts it, some properties of the window, such as orientation, are inherited from the corresponding properties of the hosting element (Figure 19). These relations therefore affect the semantic data type of symbol properties. Both the window and the wall in this example are each represented by a discrete symbol with its own properties. Most of these properties are primary data, i.e. essential for the identity of each symbol: length, height, width, material composition etc. BIM software routinely also adds properties that are derivative, i.e. products of functions on primary properties, such as area and volume but also fire rating and cost. Orientation is another derivative property that in a straight wall can be calculated from the relative position of the endpoints of the wall axis. This calculation applies to the wall but is not required for the window, which by definition inherits orientation from the wall, as does any other hosted element. One could argue that other properties of the window, notably its dimensions, remain primary in spite of the hosting relation but the fact that their values must be in a range determined by the wall properties also makes them derivative, only not in the strict sense of equality that applies to orientation. They remain the same as in the unattached window so long as they do not cause any interfacing problems with the wall but, when this happens, it becomes clear that the width of the window is linked to that of the hosting wall.

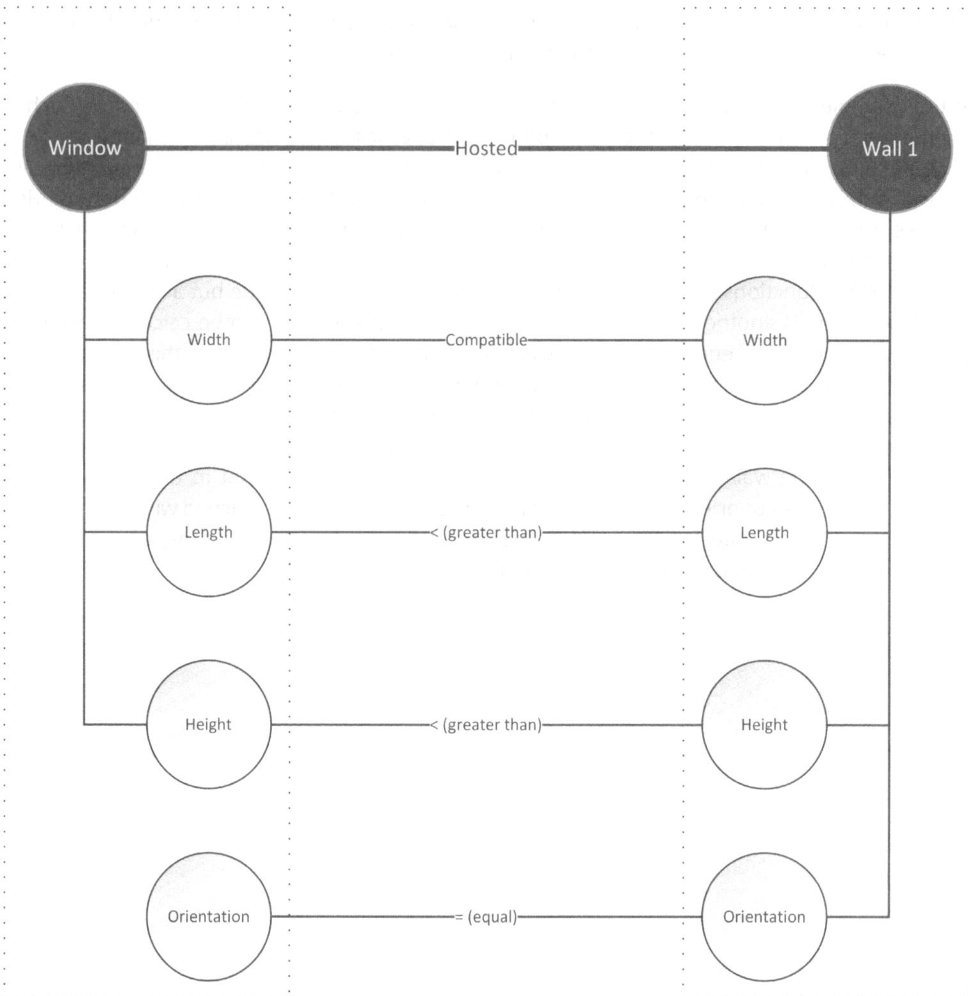

Figure 19. Relations between window and hosting wall

Similar derivation of dimensions on the basis of relations also applies to non-hosted elements. For example, the height of a wall is normally constrained by the position of the floor above and the floor underneath the wall: the wall height is derived from difference in vertical level between the two floors that bound it (Figure 20).

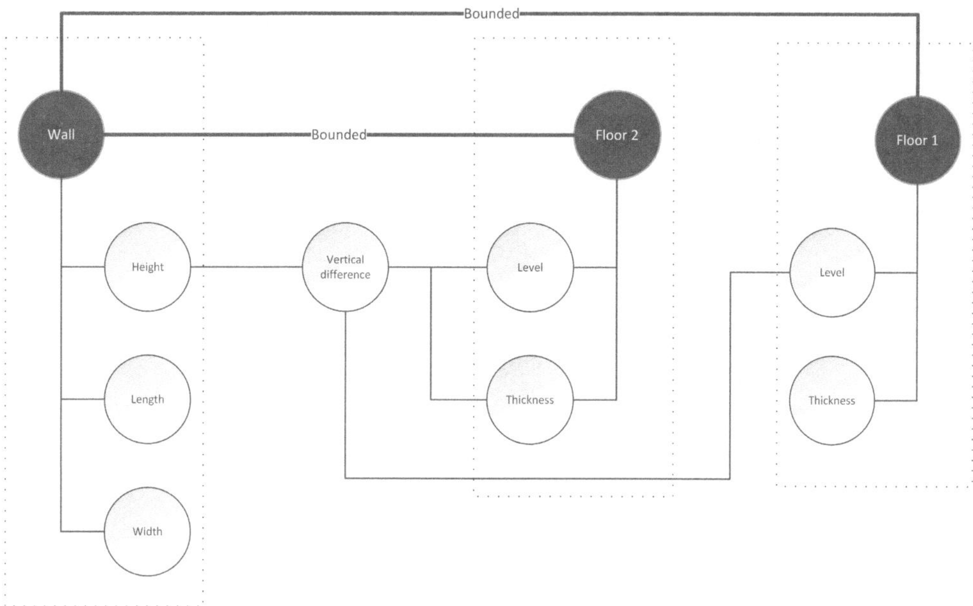

Figure 20. Symbol graph of the wall and the two floors that bound it

This relation seems straightforward but BIM software makes it more complicated in a way that reveals the intricate chain behind any relation we isolate by way of example. A wall in BIM may be constrained not by floor symbols but by *levels:* reference planes in the model setup. The wall in Figure 21 has its base on Level 1 (which also determines the position of a floor symbol) but its top is determined by a default value of the type, as indicated in the properties palette. The wall appears to connect to the floor underneath it but in fact the position of both is determined by the same level.

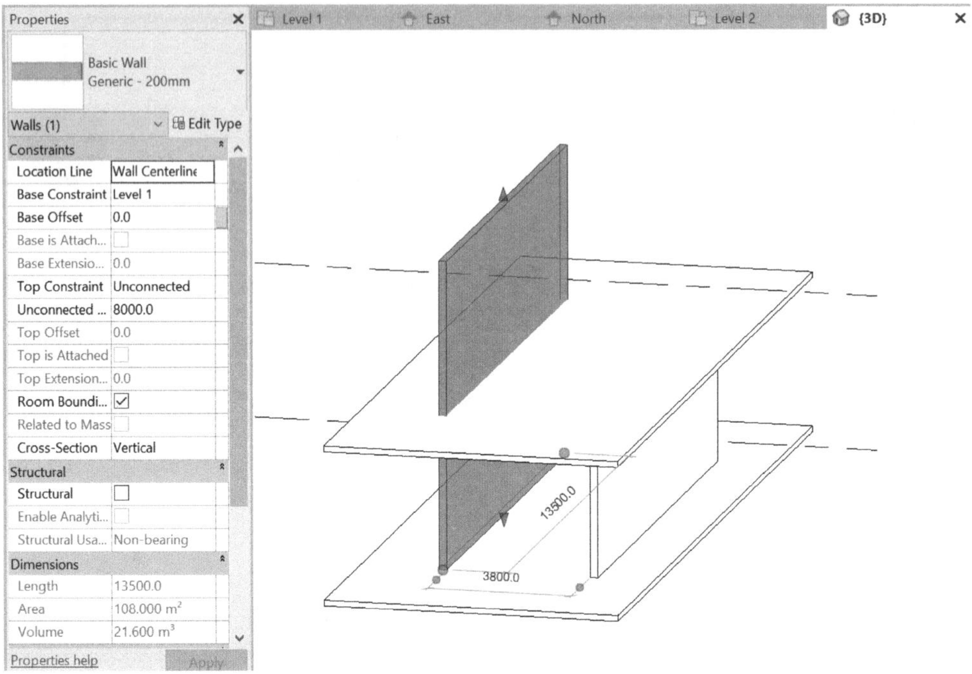

Figure 21. Wall partly constrained by levels

On the other hand, the top of the wall in Figure 22 is determined by Level 2, which also constrains the position of another floor symbol. As the properties palette reveals, this wall is moreover attached at the top. This means that if the floor above the wall is moved to another height, the wall tries to remain connected to it. If the floor below is moved, the wall sticks to the level, losing contact with the floor. If the base was also attached, then the wall would be fully constrained, as in Figure 20.

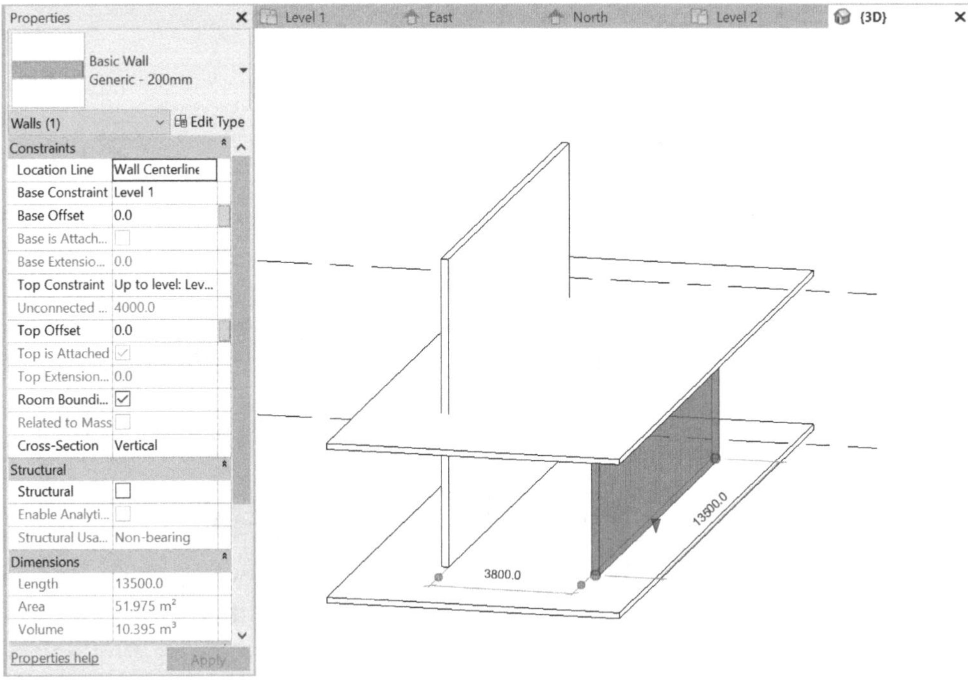

Figure 22. Wall fully constrained by levels and attached at the base

The above examples demonstrate that the semantic type of each property is often affected by constraints external to the symbols. The width of a wall, for instance, can be determined by its composition out of various layers of different materials, each with its own thickness. This makes wall width derivative and creates some dimensional and technical tolerances, as e.g. a wall can be made thinner by replacing an insulation layer with thinner, better material, without changing the wall's thermal performance. On the other hand, wall width can also be fixed by external constraints, e.g. for reasons of standardization. This makes wall width primary, while the material composition of the wall (the material layers and their thickness) becomes derivative from the fixed wall width and requirements on e.g. thermal or acoustic performance.

Some of the most important external constraints come from planning regulations. These often determine large parts of a design, e.g. the position of external walls by a setback from the plot boundaries. This means that the footprint of the building is derived from the plot shape and dimensions minus the setbacks. Similarly, most Dutch planning regulations impose a setback from the ends of the roof for dormer windows, e.g. 100 cm from the bottom and side ends, and 50 cm from the top (Figure 23). Consequently, the dimensions of the dormer are derived from those of the roof, which in turn derive from the building footprint, and external constraints, including on the roof pitch (also determined by planning regulations, either by a fixed value, such as 30 degrees, or a bandwidth, e.g. 25–40 degrees). In short, a building representation is based on such networks of relations and constraints, making many primary properties dependent on others and therefore derivative.

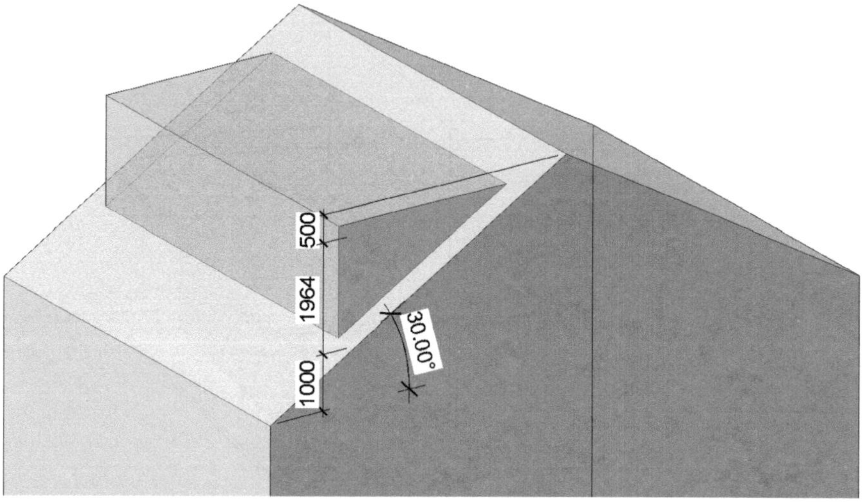

Figure 23. Dormer in Dutch house

The conclusions that can be drawn from the above are:

1. The semantic type is sensitive to the context: what in an isolated symbol is a primary property may become derivative in a representation where the symbol connects to others.
2. These others include symbols in the same representation, as well as external information entities, such as constraints from standards or planning regulations. For IM purposes, these too should be explicitly included in the representation.

Key Takeaways

- *A information instance consists of one or more data which are well-formed and meaningful*
- *Data are lacks of uniformity in what we perceive at a given moment or between different states of a percept or between two symbols in a percept*
- *Data can be primary, anti-data, derivative, operational or metadata*
- *There are significant differences between analogue and digital building representations concerning data types, with symbols like dimension lines being primary in the one and derivative in the other*
- *In BIM, lacks of uniformity can be identified in the properties and relations of symbols*
- *Information instances can be categorized by the semantic type of their data and by their scope in the representation*
- *Semantic type depends on the context, which may turn primary data into derivative*

Exercises

1. Identify the semantic data types in the infobox of a Wikipedia biographic lemma (the summary panel on the top right), e.g. https://en.wikipedia.org/wiki/Aldo_van_Eyck (Figure 19),[6] and in the basic page information of the same lemma (e.g. https://en.wikipedia.org/w/index.php?title=Aldo_van_Eyck&action=info)
2. Explain the information instances produced in BIM when one inserts a door in an existing wall. Use the following notation:
   (scope; symbol; name of property or relation; value of property or relation; time; semantic data type)
   If the instances concern multiple symbols, use the notation to describe each symbol separately.
3. Explain the information instances produced in BIM when one moves an existing door to a slightly different position in an existing wall. Use the above notation for each concerned symbol separately.
4. In BIM it is claimed that one can add information dimensions to the three geometric dimensions, turning 3D into *n*D: 4D comes with the addition of time (e.g. when the symbolized entity is constructed), 5D with the addition of cost, 6D with sustainability, 7D with facility management, 8D with accident prevention (or safety) etc. However, for something to qualify as a dimension, it should be primary and not derivative, otherwise area and volume would be dimensions, too.[7]
   Describe how the values of these four dimensions emerge and change throughout the lifecycle of a building element or component, such as a door, window, floor, ceiling etc., and which primary or derivative information attracts attention in various stages and activities after development (procurement, transport, realization, maintenance, refurbishment, renovation, demolition etc.). Present your results in a table.

5. IFC (Industry Foundation Classes) is a standard underlying BIM, in particular concerning how each entity is represented. Identify the semantic data types in the IFC wall base quantities, i.e. quantities that are common to the definition of all occurrences of walls (http://www.buildingsmart.org/ifc/dev/IFC4_3/RC2/html/schema/ifcsharedbldgelements/qset/qto_wallbasequantities.htm). Pay particular attention to derivative quantities present in the specification. If each of the quantities becomes a symbol property in BIM, calculate how much of a typical model consists of derivative data, both in percentage and megabytes (assuming that what holds for walls also holds for all entities in BIM).

Figure 19. Infobox in Wikipedia

Notes

1. Zins, C., 2007. Conceptual approaches for defining data, information, and knowledge. *Journal of the American Society for Information Science and Technology.* **58**(4) 479-493 DOI: 10.1002/asi.20508
2. There are several fundamental sources on the MTC, starting with the original publication: Shannon, C., 1948. A mathematical theory of communication. *Bell System Technical Journal,* 27(July, October), 379-423, 623-656; Shannon, C.E., & Weaver, W., 1998. *The mathematical theory of communication.* Urbana IL: University of Illinois Press; Cover, T.M., & Thomas, J.A., 2006. *Elements of information theory* (2nd ed.). Hoboken NJ: Wiley-Interscience; Pierce, J.R., 1980. *An introduction to information theory: symbols, signals & noise* (2nd, rev. ed.). New York: Dover.
3. The classification of theories of information is after: Sommaruga, G., 2009. Introduction. G. Sommaruga (ed), *Formal Theories of Information: From Shannon to semantic information theory and general concepts of*

information. Berlin, Heidelberg: Springer.

4. Floridi's theory has been published in: Floridi, L., 2008. Trends in the philosophy of information. P. Adriaans & J. v. Benthem (eds), *Philosophy of information.* Amsterdam: North-Holland; Floridi, L., 2009. Philosophical conceptions of information. G. Sommaruga (ed), *Formal Theories of Information: From Shannon to semantic information theory and general concepts of information.* Berlin, Heidelberg: Springer; Floridi, L., 2016. Semantic conceptions of information. *The Stanford Encyclopedia of Philosophy.* https://plato.stanford.edu/entries/information-semantic/
5. In later publications Floridi has used the term *secondary data* instead of anti-data but the new name seems rather confusing, suggesting data of a lesser importance rather than the converse of primary data.
6. Source: https://en.wikipedia.org/wiki/Aldo_van_Eyck; photograph credit: Aldo van Eyck in 1970 by Bert Verhoef, licensed under CC BY-SA 3.0 NL
7. Koutamanis, A., 2020. Dimensionality in BIM: Why BIM cannot have more than four dimensions? *Automation in Construction*, **114**, 2020, 103153, https://doi.org/10.1016/j.autcon.2020.103153.

CHAPTER 7

Information management

This chapter introduces the general goals of information management and connects them to building representations, semantic types and AECO processes in order to distill the main goals of building information management.

THE NEED FOR INFORMATION MANAGEMENT

With the information explosion we have been experiencing, it is hardly surprising that IM seems to have become a self-evident technical necessity. Handling the astounding amounts of information produced and disseminated every day requires more robust and efficient approaches than ever. Nevertheless, IM is considered mostly as a means to an end, usually performance in a project or enterprise: with effective IM, one can improve the chances of higher performance. Consequently, IM usually forms a key component of overall management.

This is widely acknowledged in building design management (DM). Even before the digital era, the evident dependence of AECO on information that came from various sources and concerned different but interconnected aspects of a building had led to general agreement that this information and the way it is handled can be critical for communication and decision making. DM often focuses on information completeness, relevance, clarity, accuracy, quality, value, timeliness etc., as prerequisites to enabling greater productivity, improving risk management, reducing errors and generally raising efficiency and reliability. The dependence on information is such that some even go so far as to suggest that DM is really fundamentally about IM: managing information flows so that stakeholders receive the right information at the right time.[1]

In practical terms, however, there is little clarity concerning what should be managed and how. DM sources often merely affirm that information is important and should be treated with care. What makes information usable, valuable, relevant etc. is assumed to be known tacitly. Information is vaguely defined as data in usable form but is also equated to the thousands of drawings and other documents produced during the lifecycle of a building — the carriers of information. If the right document is present, then it is assumed that stakeholders also possess the right information and are directly capable of judging the veracity, completeness, coherence etc. of what they receive. However, equating information with documents not only prolongs outdated analogue practices, it also places a heavy burden on users.

It is arguably typical of AECO and DM that, in the face of operational and especially technical complexity, they invest heavily in human resources. This goes beyond the interpretation of documents in order to extract information; it also extends to the invention of new roles that assume a mix of new and old tasks and responsibilities. So, in addition to project and process managers, one encounters information managers as well as BIM managers and CAD managers, BIM coordinators and CAD coordinators, working together in complex, overlapping hierarchies. These new roles are usually justified by the need for support with new technologies, which may be yet unfamiliar to the usual participants in an AECO project. This, however, increases the distance between new technologies and their real users, limiting learning opportunities and prolonging the treatment of technologies as new and unfamiliar (something that contrasts sharply with what we do in our private encounters with new technologies, as discussed in the section on digitization). Even worse, all these roles increase complexity and reduce transparency by adding more intermediaries in the already multi-layered structure of AECO.

New roles are inevitable with technological innovation. Sometimes they are temporary and sometimes permanent. In the early days of motorcars, for example, chauffeurs were more widely employed to drive them than today. On the other hand, webmasters have become necessary by the invention and popularity of the World Wide Web and remain so for the foreseeable future, despite the growing web literacy among general users. What matters is that any such new roles should be part of a sound and thorough plan of approach rather than an easy alternative to a good approach. A good plan should determine what is needed and why, allowing for increasing familiarity and even proficiency of many users with various technologies, to a degree that, after some point, they might require little day-to-day support. In our case, one may safely expect that AECO professionals will eventually become quite capable not only of using BIM directly but also of coordinating their BIM activities, with little need for technical intermediaries. To achieve this, AECO needs practical familiarization with the new technologies but above all clear comprehension of what these technologies do with information. Based on that, one can develop a sound IM approach that takes into consideration both domain needs and the capacities of digital technologies in order to determine changes in the tasks, responsibilities and procedures of existing AECO roles, and develop profiles for any additional roles.

INFORMATION SOURCES

INCLUSIVENESS

IM is both an activity and a well-defined discipline of professionals who support this activity. The discipline of IM has a broad scope and, as a result, is quite inclusive.[2] It pays no attention to issues of representation and accepts as information sources all kinds of documents, applications, services and schemes. This is due to three reasons. Firstly, IM covers many application areas and must therefore be adaptable to practices encountered in any of them. Secondly, in many areas there is a mix of analogue and digital information, as well as various channels. For example, financial client transactions with a shop can involve cash and debit or credit cards, either physically or via the web. IM provides tools for bringing such disparate material together into more coherent forms, ensuring that no outdated or inappropriate information is used and preventing that information is missing, inaccessible or deleted by error. These tools include correlation with contexts (e.g. time series displays relative to other data), classification and condensation (aggregation, totalling, filtering and summarization). Thirdly, IM has a tenuous relation to computerization, often relying on it but also appearing weary of putting too much emphasis on digital technologies as a general solution.

The inclusiveness of IM with respect to information sources means that it may end up not only tolerating the redundancy of analogue and digital versions of the same information but also supporting outdated practices and conventions, even prolonging their life through superficial digitization, on the assumption that the application area wants it. This reduces IM to mere document management, i.e. making sure that the necessary documents are retained and kept available. Such inclusiveness is arguably an easy way out of most domain problems. At present, there may be enough computer power and capacity to store and retrieve any document produced in a project or enterprise — in our case, throughout the whole lifecycle of a building. However, the information explosion of the digital era and big data approaches suggest the opposite: we already need more intelligent solutions than brute force. Can we upscale the haphazard, inclusive recording of the history of a building to all buildings in the world? At this moment, we may have the illusion that we still have control over the huge amounts of information in production and circulation but this is because AECO currently approaches information with respect to the limited demands of normative practices. Beyond these demands, there is already too much information that is ignored, neglected and even discarded. Moreover, new developments like the IoT could change the overall picture soon, as smart things start communicating with each other with great intensity. For AECO this can be quite critical because buildings are among the prime candidates for accommodating a wide range of sensors and actuators, e.g. for controlling energy consumption, ensuring security or regulating air quality to prevent the spread of epidemics.

STRUCTURED, SEMI-STRUCTURED AND UNSTRUCTURED INFORMATION

BIM is important for IM because it marks a transition not only to symbolic representation but also to holistic, *structured* information solutions for AECO. With regard to structure, there are three main data categories:

- *Unstructured data* are the subject of big data approaches: sensor measurements, social media messages and other data without a uniform, standardized format. Finding relevant information in unstructured data is quite demanding because queries have to take into account a broad range of locations where meaningful data may reside and a wide variety of storage forms (including natural language and images).
- *Semi-structured data* are a favourite of IM: information sources with a loosely defined structure and flexible use. Analogue drawings are a typical example: one knows what is expected in e.g. a section but there are several alternative notations and few if any prohibitions concerning what may be depicted and how. IM thrives on semi-structured sources, adding metadata, extracting and condensing, so as to summarize relevant information into a structured overview.
- *Structured data* are found in sources where one knows precisely what is expected and where. Databases are prime examples of structured information sources. In a relational database, one knows that each table describes a particular class of entities, that each record in a table describes a single entity and that each field describes a particular property of these entities in the same, predefined way. Finding the right data in a structured source is therefore straightforward and less challenging for IM.

In contrast to analogue drawings, BIM is clearly structured, along the lines of a database. Each symbol belongs to a particular type and has specific properties. This structure is one of the driving forces behind BIM, in particular with respect to its capacity to integrate and process building information coherently. Given the effort put into developing structured models in BIM, it makes little sense to abandon the advantages they promise. This makes BIM the main environment for IM in AECO and calls for approaches that should:

- *Avoid having other primary information sources next to BIM.* All building information should be integrated in BIM and any related data linked to it. Currently, there is general agreement that the price of a component, e.g. a washbasin, should be a property of the corresponding symbol. However, the same should apply to all data relevant to AECO, e.g. packaging information for this component. The dimensions of the box in which the washbasin is brought to the building site, the packaging materials it contains etc. are useful for logistic purposes, as well as for waste management. Trying to retrieve this information from the manufacturer's catalogue is significantly less efficient than integrating the relevant data among the symbol properties. The same applies to a photograph of some part of the building during construction or use. This too should be connected to BIM as a link between the digital file of the photograph and relevant symbols in the model (Figure 1) or even mapped as a decal on the symbols (Figure 2).

- *Desist from promoting BIM output to the level of a primary source.* Any view of a model, from a floor plan to a cost calculation, can be exported as a separate document (PDF, spreadsheet etc.). Such an export may have its practical uses but one should not treat it as a source separate from the model. Any query about the building should start from the model, bypassing exports and similar output. Using IM to ensure consistency between exports and the model is meaningless. This applies even to legally significant documents like contracts because these too can be expressed as views of the model (i.e. textual frames around data exported from the model).

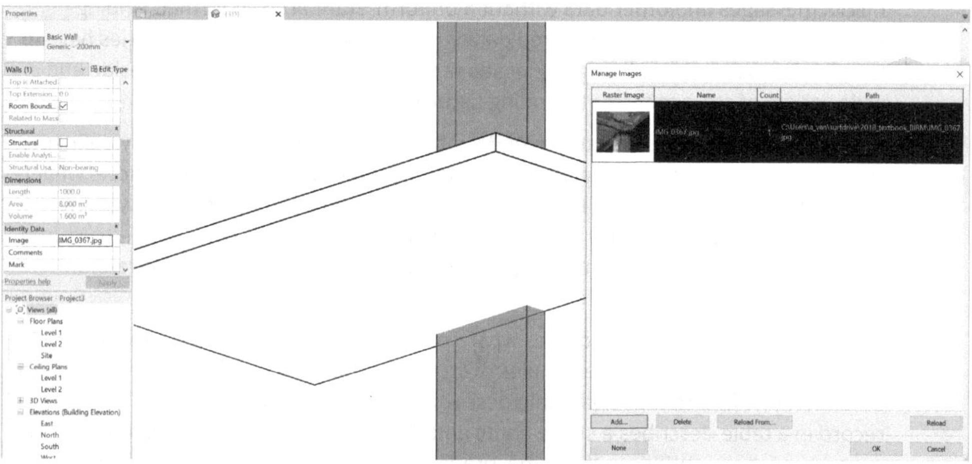

Figure 1. Photograph of current state linked as image to relevant components in Revit

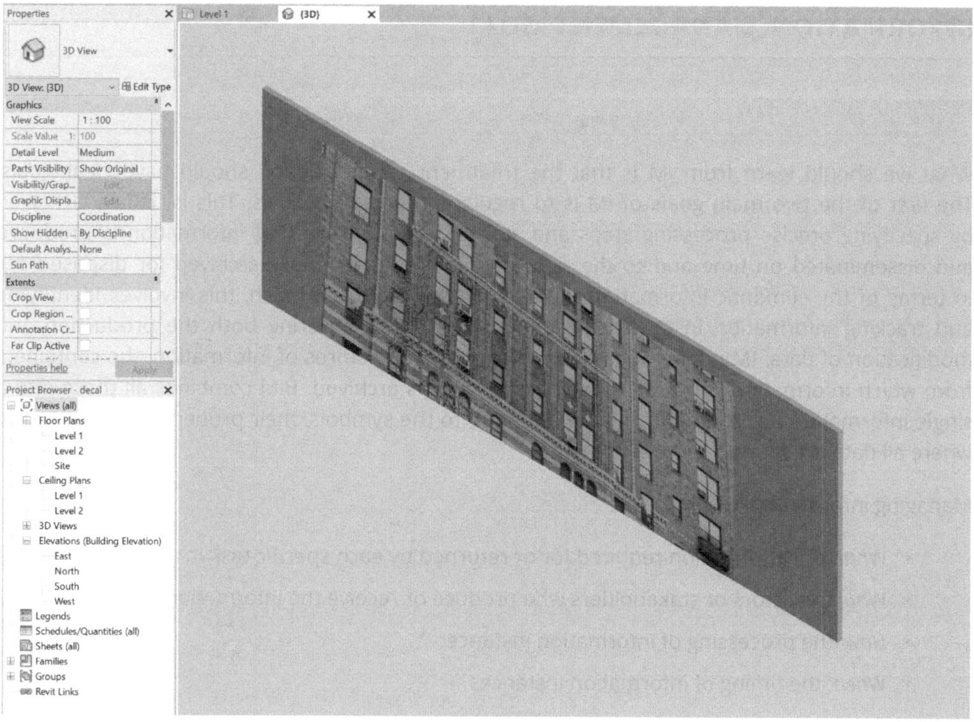

Figure 2. Photograph of current state mapped as decal in Revit

From the above, a wider information environment emerges around the model, populated largely by data linked to the model, preferably to specific symbols. IM can assist with the organization of this environment but it should not be allowed to cut corners, e.g. answer queries on the basis of satellite files. IM reliability depends on transparent links between queries, external files and the model, specifically the primary data in symbols and their history.

It is perhaps ironic that while the world is focusing on big, unstructured data, AECO should insist on structured data. One explanation is latency: AECO has been late with the development of structured information solutions because it continued to use analogue, semi-structured practices in digital facsimiles. As a consequence, AECO has yet to reap the benefits of structured data approaches, let alone find their limits.

The emphasis on the structured nature of BIM also flies in the face of IM and its inclusiveness. In this respect, one should keep in mind what was discussed in a previous section: IM is a means, not an end, and its adaptability has historical causes. It is not compulsory to retain redundant information sources next to BIM, simply because IM can handle redundancy and complexity. If the structured content of BIM suffices, then IM for AECO simply becomes easier and parsimonious.

INFORMATION MANAGEMENT GOALS

INFORMATION FLOW

What we should learn from IM is that the treatment of information should have clear goals. The first of the two main goals of IM is to regulate information flows. This is usually achieved by specifying precise processing steps and stages, which ensure that information is produced and disseminated on time and to the right people, until it is finally archived (or disposed of). In terms of the semantic information theory underlying our approach, this involves identifying and tracking information instances throughout a process, covering both the production and modification of data. IM puts emphasis on the sources and stores of information: the containers from which information is drawn, in which it rests or is archived. BIM combines all these into a single information environment, shifting attention to the symbols, their properties and relations, where all data are found.

Managing information flow involves:

- *What:* the information required for or returned by each specific task in a process
- *Who:* the actors or stakeholders who produce or receive the information in a task
- *How:* the processing of information instances
- *When:* the timing of information instances

What is about the paradigmatic dimension: symbols in BIM and external sources linked to them. For both internal and external information, it is critical to distinguish between *authorship* and *custodianship*: the actors who produce some information are not necessarily the same stakeholders who safeguard this information in a project, let alone in the lifecycle of a building. A typical example is the brief: this is usually compiled in the initiative stage by a specialist on the basis of client and user input, as well as professional knowledge. In the development stage, custodianship often passes on to a project manager who utilizes the information in the brief to guide and evaluate the design, possibly also adapting the brief on the basis of insights from the design. Then in the use stage, it becomes background to facility and property management, before it develops into a direct or indirect source for a new brief, e.g. for the refurbishment of the building. Making custodianship specific and unambiguous in all stages is of paramount importance in an integrated environment like BIM, where overlaps and grey areas are easy to develop.

How information flows are regulated relates to the syntagmatic dimension of a model: the sequence of actions through which symbols, their properties and relations are processed. The information instances produced by these actions generally correspond to the sequence of tasks in the process but are also subject to extrinsic constraints, including from the software (the implementation environment): the presence of bounding walls is necessary for defining a space in most BIM editors, although in many design processes one starts with the spatial design rather than with construction. IM needs to take such conflicts into account and differentiate between the two sequences.

A useful device for translating tasks into information actions is the tripartite scheme *Input-Processing-Output (I-P-O)* that underlies any form of information processing. For any task, some actors deliver information as input. This input is then processed by other (or even the same) actors, who return as output some other information. Then, this output usually becomes input for the next task. IM has to ensure that the right input is delivered to the right actors and that the right output is collected. By considering each decision task with respect to I-P-O, one can identify missing information in the input and arrange for its delivery.

The syntagmatic dimension obviously also relates to *when:* the moments when information instances become available. These moments usually form a coherent time schedule. The time schedule captures the sequence of actions and transactions, linking each to specific information instances. Here again one should differentiate between the sequence of tasks, which tends to be adequately covered by a project schedule, and the sequence of information actions, which may require additional refinement. This difference is the subject of the next part in this book.

INFORMATION FLOW IN BIM

We are used to viewing the early part of a design process as something almost magical: someone puts a few lines on a scrap of paper and suddenly we have a basis for imagining what the building will look like. The same applies to BIM: one starts entering symbols in a model and suddenly the design is there for all to see and process. Building information flows seem to emerge out of nothing but this is far from true. The designers who make the first sketches or decide on the first elements in a model operate on the basis of general knowledge of their disciplines, more precise knowledge of the kind of building they are designing and specific project information, including location characteristics and briefs. In other words, building representations are the product of cognitive processes that combine both tacit and overt information.

It is also widely assumed that the amount of information in a design process grows from very little in early design to substantial amounts by the end, when a building is fully specified. This actually refers to the specificity of conventional building representations, e.g. the drawing scales used in different design stages. In fact, even before the first sketch is made, there usually is considerable information available on the building. Some of it predates the project, e.g. planning regulations and building codes that determine much of the form of a building and key features of its elements, such as the pitch of the roof and the dimensions of stairs. Other information belongs to the project, e.g. the brief that states accommodation requirements for the activities to be housed in the building, the budget that constrains cost and location-related principles like the continuation of vistas or circulation networks through the building site. Early building representations may conform to such specifications but most related information remains tacit, either in other documents or in the mind of the designers. For example, the site layout on which one starts drawing or modelling rarely includes planning regulations, even though the designers are normally aware of these regulations and their impact on the design.

In managing both AECO processes and information, one should ensure that tacit information becomes explicit and is connected to tasks. In BIM, this means augmenting the basic model setup (site plan, floor levels, grids etc.) with constraints from planning regulations (e.g. in the form of the permissible building envelope), use information from the brief and constraints on the kind of building elements that are admissible in the model (e.g. with respect to the fire rating of the building). Integration of such information amounts to *feedforward:* measurement and control of the information system before disturbances occur. Feedforward is generally more efficient and effective than feedback, e.g. checking if all building elements meet the fire safety requirements after they have been entered in the model.

It has also been suggested that early design decisions have a bigger impact on the outcome of a design process than later decisions. Having to decide on the basis of little overt information makes these decisions difficult and precarious. This conventional wisdom concerning early decisions may be misleading. Admittedly, early design decisions tend to concern basic features and aspects, from overall form to load-bearing structure, which determine much of the building and so have a disproportionate influence on cost and performance. However, such decisions are not exclusive to early design: the type of load-bearing structure can change late in the process, e.g. in relation to cost considerations, procurement or the unanticipated need for larger spans. Late changes can be even more expensive because they also necessitate careful control of all interfacing between load-bearing and other elements in the design. Moreover, small, local decisions can also be critical, whether in an early or late stage: if some doors in a building are too narrow, wheelchair circulation may become cumbersome or even impossible, leading to costly restrictions or adaptations. From an IM perspective, what matters is that all relevant information is made explicit in BIM, so as to know which data serve as input for a task and how to register the output of the task. Explicitness of information allows us to map decision making in a process and understand the scope and significance of any decision, regardless of process stage.

INFORMATION QUALITY

The second main goal of IM is to safeguard or improve information quality.[3] Quality matters to IM in two respects. Firstly, for information utility: information produced and disseminated in a process should meet the requirements of its users. Secondly, concerning information value: information with a higher quality needs to be preserved and propagated with higher priority. IM measures quality pragmatically, in terms of relevance, i.e. fitness for purpose: how well the information supports the tasks of its users. In addition to pragmatic information quality, IM is also keen on inherent information quality: how well the information reflects the real-world entities it represents. It should be noted that IM is not passive with regard to information quality. It can also improve it, both at meta-levels (e.g. by systematically applying tags) and with respect to content (e.g. through condensation).

In both senses, information quality is determined within each application domain. IM offers a tactical, operational and technical framework but does not provide answers to domain questions. These answers have to be supplied by the application environment in order for IM to know which information to preserve, disseminate or prioritize. In our framework, information quality concerns the paradigmatic dimension: the symbols of a representation and their relations. As this dimension tends to be quite structured in symbolic representations, one can go beyond the pragmatic level of IM and utilize the underlying semantic level to understand better how information quality is determined.

The first advantage of utilizing the semantic level lies in the definition of acceptable data as being well-formed and meaningful. This determines the fundamental quality of data: their acceptability within a representation. A coffee stain cannot be part of a building representation but neither can a line segment be part of a model in BIM: it has to be an explicit symbol of something. That symbol may have the appearance of a line segment (i.e. uses the line segment as implementation mechanism, as is the case for a room separation in Revit) but the meaning of the symbol is not inferred by its appearance — quite the opposite: the appearance is determined by the meaning. Any data that do not fit the specifications of a symbol, a property or a relation cannot be well-formed or meaningful in BIM. Such data are indications of low quality that requires attention. If quality cannot be improved, these data should be treated as noise.

Data that pass the fundamental semantic test must then be evaluated concerning *relevance* for the particular building or project and its tasks. To judge relevance, one needs additional criteria, e.g. concerning specificity. For example, it is unlikely that a model comprising generic building elements is satisfactory for a task like the acoustic analysis of a classroom because the property values of generic elements tend to be too vague regarding factors that influence acoustic performance.

The semantic level also helps to determine information value beyond utility: prioritizing which information should be preserved and propagated depends on semantic type. As derivative data can be produced from primary when needed, they do not have to be prioritized — in many cases, they do not have to be preserved at all. Operational data and metadata tend to change little and infrequently in BIM, so these too have a lower priority than primary data. Finally, anti-data have a high priority, both because they necessitate interpretation and action, and because such action often aims at producing missing primary data.

Parsimonious IM concerning information quality in a symbolic representation like BIM can be summarized as follows:

1. Preservation and completion of primary data
2. Establishing transparent and efficient procedures for producing derivative data when needed
3. Identification and interpretation of anti-data, including specification of consequent actions
4. Preservation of stable operational and metadata

The priority of primary data seems to conflict with IM and its improvement of information quality through condensation, i.e. operations that return pragmatically superior derivative data and metadata. Such operations belong to the second point above: if the primary data serve as input for certain procedures, then these procedures have to be established as a dynamic view or similar output in BIM. If users need to know the floor areas of spaces, one should not just give them the space dimensions and let them work out the calculations themselves but supply instead transparent calculations, organized in a legible and meaningful way. This does not mean that the results of these calculations should be preserved next to the space dimensions from which they derive.

Moving from the semantic to the pragmatic level, *veracity* is a key criterion of quality: fitness for purpose obviously requires that the information is true. In addition to user feedback, veracity can be established on the basis of comparison to additional, reference data, e.g. laser scans that confirm that a model represents faithfully, accurately and precisely the geometry of an existing building.

Before relevance or veracity, however, one should evaluate the structural characteristics of primary information: a model that is not complete, coherent and consistent is a poor basis for any use. *Completeness* in a building representation means that all parts and aspects are present, i.e. that there are no missing symbols for building elements or spaces in a model. BIM software uses *deficiency detection* to identify missing symbols. Missing aspects refer to symbol properties or relations: the definition of symbols should include all that is necessary to describe their structure, composition, behaviour and performance.

Completeness is about the presence of all puzzle pieces; *coherence* is about how well these pieces fit together to produce a seamless overall picture. In a building representation this primarily concerns the interfacing of elements, including possible conflicts in space or time. *Clash detection* in BIM aims at identifying such conflicts, particularly in space. Relations between symbols are of obvious significance for coherence, so these should be made explicit and manageable.

Finally, *consistency* is about all parts and aspects being represented in the same or compatible ways. In a symbolic representation, this refers to the properties and relations of symbols. If these are described in the same units and are present in all relevant symbol types, then consistency is also guaranteed in information use. Colour, for example, should be a property of the outer layer of all building elements. In all cases, the colour should derive from the materials of this layer. This means that any paint applied to an element should be explicit as material with properties that include colour. Moreover, any colour data attached to this material layer should follow a standard like the RAL or Pantone colour matching systems. Allowing users to enter any textual description of colour does not promote consistency.

Key Takeaways

- *IM is more than a technical necessity: it is also a means of improving performance in a project or enterprise and therefore a key component of overall management*
- *IM is inclusive and accepts all kinds of information, from structured, semi-structured and unstructured sources*
- *As a structured information system, BIM simplifies IM*
- *IM has two main goals: regulate information flow and safeguard or improve information quality*
- *Custodianship of information is critical for information control*
- *Information flow relates to the syntagmatic dimension of a representation and draws from the sequence of tasks in a process, as well as from extrinsic constraints*
- *In managing information flow one needs to make explicit what, who, how and when*
- *The I-P-O scheme helps translate tasks into information actions*
- *Even before a design takes shape, there are substantial amounts of information that should be made explicit in a model as feedforward*

- *Information quality concerns the paradigmatic dimension and can therefore build on the semantic typology of data*
- *In addition to semantic and pragmatic criteria, information quality also depends on completeness, coherence and consistency*

Exercises

1. Use the I-P-O scheme to explain how one decides on the width of an internal door in a design. Cluster the input by origin (general, specific, project) and describe the relations between input items.
2. Use the I-P-O scheme to explain what, who, how and when in deciding the layout of an office landscape, particularly:
    1. Which workstation types are to be included, including dimensions and other requirements.
    2. How instances of these types are to be arranged to achieve maximum capacity.
3. In a BIM editor of your choice make the permissible building envelope for a building in a location of your choice. Describe the process in terms of input, information instances produced and resulting constraints for various kinds of symbols in the model.
4. Evaluate the completeness, coherence and consistency of the permissible building envelope model you have made.
5. Analyse how one should constrain types of building elements in relation to performance expectations from the use type of building: compare a hotel bedroom to a hospital ward on the basis of a building code of your choice. Explain which symbol properties are involved and how.

Notes

1. The views on DM derive primarily from: Richards, M., 2010. *Building Information Management – a standard framework and guide to BS 1192.* London: BSI; Eynon, J., 2013. *The design manager's handbook.* Southern Gate, Chichester, West Sussex, UK: CIOB, John Wiley & Sons; Emmitt, S., 2014. *Design management for architects* (2nd ed.). Hoboken NJ: Wiley
2. The presentation of IM is based on: Bytheway, A., 2014. *Investing in information.* New York: Springer; Detlor, B., 2010. Information management. *International Journal of Information Management,* **30**(*2*), 103-108, doi:10.1016/j.ijinfomgt.2009.12.001; Flett, A., 2011. Information management possible?: Why is information management so difficult? *Business Information Review,* **28**(*2*), 92-100, doi:10.1177/0266382111411066; Rosenfeld, L., Morville, P., & Arango, J., 2015. *Information architecture: for the web and beyond* (4th ed.). Sebastopol CA: O'Reilly Media.
3. IM definitions of information quality derive from: Wang, R.Y., & Strong, D.M., 1996. Beyond accuracy: what data quality means to data consumers. *Journal of Management Information Systems,* **12**(*4*), 5-33.

doi:10.1080/07421222.1996.11518099; English, L.P., 1999. *Improving data warehouse and business information quality: methods for reducing costs and increasing profits.* New York: Wiley.

PART IV

MANAGEMENT

In this part, we conclude the exploration of how digitization and information impact on AECO by focusing on the relation between information and management: how IM contributes to performance by improving not only clarity and transparency but also consistency, efficiency and effectiveness. Previous parts have explained:

- How digitization has changed expectations and attitudes concerning information.
- The structure of digital symbolic representations and their differences from analogue representations.
- What data and information are, and the principles of digital information management.

The viewpoint of this part is primarily managerial. While it is tempting to focus on specific AECO aspects and disciplines, and consider information in a narrower frame, for example study the relations between design, creativity and representation, there are several important reasons for adopting a managerial viewpoint. First and foremost, management is normally about the whole of a process or project. From this holistic perspective, information is less what each actor produces or consumes and more what enables actors and stakeholders to interact with each other concerning common goals and constraints; it is what returns an overview of the whole and an understanding of parts one is only indirectly linked to. In short, the true value of information in a process becomes apparent when considered in the wider frame of someone with a general mandate and overall interests.

Armed with an understanding of symbolic representations, graphs and semantic data types from the previous parts, we consider what we do with information when and where it matters in a process. Unfortunately, as the next chapter explains, the answer is: not much. Our cognition appears to be built in a way that allows us to operate effectively and efficiently in many common situations but also makes us biased and failure-prone in other, more demanding situations. Cognitive limitations are hard to overcome but we should at least provide the means for recognizing them and correcting their mistakes. The book contributes towards this objective by stressing the duality of process and information management, and making it operational, transparent and supportive of reflective and analytical thinking.

CHAPTER 8

Decisions and information

The chapter introduces the dual-process theory and explains its relevance to decision making in AECO. It presents the foundations of the theory and a number of illusions, biases and fallacies that derive from our cognitive limitations.

DUAL-PROCESS THEORY

One of the striking scientific developments around the turn of the century was that several compatible and often complementary views of mental duality emerged independently, in different contexts and disciplines, ranging from social psychology and neuropsychology to decision theory and economics. The notion of many different systems in the brain is not new but what distinguishes the dual-process theory from earlier views is that it builds on a better understanding of the brain's biologic and cognitive structure to suggest that there are two different types of thinking, each with different functions, strengths and weaknesses:

1. *Type 1* processes: these are autonomous, unconscious, automatically executed when relevant stimuli are encountered, unguided by higher-level control systems, fast, low-effort, often parallel and with a high processing capacity. Examples of Type 1 processes are simple mental calculations, such as 2 + 3, the recognition of a common animal species like a dog, the detection of hostility in a person's voice and the identification of a roof in an elevation drawing.
2. *Type 2* processes, which are the opposite: controlled, analytical, slow, high-effort, generally serial and with a limited processing capacity. Examples of Type 2 processes are demanding mental calculations, such as 3943 × 2187, filling in an insurance form for a motor vehicle accident and looking for inward-opening swing doors wider than 67 cm in a floor plan of a large building.

For their immediate responses in a variety of situations, Type 1 processes rely on encapsulated knowledge and tightly compiled learned information, accumulated through exposure and personal experience common to the majority of people. Some of the best examples concern *affordances:* the actionable properties an environment presents to us, such as that we can walk on a pavement or go through a door. These are things anyone can do, usually equally well. Other things are restricted to a minority of individuals and are often an indication of expertise, for example in a hobby like fishing or a sport like table tennis. Nevertheless, they are all acquired and encoded in a similar manner. In fact, expertise in dual-process theory is seen as an extension of common capacities through practice: in the same way a child learns to recognize animal species, an expert learns to recognize familiar elements in new situations and deploy ready interpretations and actions. It should be noted that expertise is not a single skill but a large collection of small skills: an expert footballer is capable of simultaneously (or in quick succession) doing many small things both individually and in a team, from controlling a ball coming at different speeds and from different directions to passing the ball to teammates according to an agreed plan, taking into account their individual capacities and position in the field.

Type 2 processes are distinguished into two categories. The first consists of *reflective* processes, which evaluate Type 1 thinking and its results on the basis of beliefs and goals. Reflection often involves cognitive simulation and can be triggered by the outcome of Type 1 processes, such as the feeling of doubt that arises from frequent failure, for example constant slipping on a frozen pavement. It is also linked to interpersonal communication and the need to explain or justify proposed joint actions and goals, such as the tactics of a football team. Once activated, reflective processes can interrupt or override Type 1 processing, suppress its responses and reallocate expensive mental resources from failing Type 1 processes to searches for alternative solutions through Type 2 thinking.

These solutions are the subject of the second category in Type 2 thinking, *algorithmic* processes: strategies, rule systems, general and specific knowledge, usually learned formally and therefore bounded by culture. For example, unlike a simple DIY job, a loft conversion requires more meticulous organization, which can be based on empirically acquired knowledge, a textbook on home improvement or Internet tutorials. If the project is undertaken by AECO professionals, it inevitably also draws from their training in design, construction, time planning and site management. One of the basic functions of algorithmic processes is *cognitive decoupling:* the distinction between representations of the world used in Type 1 processes and representations required for the analysis of imaginary or abstract situations. Cognitive decoupling concerns both substituting the naïve representations implicit in daily life, such as that of a flat earth, and allowing for imaginary situations, such as a cubic earth, which form settings for hypothetical reasoning.

It should be pointed out that Type 2 processes do not necessarily return better results than Type 1 ones. Being highly demanding, mentally expensive, subject to personal intelligence and knowledge, and founded on Type 1 biases or professional thinking habits, they may also lead to failure. Being usually acquired through formal learning, they may also be limited or failure-prone because of theoretical and methodical issues. For example, before the Copernican revolution, learned astronomers made fundamental mistakes because they based their work on erroneous earth-centric models, not because they made errors in their calculations. What Type 2 processes certainly do is avoid the biases of Type 1 thinking and therefore have smaller error margins, moreover neither too high nor too low with respect to the truth. Kepler's laws of the heliocentric model and Newtonian mechanics form a sound basis for calculating planetary motion with sufficient precision and accuracy, regardless of the means used for the calculation.

Dual-process theory has a number of advantages that explain its acceptance and popularity in many application areas. One advantage is that it makes evident why we are are so good at some tasks and so poor at others. For example, we are good grammarians: children at the age of four are already capable of forming grammatically correct sentences. By contrast, we are poor statisticians: we are clever enough to have invented statistics but nevertheless fail to apply statistical thinking in everyday situations that clearly demand it, such as games of chance. The reason for this is that Type 1 processes represent categories by prototypes or typical examples. As a result, they rely on averages and stereotypes, avoiding even relatively easy calculations for drawing conclusions about individual cases from what is known about relevant categories. Interestingly, most people have little difficulty making these Type 2 calculations when asked to do so.

Such variability in cognitive performance should not be mistaken for inconsistency. It is instead an indication of conflicts that are inherent in our cognitive mechanisms. Dual-process theory has the advantage that it includes these conflicts in its core, as opposed to treating them as a loose collection of anomalies to be resolved afterwards, as exceptions to the rules. The most fundamental conflict is that Type 1 processes which undeniably serve us well in most situations are also the cause of frequent and persistent failures, some of which are discussed below. A related conflict is the constant struggle between Type 1 and Type 2 thinking for dominance and mental resources. At practically every moment of the day, we need to choose between what we do automatically and what requires analytical treatment. Sometimes what attracts our attention is an established priority, such as as an exam question. At other times, it is a sudden occurrence or a new priority, for example a sudden opening of a door or a cramp in the writing arm. At yet other times, it is anti-data, such as a pen that fails to write. We are constantly asked to prioritize in a continually changing landscape of often apparently unrelated tasks that nevertheless affect our performance both overall and with respect to specific goals. Unfortunately, we often fail because of Type 1 biases and underlying cognitive limitations.

COGNITIVE ILLUSIONS, BIASES, FALLACIES AND FAILURES

INATTENTIONAL AND CHANGE BLINDNESS

A typical failure caused by our cognitive limitations is *inattentional blindness:* we systematically fail to notice unexpected things and events, especially when we are concentrating on another, relatively hard task. This is why we may fail to see a cyclist appear next to the car we are driving in heavy traffic (unless of course cyclists are an expected part of this traffic, as in most Dutch cities). Inattentional blindness is hazardous in traffic but the same neglect for unexpected things around us is actually helpful in many other situations because it allows us to reserve our limited cognitive capacities for important tasks at hand. When taking an exam, for example, we do not want to be distracted by extraneous stimuli, such as noise coming from outside, unnecessary movement in the room or incoming messages on social media.

Closely related is *change blindness:* the failure to see obvious changes in something unfolding in front of our eyes, primarily because we are concentrating on something else, usually a narrative (a subject discussed in more detail later in this chapter). Typical examples are continuity errors in films, which most viewers miss until someone points them out, making them immediately and permanently glaringly obvious to all. Just like inattentional blindness, change blindness is due to our memory limitations: perception is followed by recognition of meaning, which is what we encode in memory rather than every detail of the percept. What we retain in memory is an image or narrative that is above all coherent and consistent with its meaning. This also means that we may embellish the memory with fictitious details that fit the meaning and the emotions it elicits. Vivid details are often an indication of such reproduction *after* the memory was formed.

PLANNING AND SUNK-COSTS FALLACIES

A popular subject in news stories are projects poorly conceived by clients and developers, inadequately understood by politicians and authorities that endorse them, and unquestioningly attempted by designers and engineers, with dramatic failures as a result. Such projects are often linked to the *planning fallacy:* we tend to make designs, plans and forecasts unrealistically close to best-case scenarios, neglecting to compare them to the outcomes of similar projects, therefore repeating mistakes that have led to previous failures. Common reasons behind the planning fallacy are the desire to have a design approved, pressure to have a project completed and a general tendency to act fast so as not to delay. These push decision makers to quick, overoptimistic, typically Type 1 decisions that remain unchecked.

Interestingly, these attitudes persist when the failure becomes apparent, usually by the height of sunk costs. Rather than accept defeat and cut their losses, many stakeholders insist on throwing good money after bad, desperately continuing the project, in the vain hope to change its fortunes around. The escalation of commitment caused by the *sunk-costs fallacy* is often celebrated for merely reaching some goals, ignoring the devastation it has brought along. It seems that the height of the sunk costs actually increases commitment, as well as the misguided appreciation of partial goals (often just the completion of the project), which confuses stubbornness and incompetence with heroism.

In principle, optimism in the face of danger or failure is a positive characteristic. It encourages us to persist against obstacles and, in many cases, to overcome them. A defeatist attitude under difficult conditions is obviously unhelpful for survival but the same also holds for insistence that is uninformed and uncontrolled by rational analysis. For example, any decision to repair a damaged car should depend on the technical and economic feasibility of the repairs, in relation to the value and utility of the car. Endless expensive repairs of a car that can be easily replaced by another rarely make sense.

INSIDE AND OUTSIDE VIEW

Such fallacies are reinforced by the tendency of stakeholders to stick to *inside views:* views shared by the project participants, relying too much on information produced in the project by the participants themselves. By repeatedly using and sharing this information, such as an early budget or time plan, they end up believing it unquestioningly, even when new developments should cast doubt on earlier decisions and lead to major adjustments in the project (relation to change blindness). Consequently, participants subscribing to an inside view tend to underestimate problems and dangers that are evident from an *outside view,* i.e. one that covers the whole class to which the project belongs and the statistics of this class. Failing to adopt outside views reduces the validity of any basic decision in a project. It also causes unwarranted, pervasive optimism: the mistaken belief that this project is surely not subject to the causes of failure in other, very similar projects.

ILLUSIONS OF KNOWLEDGE, CONFIDENCE AND SKILL

Planning fallacies and inside views are linked to the *illusion of knowledge:* we think that we know more than we actually do because we understand *what* happens and mistake it for an understanding of *why* it happens. The consequence is that we rarely doubt our beliefs and assumptions, and, when confronted with a task, we plunge into direct action before we fully understand the situation. The more complex the task, the more profound the illusion and the more dangerous its effects.

A complementary illusion is that of *confidence:* we tend to delegate tasks to actors on the basis of what they believe they can do. Even without relevant qualifications or a convincing track record, a person can be confident about their competence to do something and claim it. Even worse, others are inclined to accept the claim: we treat the confidence of a person in their abilities as a true measure of their skill or expertise and therefore overestimate their capacities. However, as talent shows make abundantly and embarrassingly obvious, incompetent people are often overconfident about their abilities. They audition for something that they clearly cannot do, not as a joke but because they genuinely believe in themselves. Moreover, the *illusion of skill* from which they suffer means that they are less inclined to improve their skills. By contrast, highly skilled persons, such as top athletes and celebrated musicians, always look for ways to improve themselves, e.g. through constant, demanding and often innovative training. Similarly, true experts are aware of their limitations and scope (unlike users of questionable or arbitrary expert-like heuristics), and constantly try to augment or refine their interpretations and solutions in every new situation they encounter.

The illusions of knowledge, skill and confidence are not confined to extreme cases, like the ones in talent shows. Most people suffer from it, typically undertaking jobs they botch and abandon, e.g. in DIY. More importantly, they tend to attribute good performance to superior skills or expertise rather than luck and bad performance to accidental or unforeseen conditions that are beyond their control or to the incompetence or obstruction of others. Even seasoned professionals may be confident that they can achieve the necessary goals in a project, despite having failed to deliver in previous projects. However, experience is not the same as expertise or ability. The true hallmark of knowledge and skill is a persistently high performance, as attested by our expectations from e.g. professional musicians and surgeons.

SUBSTITUTION

One of the clever strategies of Type 1 thinking is that difficult problems are routinely substituted by simpler ones. Rather than taking the trouble of calculating a sum like 3943 × 2187 precisely, we approximate by calculating 4 × 2 and then adding zeros for the thousands. This is acceptable in many situations but can be misleading in others. For example, when people are asked how happy they are, they invariably base their answer on their current mood and give an answer that reflects only very recent events and conditions. Regrettably, the fluency by which Type 1 thinking finds solutions to the simple problems makes us think that we have found adequate solutions to the complex ones they have substituted. Consequently, we seldom attempt to solve or even understand the complex problems. Instead, we resort to approximations and received wisdom, and so frequently fail to utilize the tools, knowledge and information at our disposal. Simplifying a mental calculation may be a clever strategy but doing so in a spreadsheet or a calculator is pointless, especially if precision is required.

FRAMING

Fallacies and illusions often relate to *narrow framing:* focusing on the individual project rather than the enterprises involved in it or focusing on a single problem rather than the whole project. What appears to be the right decision in a narrow frame is often patently wrong when considered more broadly, in relation to other issues and options or for a longer term. However embarrassing, the termination of a failing project may be right for the enterprise and its fortunes, as it allows allocation of resources elsewhere instead of increasing sunk costs. Crucially, a situation can be framed positively or negatively. Our reactions to e.g. the Internet are influenced by how it is presented: either as a source of hidden dangers or a universe of new opportunities. Similarly, a budget overrun by 46,3 million euros for a major, demanding building may raise few eyebrows among people familiar with much worse cases in infrastructure and defence projects but the same overrun expressed as 26% of the original budget sounds more serious.[1]

One of the most significant recent developments in decision theory goes beyond the realization that framing and the context it creates influence decision taking: it actively deploys a *choice architecture* that structures this context and *nudges* decisions towards better choices without forcing any outcomes. This involves using suitable defaults (e.g. opting out of organ donation instead of opting in) and making the various options more comprehensible (by providing clear information on what they entail in both short and long term) to prevent people from taking simplistic solutions when the number of choices and complexity of problems increase. Nudging accepts the possibility that people make errors and develops means to suppress them. In addition to the above feedforward mechanisms, a choice architecture should also provide feedback that informs people on the consequences of their decisions, warns them if things go wrong and allows them to learn about the tasks they are facing and their own behaviour and performance.

NARRATIVES, COHERENCE AND CAUSES

We have all experienced it in one form or another: we have attended a presentation that convinced us but afterwards it was unclear why; we have enjoyed watching a film only to realize later that the plot was full of holes. The success of a narrative is often due to the *halo effect:* a presentation delivered by someone we like, respect or admire is received positively by Type 1 thinking, often impeding Type 2 processes from analysing its content. But even without this effect, our love of narratives and the coherence they bring to our perceptions and experiences are decisive. Type 1 thinking looks for coherence in a story and confuses it with quality of evidence: if the narrative is coherent, it is plausible and therefore acceptable. Its probability matters little; it suffices that it is a simple, concrete story about a few striking events, with enough detail to make it realistic.

This is the kind of stories that convinces and appeals to us in real life, in literature or in films. These stories usually tell us that practically everything is due to talent, stupidity or intention. They can therefore be didactic or inspirational, allowing us to marvel at the leadership of a great military hero or a titan of industry. The role of luck and circumstance is often ignored, in a way that makes us believe not only that we understand the past and the present but also predict and control the future. On the positive side, this allows the development of beliefs and confidence in them, so that we are not easily daunted by adversity or yet unsolved problems. The "never mind, we'll find a solution; let's crack on now" mentality can be beneficial for survival but not necessarily helpful with problems that require careful analysis and planning, such as big construction projects.

Unfortunately, narratives may contain invented causes that help facts connect and make sense together. This also implies selectivity as to which facts are included. As information is costly to obtain, store and process in our brains, we apply the same simplification as in our memories: we reduce narratives into something simple that makes sense and reveals agents, intentions and causes with clear characteristics and relations. Interestingly, we then embellish narratives (similarly to memories) with details that make them more believable, consistent and coherent — details that may have been invented or imagined, at the cost of others that reveal the complexity or randomness of reality. This retrospective distortion of facts enhances the illusion of fully understanding reality and being able to predict it, and sustains a dangerous eagerness to accept overgeneralizations like "generation X", zodiac signs or perfect curves that profess to be analytical, despite their lack of foundation in real data.

Part of the appeal of narratives lies in their linear structure, which reinforces three biases that make us jump to conclusions: our minds are built to assume causality on the basis of precedence in time, to infer causes from coincidence and to detect meaning in patterns. These Type 1 cornerstones allow us to connect events like the flicking of a switch to a light turning on, identify malfunctions in a machine by the sounds it makes and recognize familiar persons in a crowd by the way they move. On the negative side, they lead to *illusions of cause* when we infer relations and patterns in random data. The illusion may affect even experts who, when confronted with randomness or unknown patterns, do not pause to consider alternatives but remain in Type 1 mode and seek confirmation of what they know or expect. Spurious correlations are quite easy to find given enough data but unfortunately not all of them are as obviously ridiculous as the link of US spending on science, space and technology to the number of suicides by hanging, strangulation or suffocation; margarine consumption to the divorce rate in Maine; the age of Miss America to murders by steam, hot vapours or hot objects; the consumption of mozzarella cheese to civil engineering doctorates; or superstitions like an athlete always wearing the same "lucky" socks.[2]

Narratives are also inherently unfair, as we realize from the need to change the narratives of the colonial past: the old depictions and descriptions of persons and events were at best partial and selective, providing coherence and simplicity by downplaying the complexity of a world that often seems inexplicable because it contains things we consider improbable or fixed. Change blindness makes us fail to notice things that change if they fall outside the narrative and so eliminate them from the story, which is then presented in a way that reinforces the remaining points. In this way, other facts and perspectives remain hidden, only to resurface too late, when the partiality and unfairness of the narrative has become painfully obvious.

DUAL PROCESSES AND INFORMATION

A widely accepted explanation for our frequent, systematic cognitive failures is that the otherwise highly efficient Type 1 processes stem from our evolution and adaptation to a world quite different to today's highly technological, fast and busy environment. Back then, our cognitive systems developed ways to allocate their limited resources for the requirements of fundamental tasks at walking or running speed, not for demanding problems in mathematics or the much higher speed of motorized traffic. The world has since changed, as have our activities and priorities it it, but Type 1 processes remain the same, making us prone to biases and errors. What makes us able to use simple construction tools to build a garden wall is not what is required in planning and executing the realization of a skyscraper.

Unfortunately, our capability at many everyday tasks makes us overconfident about our cognitive abilities in general. We confuse the fluency of Type 1 processes with deep understanding and treat it as a general performance guarantee. This causes the cognitive illusions that make us underperform with worrying regularity. Even worse, we seem unable to appreciate the significance of these illusions and the frequency or magnitude of our failures. Law courts, for example, insist on putting too much weight on eyewitness accounts, despite known limitations of our memory and especially the tendency to reconstruct memories and complement them with fictitious details that enhance their meaning.

Most scientists agree that our cognitive limitations cannot be avoided. All we can do is be aware of them and remain alert to situations and conditions that require activation of Type 2 reflective processes: learn to recognize and neutralize biases, so as to avoid the pitfalls of intuitive, automatic decisions and actions. To do so, we require information that helps us both fully understand the situation and identify better solutions through Type 2 algorithmic processing. Making explicit the information surrounding every task in a process is therefore a prerequisite to any improvement in our decision making. Finding this information and processing it towards better solutions often involves the use of technologies that aid memory, such as writing, or processing, such as calculators. It follows that digital information technologies are a key part of the further, hybrid evolution of human thinking. Matching their structure and potential to our cognitive capacities is the starting point for understanding how IM can support decision making.

AECO AND DUAL-PROCESS THEORY

Among the examples of failure mentioned in dual-process literature, AECO has a prominent place: its history is full of examples of the planning fallacy. Defence, industrial, ICT and infrastructure projects may result in higher overruns but the AECO examples are far more frequent and widespread. The reasons behind the planning fallacy appear to be endemic in AECO and regularly lead to hasty designs or project plans, build on largely unfounded Type 1 decisions. As one would expect, the disregard for realism and reliability does not change when projects start to fail or are affected by sunk costs. AECO stakeholders stubbornly keep investing in failures, focusing on project goals and anchoring on plans that are clearly faulty. Despite the availability of data, knowledge and advanced tools, many decisions are taken on the basis of norms and rules of thumb, which encourage superficial treatment of building performance and process structure. The result is that costs increase disproportionately, while even minor cuts or concessions dramatically reduce quality and scope. In the end, it seems that all that matters is that the buildings are realized, however expensive or poor. Even when we avoid outright failure, we generally produce buildings with the same severe limitations, through the same processes that have returned so many earlier mediocrities or failures.

The planning fallacy in AECO is reinforced by strong inside views. The dictum "every building is unique" is misleading because it ignores similarities not only between the composition and performance of buildings at various levels (from that of individual parts like doors and corridors to common configurations like open-plan offices) but also between the processes of development, realization and use in different projects. It leads to an arrogant, persistent repetition of the same mistakes, coupled to lack of interest in thorough analyses that can reveal what goes wrong. It seems than the main priority of AECO is to keep on producing, even though the high turnover in construction is linked to a rather low mark-up for many stakeholders.

Under these conditions, substitution is rife in AECO. Practically everything is kept as simple as possible, regardless of what is actually needed. This especially affects forecasts, such as cost estimates, and analyses, which are reduced to mere box ticking against basic norms like building codes. Compliance clearly weighs more heavily than real performance and this adds to the persistence of outdated approaches and technologies. While other production sectors increasingly invest in advanced computerization, AECO insists on doing too much manually, simultaneously heavily relying on cheap labour.

Such issues are exacerbated by the frequently loose structure of AECO processes, which include large numbers of black boxes with uncertain connections between them. These black boxes generally relate to the illusion of confidence, which underlies the delegation of aspects and responsibilities to specific actors. It is often enough that these actors represent a discipline relevant to an aspect; if they also emanate confidence in their knowledge and decisions, we tend to take it for granted that they know what they are doing and so impose few if any checks on their contributions — checks on which any sensible manager should insist anyway, given the high failure rate in AECO projects and the blame games that follow failure.

As for narratives and their capacity to obscure true causes, the halo effect has a strong presence in AECO, as attested by the attention given to famous architects and the belief that their designs are good by default. Any failure by a grand name is either a heroic one, attempted against all odds, or the result of unjust lack of acceptance or support by others. The culture of learning from prominent peers means that lesser AECO professionals are also fully aware of the power of a coherent narrative and therefore often choose to focus on simple, strong ideas rather than detailed, fully worked-out designs and plans. This is facilitated by ritual processes, formulated as prescriptive, box-ticking sequences of actions, products and stages: a process can usually proceed only if the previous steps have been completed, for example, if there are drawings of the design at the agreed scale, budgets and time schedules. The presence of these carriers is more important than the quality of their content, which remains unchecked until a problem emerges later on. So long as the coherence of the core narrative holds, we see what we want to see, oblivious to our inattentional or change blindness. This also leads to illusions of cause: we often attribute problems and failures to the immediately previous stage of a project, instead of searching for true causes throughout the project.

The fallacies and illusions in AECO are closely related to narrow and biased framing that isolates problems and solutions. For example, policy makers propose intensified, denser and higher housing construction in the Dutch Randstad in order to meet demand, without linking this to other issues, such as environmental concerns (e.g. the negative effects of urban heat islands) or transportation problems. These issues are subjects of other ongoing debates and current policies, which are kept separate, even though they are obviously related to urbanization and will be directly affected by housing development. By keeping them out of the housing demand frame, their resolution is deferred to a later stage, when the effects of this urbanization wave may have become painfully apparent and possibly irreversible. The danger is that they will be addressed only then, again in a piecemeal, narrow-frame fashion.

In short, despite the nature of its problems and solutions, AECO thinking appears dominated by Type 1 processes. Quick decisions based on norm, habit, principle or goal proliferate, notwithstanding the availability of detailed specifications (e.g. construction drawings) that could be used for precise evaluations of validity and feasibility. Moreover, such specifications and evaluations usually come after the decisions are taken and are constrained by resulting narratives: what does not fit the basic message that should conveyed in a project is frequently underplayed.

THE SOCIAL AND INFORMATION SIDES

An ingrained bias in process management is the frequent overemphasis on the social side: the stakeholders and actors, their interests, what they should do and when, and how to align them towards common goals and joint products. While this side of management is obviously significant, it also entails the danger of black boxes, formed out of generic, vague assumptions and expectations. We roughly know the capacities and remit of each participant in a project, so we feel disinclined to specify their contributions to the project or the connections between contributions in detail. Instead, we assume that everyone will do their bit and problems will be solved automatically, perhaps even before we realize their existence.

However, as the dual-process theory explains, this view is a highly suspect product of Type 1 thinking. The consequences of uncontrollable black boxes and undefined connections can be quite grave. A manager can always adopt a laissez-faire attitude and wait for crises to emerge in a project, in the knowledge that crises trigger action. Unfortunately, not all problems qualify as crises. In many cases, failure is the sum of many smaller problems that remain systematically unsolved (a characteristic malaise in AECO). But even when the problems are big enough for the crisis to be recognized, it may be too late for effective and economic solutions (as the sunk-costs fallacy indicates). The obvious solution is to structure processes clearly and consistently as a sequence of specific tasks for particular actors (the subject of the chapter on process diagrams), so that we can deploy constructive Type 2 reflection. However, the resulting critical review of a process is not enough. We additionally need to understand and control the process in terms of its main currency, information: what connects stakeholders, actors and tasks, what is consumed and produced in each task.

By managing information in addition to social interactions, we ensure that each task receives the right input and returns the right output, that tasks are unambiguously linked (as the output of one becomes input to another) and that all tasks are consistently and coherently specified.

Each participant can consequently know what is required of them, and what they should have to do their job. This makes the management of a process transparent and controllable, devoid of black boxes and grey areas. In this sense, the information side validates the social side, revealing possible gaps and inconsistencies, and removing unnecessary vagueness from the process.

Decision making in AECO is ostensibly based on expertise and often takes place in settings that justify the emphasis on expertise: confusing and dynamic situations, unclear goals and poorly defined procedures, a looming larger context and time pressure. These are typical of conditions in the field, where true experts, such as firefighters, pilots and nurses, must take rapid, difficult decisions under pressure and uncertainty. One could argue that similar conditions exist in many AECO situations, from design reviews to construction sites. However, the similarity is generally superficial or even artificial. There are very few situations in AECO that qualify as true emergencies. In most cases, it is the emphasis on the social side of management and the power games it involves that define the conditions, underplaying the information side and its significance for decision making. In essence, emergency conditions are created in AECO through poor preparation, inadequate procedures and lack of analyses or development in depth. Such inadequacies create the illusion that decisions must be taken on principle or on the basis of expertise and in total disregard to the huge amounts of information AECO professionals typically produce in documenting a situation and developing a design or plan. Relegating this information to a mere background for the personalities involved in a project makes little sense for the functioning of decision makers, as well as with respect to the information-intensive character of AECO.

Even when expertise is called for, it is not a matter of gut feeling alone. Analyses of decision making by experts suggest that it is a two-stage process: it does start with intuition (recognition of how one needs to respond to a situation) but this is followed by deliberate evaluation (simulation of response and its outcomes). In this blend of intuition and analysis, the simulation can be mental but is nevertheless based on information, including both general rules and specific characteristics of the particular situation. A firefighter, for example, needs to know the materials and structure of a building on fire in order to predict how the envelope and the load-bearing structure may behave or how smoke may develop in egress routes. The more relevant information is available, the better for the decision making. Furthermore, experts often rely on explicit information tools for aiding their memory and structuring their procedures, such as data charts and checklists.

The conclusion we can draw from this is that even if we treat every participant in an AECO project as an expert, capable of amazing Type 1 feats, there is every reason to invest in IM for a number of critical reasons:

- Clear information structures and flows allow managers to understand what takes place and guide the process.
- Reliable and meaningful information around each task helps other participants evaluate and adjust their own actions, generally without the need for interventions by manager.
- Any such intervention can be made less confrontational, as well as more operational, if conveyed through information.

RECOMMENDED FURTHER READING

Four books that explain dual-process theory in order of accessibility to a wider audience:

- Kahneman, D. (2013). *Thinking, fast and slow.* New York: Farrar, Straus and Giroux.
- Chabris, C. F., & Simons, D. J. (2010). *The invisible gorilla: and other ways our intuitions deceive us.* New York: Crown.
- Stanovich, K. E. (2011). *Rationality and the reflective mind.* New York: Oxford University Press.
- Evans, J. S. B. T., & Frankish, K. (2009). *In two minds: dual processes and beyond.* Oxford: Oxford University Press.

Nudge theory and choice architecture are presented in: Thaler, R. H., & Sunstein, C. R. (2021). *Nudge: the final edition*. New Haven: Yale University Press.

A enlightening analysis of true expertise is: Klein, G. A. (1998). *Sources of power: how people make decisions.* Cambridge MA: MIT Press.

The benefits of checklists for medical and other experts are presented in: Gawande, A. (2010). *The checklist manifesto: how to get things right.* New York: Metropolitan Books.

y Takeaways

- *Thinking comes in two different types, Type 1(fast but biased) and Type 2 (analytical but slow and expensive)*
- *Type 2 processes can be reflective (evaluation of Type 1 results) or algorithmic (strategies, rule systems etc., often bas on cognitive decoupling)*
- *Failures due to Type 1 thinking include: inattentional and change blindness; planning and sun-costs fallacies; inside views; illusions of knowledge, confidence, skill and cause; inappropriate substitution; narrow framing; false coherenc invented causes and partiality in narratives*
- *The activation and execution of Type 2 processes depends on information*
- *AECO exhibits many failures that suggest a dominance of Type 1 thinking*
- *Management has a social and an information side*
- *True expertise relies on information*

ercises

1. Analyse a project known from literature to have suffered from planning or sunk-cost fallacies:
    1. What were the causes of the failure in terms of the dual-process theory?
    2. What would be the right frame and outside view for the project?
    3. Which information is critical in this frame and view?
2. Study the MacLeamy curve (any variation):
    1. Is it a law, a generalization (like Moore's "law") or an overgeneralization?
    2. Which information is necessary for constructing the curve?
    3. Give three examples that do not fit the curve, including specific information and the resulting curve.

Notes

1. The budget overrun example concerns the Amare cultural complex in The Hague, as calculated by the local Court of Auditors: https://www.rekenkamerdenhaag.nl/publicatie-onderwijs-en-cultuurcomplex/.
2. For a number of amusing spurious correlations, see http://tylervigen.com.

CHAPTER 9

Process diagrams

This chapter explains how a process can be described as a graph of tasks that affords overview and supports reliable planning and effective guidance for each task and the whole process. By doing so, process diagrams address many questions on the social side of management. The chapter presupposes knowledge of graphs and in particular of directed graphs (see Appendix I).

PROCESS DESCRIPTIONS

As we have seen in the chapter on IM, there is a strong correspondence between the sequence of tasks in a process and the sequence of information actions: process management and IM overlap. Therefore, the first step towards effective IM in any process is understanding the process itself: what people do and how their actions, decisions, interactions and transactions relate to the production, dissemination and utilization of information. Starting IM by analysing the process also has advantages for the deployment of IM measures: most people and organizations are more process-oriented than information-oriented. As a result, they may have difficulty identifying and organizing information actions without a clear operational context. Using a process model as basis makes clearer why and how one should manage information.

The various ways of describing processes fall under two main kinds:

1. *Textual* descriptions, such as reports, often including tables and lists that summarize key points
2. *Diagrammatic* descriptions: visual displays of the process structure, either focusing on the overall picture or providing step-by-step descriptions of the process flow

The two kinds are complementary: textual descriptions can be detailed specifications, while diagrammatic ones afford overview. This fundamental difference makes textual descriptions better suited for the level of single tasks and diagrammatic ones the unmissable starting point for the whole process. Doing away with diagrammatic descriptions and relying solely on texts is inadvisable because of the resulting difficulty in constructing mental overviews. Recognizing dependencies between multiple tasks, redundancies, omissions and other process characteristics is quite demanding for any reader of a text. It can lead to unnecessary errors in interpretation, including through illusions of cause from presumed precedence or coincidence in time, especially in sequential processes (which abound in AECO). Diagrammatic descriptions help us overcome such cognitive limitations by serving as mnemonic aids for understanding and managing processes: they can be seen as checklists of tasks and of relations between tasks that unburden actors' memories and prevent them from missing critical steps or available options at any step in a process.

This chapter builds on the potential of graphs to answer two fundamental questions:

1. *How* process diagrams should be made: the syntactic and semantic rules they should follow to capture the composition and structure of tasks in a process with the right abstraction and consistency
2. *Which problems* can be addressed in these diagrams, with emphasis on the unwanted products of Type 1 thinking, so that the social side of management becomes both more specific and free from cognitive illusions and fallacies

FLOWCHARTS

Basic flowcharts suffice for describing practically any AECO process as a sequence of tasks towards a specific outcome. These diagrams are directed graphs (*digaphs*), in which objects are represented by *nodes* of various kinds, while relations are described by *arcs* (Figure 1). The direction of the arcs indicates the direction of flow in the process. Bidirectional arcs should be avoided because they usually fuse different relations, obscuring differences in time and purpose between denoted actions, e.g. between an evaluation and the feedback that follows. Separate representation of each such action is essential for understanding and managing process flow.

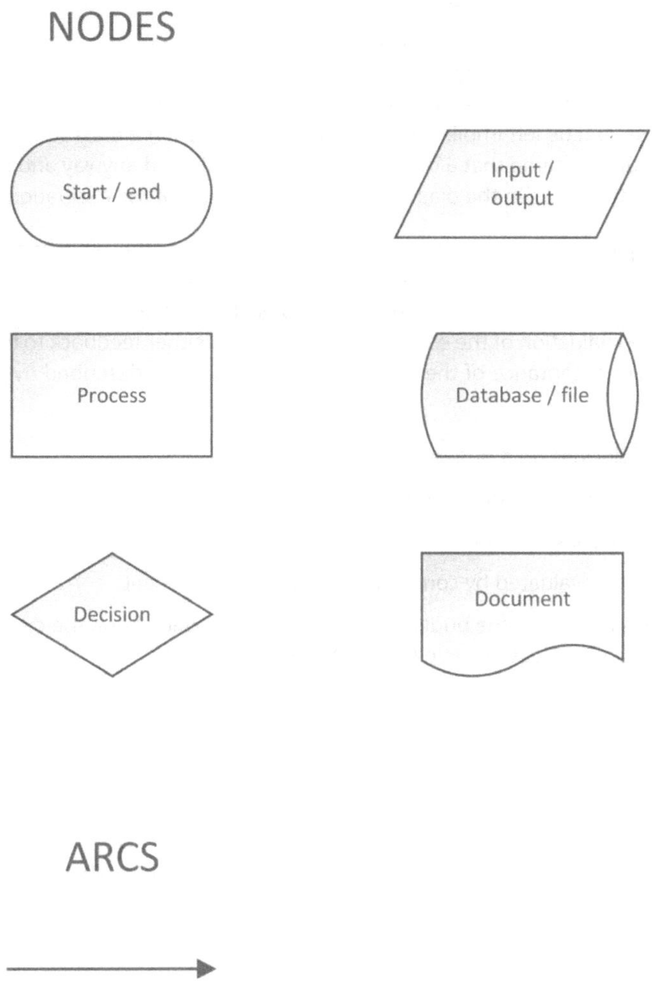

Figure 1. Nodes and arcs in a flowchart

To make an usable flowchart of a process, one should adhere to a few basic rules:

- *Uniqueness:* each thing should be represented by a single node in the diagram. The uniqueness rule makes explicit the actors, stakeholders and tasks in a process, the scope of each, process flow and, through these, the overall complexity of a process. It also permits the use of graph-theoretic measures, such as the degree of a node, in analysing the process.
- *Decision degrees:* the in- and out-degrees of each decision node should be at least 2. This means that there are at least two things to be compared in order to take the decision, for example a design and a brief, and at least two decisions that could be taken, for example

design improvement or approval.

- *Specificity and comprehensiveness:* a process flowchart is not an abstract depiction of vague intentions, like many conceptual diagrams. Each node and arc should be meaningful as an unambiguous actor, task or relation. No directly relevant task or relation should be left implicit or otherwise absent from the diagram. For example, it is not helpful to assume that a design is somehow evaluated anyway and neglect including the evaluation tasks in the diagram or omit the criteria of the evaluation.

Figure 2 is a simple example of a process in building design: the estimation of construction cost in early design, on the basis of gross floor area. The process involves three actors: a client, an architect and a cost specialist. These are responsible for the budget, the design, the cost estimation and the evaluation of the estimate, which leads to either feedback to the design (usually to lower the cost) or acceptance of the design as it is. The process described by the diagram is as follows:

1. The client decides on a budget for the building
2. The architect makes a design for that budget
3. The cost specialist estimates the costs of that design
4. The design is evaluated by comparing its costs to the budget
5. If the costs are within the budget, the design is approved; if not, the design must be improved and evaluated again (repeat from step 2)

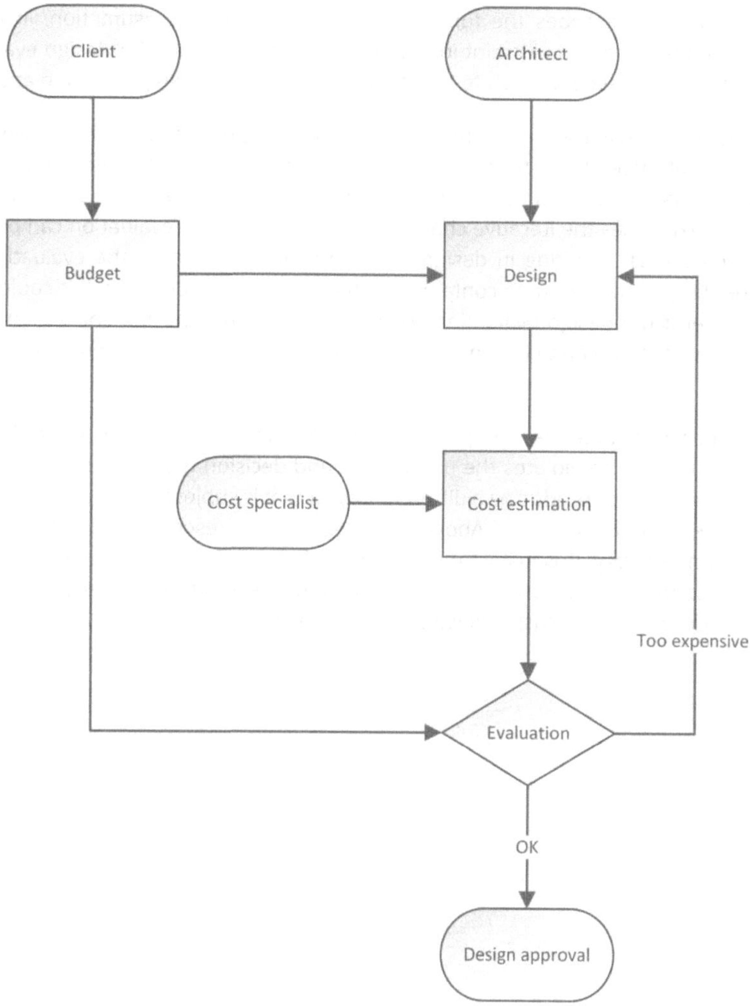

Figure 2. Cost estimation process diagram

The comparison between this list of steps and the process diagram is telling: there is nothing in the list that cannot be inferred from the diagram. Reading the diagram is faster than reading the list and the process structure is easier to recognize in the diagram than in the list, especially concerning relations between tasks. If the list was replaced by a less structured text, the differences would become even greater.

The example is purposely kept simple in order to illustrate the basic principles of process diagramming. A client obviously issues more instructions and requirements, e.g. a design brief, while the design must also take into account other goals and constraints, such as the applicable building codes and planning regulations, location features etc. Even in this simple form, however, the diagram accurately describes the fundamental structure of cost estimation, including the double role of the budget as a constraint in designing and as a criterion for design evaluation, as well as the generate-and-test approach to design (with analysis between generation and testing).

Due to the uniqueness rule, there is a single node for the design. Evaluation is followed not by a new design node but by feedback to the design. This makes clear that the decision is to improve the design rather than produce a completely new design, possibly by a new architect or with a new budget. This expresses the iterative character of design: the cost evaluation can be repeated a number of times, each resulting in design improvements, until finally the evaluation returns approval of the design. The example contains feedback only to the design but it could also feed back to the budget if the design evaluation suggested that higher investment, e.g. an energetic solution that raised construction costs but lowered operation costs, would return significant life-cycle benefits.

A process diagram without feedback loops is by definition suspect. Figure 3 is a negative example (a poor diagram), which also violates the uniqueness and decision degrees rules: it is as if many architects are involved, each producing a different design that is subjected to a different evaluation with unclear criteria and outcomes. Above all, however, it presents an iterative process as sequential, with an arbitrary, unsatisfactory conclusion that comes only because the diagram ran out of space. In comparison, Figure 2 leaves no fundamental matters unspecified, including by means of feedback to an earlier task following a transparent decision.

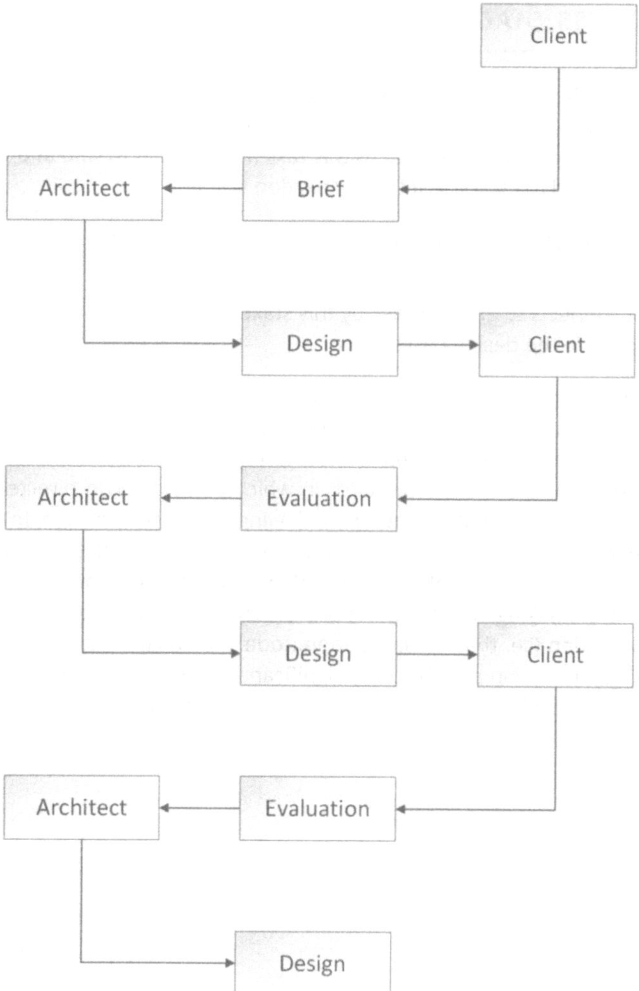

Figure 3. Inappropriate process diagram: among other mistakes, it describes an iterative design process as sequential

In short, the diagram in Figure 2 affords overview of the process in the same way that a metro map allows travellers to see every station and line in a city, the location of each station, its connections to others via different lines and the patterns that emerge in each line and any part of the metro network. The process diagram allows us to zoom in on any task, understand its immediate context, track how we come to that task and where we go from there, as well as identify general characteristics of the process, for example if it is sequential or iterative.

TESTING PROCESS DIAGRAMS

A basic way of testing the structure and content of basic diagrams is from the perspective of each actor and stakeholder. Starting from the beginning of the process, we need to consider at each node if this actor or stakeholder is related to this task (i.e link *what* to *who* and consequently also *how*). If yes, then we need to establish if the connection is:

- *Direct*: it is a task that should be undertaken by this particular actor, e.g. the design by the architect
- *Indirect*: it connects to another task by this stakeholder, e.g. the architect needs the budget to guide the design costs

Once this is completed and the diagram accordingly corrected, the involvement of each actor and stakeholder can be tracked in the process (i.e. extend to *when*). To do this, we need to examine the subgraph that contains all directed walks that start from the node of the actor or stakeholder. Figure 4 is the subgraph of the cost specialist, in which there are two directed walks to design approval: one directly after evaluation and one following feedback to design. In this subgraph, we can identify the extent of the cost specialist's involvement, examine if the sequence of the process steps is logical and, on the basis of anti-data, identify relations to other actors, stakeholders and tasks, e.g. who is making the design improvements following feedback and what are the criteria for the evaluation (i.e. that the evaluation node should connect to a budget). The results returned from this examination are obviously significant for the functioning of the particular actor or stakeholder but also useful for the manager: in many situations, missing nodes and especially arcs become apparent only in such subgraphs.

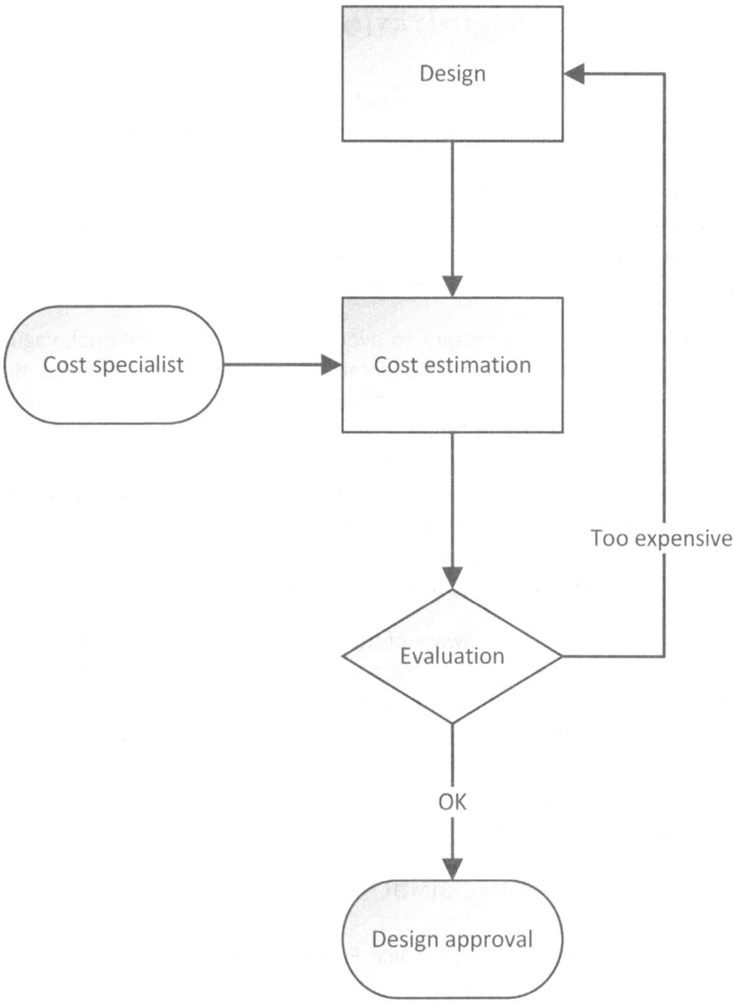

Figure 4. The subgraph of the cost specialist

Following the examination of each perspective separately, we should investigate how they come together in a simulation the process flow. This is best done by a group, in which each member assumes the role of an actor or stakeholder. In board-game fashion, the simulation goes through the process step by step, stopping at every task to consider not only if the task is fully and clearly specified but also where each actor and stakeholder is at that step of the process. The former makes clear the interactions between actors and stakeholders, including through their products. The latter helps anticipate the nature and timing of upcoming interactions, e.g. that the budget should be available before the architect starts designing. Many conflicts in a process are due to bad timing and the consequent need to make haste in order to catch up with the process flow.

OVERCOMING COGNITIVE LIMITATIONS

The overview afforded by process diagrams is not merely practical for explaining the process, so that all actors know what to do and when, and managers can organize actions towards project goals. It is also instrumental for overcoming cognitive limitations that lead to mistakes and failures. Acknowledging that project participants may suffer from cognitive biases and illusions, and trying to help avoid them is a key managerial task. For example, explicit connections between tasks help avoid illusions of cause. If the connections are accurate and no tasks are missing, one cannot easily infer fictitious causes from accidental precedence or coincidence in time.

To achieve such protection, it is important to avoid thinking in conventional, vague structures, such as preliminary, concept, technical and detail design stages. In a process diagram, such stages should never become nodes. Instead, all stages should be parsed into specific tasks and patterns, like the evaluation pattern in Figure 2, which matches any stage and therefore supports condensation. Distrust of conventional structures is important for the successful deployment of Type 2 reflective processes. These are often acquired by education and training, and therefore reflect cultural and professional habits. As a result, they may actually discourage analytical thinking by imposing rules of thumb and other summary or pseudo-analytical decision structures, which are embedded in conventions we tend to follow unthinkingly.

It is also important that managers are aware of their own cognitive limitations and how these can affect a process. Process diagrams can protect actors individually and as a group from avoidable mistakes but the same applies to mistakes managers make in the setup and control of the process. The most common of these relate to illusions of confidence and skill that cause managers to allocate tasks or even delegate custodianship of whole parts of a process without sufficient control (black boxes). Making the relations between actors, stakeholders and tasks explicit is a solid foundation for avoiding such illusions.

REFLECTIVE THINKING, COGNITIVE SIMULATION AND LEARNING POTENTIAL

A general advantage of a process diagram like Figure 2 is that it stimulates Type 2 reflective thinking. In contrast to an inspirational conceptual diagram, a flowchart like this supports analytical anticipation of actions and outcomes in an explicit manner that reveals unsolved problems and casts doubt on automatic decisions based on habit or convention. Unlike the mind-numbing Figure 3, it invites us to actively follow progress in a process, discovering possible problems on the way. By tracking the dipaths that lead to a node of interest or depart from it, we can examine if anything is missing or uncertain, if the connections between tasks seem doubtful or vague, or if the diagram contains practices that have led to failures in other projects. For example, a client may rightly worry that feedback to the design could lead to endless iterations with minimal improvements every time and therefore to considerable delays.

The diagram also supports improving the process through Type 2 algorithmic thinking. By tracking and evaluating progress, developing variations and measuring the graph we engage in cognitive simulation that allows all actors and stakeholders to test their assumptions and verify their expectations in an interactive manner. At a basic yet critical level, a process diagram can be used to verify the process frame, that is, if all options and consequences of each decision, all goals and constraints are present. For example, the budget cannot be absent from Figure 2: how else can we evaluate the costs of the design?

With the right frame, we can then consider improvements either by tweaking the process design or by projecting what-if and other scenarios, so as to connect better to project constraints or the perspectives of various participants. This helps anticipate problems and so prevent planning and sunk-costs fallacies. In the example of Figure 2, how long can we keep on with the iterations in a generally acceptable but not perfect situation? By evaluating the improvement achieved with each iteration, we can see if the design is reaching a plateau and take the decision to abandon or approve it, even if the costs are still higher than the budget. Alternatively, we can impose a ceiling on costs (as in Figure 5), so that the difference between costs and budget is not so big that the iterations become pointless. This nudges the design towards staying close to the budget, for example by constraining the selection of construction types and finishes.

Allowing for problems that could not have been anticipated is more difficult and requires awareness of Type 1 thinking limitations in both process management and the contributions of each actor. The interaction between the two is critical: the process design should stimulate reflective thinking in all respects, allowing actors to reflect not only on their own tasks but also on the whole process. Precision in the description of tasks is an important prerequisite because it stimulates meaningful questions about how and why. For instance, it can stimulate actors to question whether the cost estimate and approval in Figure 2 should be binding for the whole design project: this estimate is rather rough and relies heavily on the new design being quite similar to other buildings from which reference costs are derived. Therefore, making more detailed and precise estimations, including by refining the reference class, should be considered as soon as the design information allows it and before the difference between later, more detailed estimates and this one become an issue of contention in the project.

Working with analytical process diagrams is also important for skill development. In many activities, such as sports or music, improvement depends on instant feedback that triggers calibration: a wrong pass or a false note immediately call for evaluation and adjustment. In areas like AECO, there is a long latency period between taking a decision and realizing its effects — so long and so obscured by intervening events (therefore also subject to illusions of cause) that the relation between cause and effect may completely elude us. In the absence of instant feedback, it is perhaps not surprising that we opt for optimism and confidence. Cognitive simulation with process diagrams compresses time, making it easier to discern probable consequences of specific decisions before they occur, reconsider these decisions and their backgrounds, and so understand and learn.

FRAMING

The functions of a process diagram (providing overview, stimulating reflective thinking, supporting cognitive simulation and generally helping avoid Type 1 mistakes) require an appropriately broad frame: one that includes all relevant aspects and constraints, as well as all probable options and outcomes. In such a frame, we can easily detect dependencies between tasks and consequently take properly informed decisions at any task and prevent the spread of local mistakes to the rest of the process. However, a broad, inclusive frame goes against the conventional wisdom that reducing the complexity of a phenomenon makes it easier to understand and handle. This is something frequently done in conceptual diagrams, to the detriment of clarity. Process diagrams do not necessarily reduce the complexity of a process. Instead, they make it explicit and manageable, preventing the isolation of subproblems in narrow frames.

With respect to framing, a process diagram should go beyond stated objectives and include all things that connect directly to each task in the process, whether they occur in the process or not. In a design process, for example, the diagram should include the applicable planning regulations and possibly the local authorities behind them. The reason is that the regulations constrain many decisions on the form of the design and the local authorities may have to grant an exemption from these regulations. If an exemption is probable, the process diagram should also include feedback to the regulations. Things with an indirect relation to the process, for example the legal framework of planning regulations and the central authorities that determine it are highly unlikely to play a role in a design process (e.g. receive direct feedback from any process task). These should not be included in the process diagram.

In the digraph of the process diagram, extraneous nodes of questionable relevance can be detected by their degree. Long subgraphs starting from a source node and having an in- and out-degree sequence of ones should be considered for exclusion because they probably describe tasks that are irrelevant to the process (Figure 5). As a rule, such peripheral subgraphs, starting from a source node, should have a length of 2 or less: one actor or stakeholder node and one task node, the latter connecting to a task that certainly belongs to the process, as with the client/brief subgraph in Figure 2. If the source is a constraint, e.g. planning regulations, and the planning authorities are not involved, then the length can be 1.

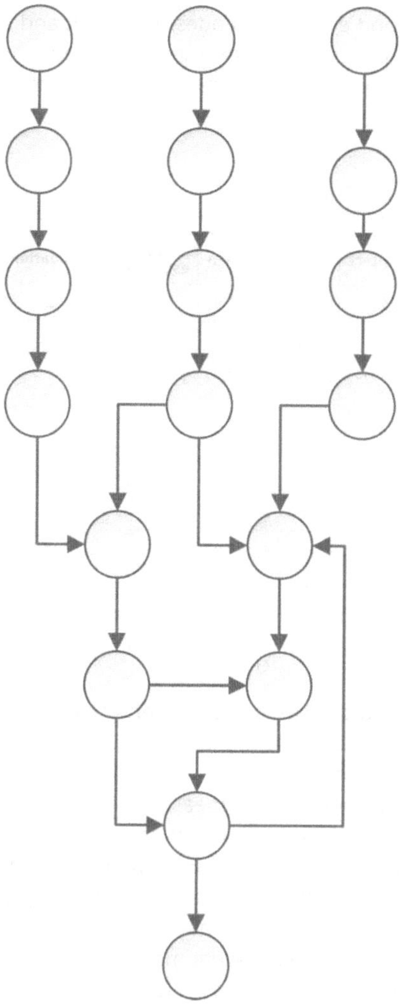

Figure 5. Suspect process diagram, with probable extraneous tasks

A related use of graph measures is to make certain that the core of the process, i.e. all essential tasks are in the center of the graph, with actors, stakeholders, preparatory and external tasks in the periphery. If the center contains non-essential or peripheral nodes, the digraph probably contains extraneous nodes.

There are two complementary ways you can measure the center and periphery of a process diagram. The first is to do it in the underlying undirected graph, i.e. the graph that is obtained if every arc is replaced by an edge (Table 1). As any process diagram is a weakly connected digraph, this returns an impression of the overall structure of the process. In this example, the center comprises the design and evaluation nodes. The client and cost specialist nodes form the periphery. The closeness measures agree with the interpretation of the center but also suggest that the architect and design approval nodes are not as central as the budget and cost estimation nodes.

Table 1. Eccentricity and closeness in the underlying undirected graph of Figure 2

	Client	Cost specialist	Architect	Budget	Design	Cost estimation	Evaluation	Design approval	Eccentricity	Closeness
Client	×	4	2	1	2	3	2	3	4	0,41
Cost specialist	4	×	3	3	2	1	2	3	4	0,39
Architect	2	3	×	2	1	2	2	3	3	0,47
Budget	1	3	2	×	1	2	1	2	3	0,58
Design	2	2	1	1	×	1	1	2	2	0,70
Cost estimation	3	1	2	2	1	×	1	2	3	0,58
Evaluation	2	2	2	1	1	1	×	1	2	0,70
Design approval	3	3	3	2	2	2	1	×	3	0,44

The second way is to measure distances in the digraph itself (Table 2). Note that as distances are measured in dipaths, there are many nodes that do not connect to each other and that the table is not symmetric with respect to the diagonal: the distance from node *X* to node *Y* is not the same as the distance from node *Y* to node *X*. The measures in our example suggest that the core of the process comprises the budget, cost estimation and evaluation nodes, with only the architect in the periphery. In terms of closeness, the evaluation node is the most central, followed by the cost estimation, while the client and the cost specialist are closer to the architect. In other words, the digraph measures give a slightly different view, more specific to the cost estimation process. Nevertheless, such differences are minute. What matters is that both tables confirm that there is nothing fundamentally wrong with the process in Figure 2.

Table 2. Eccentricity and closeness in the digraph of Figure 2

	Client	Cost specialist	Architect	Budget	Design	Cost estimation	Evaluation	Design approval	Eccentricity	Closeness
Client	×	–	–	1	2	3	2	3	3	0,64
Cost specialist	–	×	–	–	3	1	2	3	3	0,78
Architect	–	–	×	–	1	2	3	4	4	0,70
Budget	–	–	–	×	1	2	1	2	2	1,17
Design	–	–	–	–	×	1	2	3	3	1,17
Cost estimation	–	–	–	–	2	×	1	2	2	1,40
Evaluation	–	–	–	–	1	2	×	1	2	1,75
Design approval	–	–	–	–	–	–	–	×	–	–

Linear subgraphs, like the ones in Figure 5, with a degree sequence consisting largely of ones, are suspect for two additional reasons. Firstly, they may be the result of over-analytical thinking that unnecessarily splits tasks in steps that should be combined. Secondly, the absence of feedback arcs and other cross-connections suggests a schematic interpretation of the real process that does not include all options and constraints, i.e. narrow framing. To prevent decision taking in narrow frames, it is advisable to avoid sequential procedures, consisting of tasks each involving only one or two actors or stakeholders and concerning decisions on a single issue or aspect. Instead, decisions should be combined and made by larger groups. In a design evaluation, for example, one should not first evaluate the design for compliance to planning regulations, then to the building code, then to the brief and finally to the budget. Instead, all checks should be combined in a single evaluation that also includes the relations between the three criteria (Figure 6): a discrepancy with respect to the brief could be due to inescapable planning constraints, while additional costs can incur as a result of design decisions that achieve more than what the brief asks for. A combined evaluation therefore supports precise and effective feedback to the cause of a problem, such as a request for exemption from existing planning regulations because of the added value of an energetically innovative solution that adds to the building height.

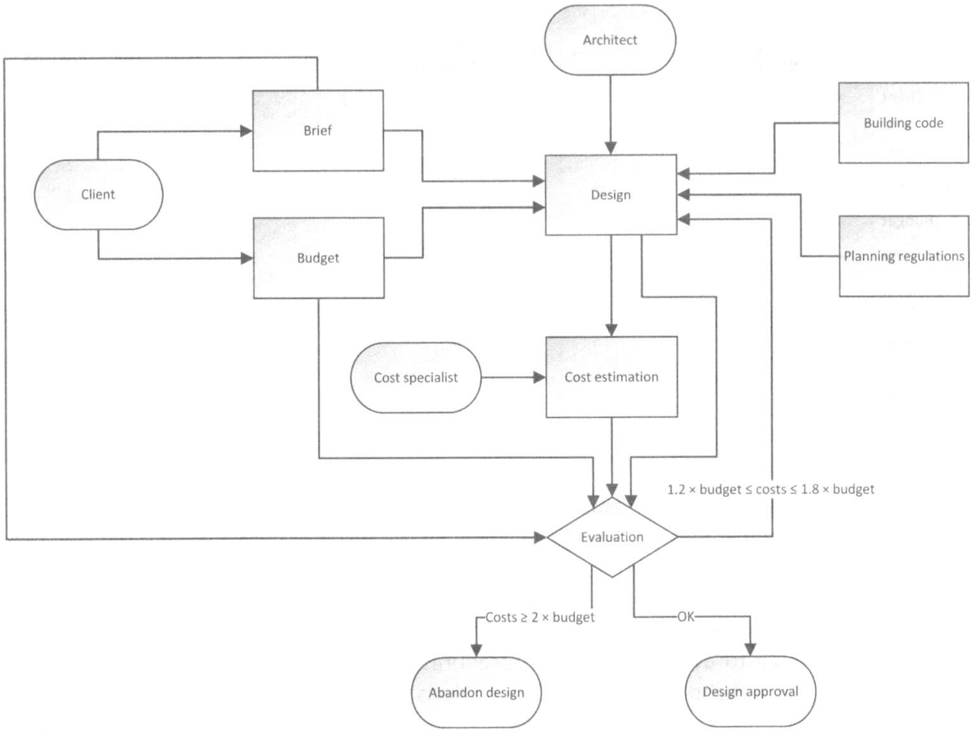

Figure 6. A more comprehensive process diagram for early design but still without feedback to the brief or budget, or evaluation of compliance to the building code and planning regulations

GROUP PROCESSES

A frequent objection to combining decisions and evaluations is the resulting complexity of the tasks (recognizable by the high in-degree of the nodes). This objection is founded on the presumed efficiency of simple tasks with narrow frames and ignores not only the dangers of narrow framing but also the low effectivity and inefficiency of sequential processes, especially if complex problems are artificially parsed into long sequences. It also follows the dangerous tendency in group decision making to put consensus above true solutions. In meetings, for example, it is customary to start debating a problem immediately and try reach a conclusion upon which all participants agree as soon as possible. This allows the most vocal participants to dictate the level and direction of the discussion. However, as we have seen, these persons may be less knowledgeable than presumed and suffer from illusions of confidence. They might therefore lead the discussion astray, while more hesitant participants hide behind them and follow their direction, creating a false feeling of rational alignment. It is recommended that, instead of initiating a meeting with an immediate debate towards general consensus, each participant should first prepare and present a separate analysis of the problem and suggestions for its solution. Informing each other in this manner is a more constructive and inclusive basis for a discussion that compares or combines different options, taking more aspects into account and considering them from more perspectives.

This approach to group decision making reflects the differences between Type 1 and Type 2 processes: for personal action, Type 1 thinking may suffice but for joint action and interpersonal communication, especially with respect to complex, partially shared goals (as in most AECO processes), Type 2 reflective processes are required. The load-bearing structure of a design can be decided in a flash of inspiration but explaining it to the other members of a design team who have to adjust to it, as well as estimating its effects (e.g. direct and indirect costs) is clearly more analytical and time consuming. It is therefore important that the process design ensures that actors arrive at combined decisions adequately prepared, with complete plans, proposals, analyses and evaluations, which are made available to all in time, before any deliberation and decision. This makes all options explicit, creating a broad frame and basing consensus on the comparison and combination of options rather than the opinions and personalities of vocal participants.

In a process diagram, this means that actors and stakeholders do not give direct input to a decision node, as the client does in the faulty example of Figure 3. That would imply a personal, possibly variable opinion, e.g. that clients change their mind about what they want without prior communication to other project participants. Instead, actors and stakeholders should connect to decisions through the products of their tasks, as the client does through the budget in Figure 2. A decision should take place by comparing the different products, e.g. a design to its brief and budget, and its outputs should include feedback to these products: if clients change their minds, this should be expressed clearly as adaptation of briefs, budgets etc. In graph terms, this means that the distance of actors and stakeholders from decision nodes should be at least 2.

In the same vein, task nodes do not output into actor or stakeholder nodes. An arc leading from e.g. a design to a client, as in the misleading diagram of Figure 3, does not mean that the design is given to the client but that a client is selected on the basis of the design — in fact, a new client, different to the one who initiated the process at the top of the diagram. A correct diagram would indicate that the design is submitted to an evaluation of its compliance to the brief, similarly to the comparison to the budget in Figure 2. The client is not directly involved in this compliance evaluation. One should not confuse the tasks in process diagrams with the social interactions that take place around the tasks. The presence of clients in meetings on brief compliance does not mean that the brief is ignored, only that the compliance evaluation is communicated directly and transparently to the clients.

The emphasis on tasks and their products in process diagrams is important for solving problems in AECO. These problems are often considered ill-defined and therefore hard to solve because there is no clear agreement on the problem, its constraints and goals. This makes difficult to agree on solutions and take joint decisions. By making tasks and products explicit, any lack of agreement becomes clear to all and nudges them towards less fuzzy problem descriptions and procedures. There is, for example, no reason why a budget should not be specific and transparent, calculated on the basis of clear parameters that can be modified in response to the design or changing social, technological or economic conditions.

ILLUSIONS OF CONFIDENCE AND SKILL

Process management is particularly sensitive to illusions of confidence concerning self-assured participants or presumed experts. A clear expression of these illusions are black boxes in a process: chunks that are delegated to a particular actor without clear understanding of what takes place there and uncertain relations to the rest of the process. Such chunks are often claimed by specific disciplines, which makes the selection of project participants for those disciplines quite sensitive. Choosing them on the basis of track record is a positive development, only marred by the lack of objective and reliable performance measurements, which render any selection even more sensitive to illusions of confidence and skill. It is quite hard to distinguish what went well in previous projects thanks to a particular actor versus other actors or contextual factors. In a successful project, practically everyone claims credit for what went well. It is even more difficult to establish what went wrong due to a specific actor, since very few are brave enough to admit responsibility. In the end, all one can tell is that some actors were involved in a project, that the project had a certain performance and that some aspects were better than others. Such vagueness does not free us from any illusion.

To safeguard a process we should therefore avoid delegating large clusters of tasks to actors or stakeholders, turning them into black boxes that are inevitably beyond control. Instead, a process description should parse activities in as specific tasks as possible. For example, rather than abstractly asking for a cost estimate, we should specify how the cost estimate should be made: the prerequisites to making an estimate (such as a design containing the necessary information), the method used for the estimation, the timing of the estimate relative to the rest of the process (making sure that the prerequisites can be met, as well as that the estimate is directly used) and how the estimate should be evaluated, including follow-up actions such as feedback to the design. It goes without saying that bundling the design, the cost estimation and the evaluation into a single node is unacceptable. Equally dangerous is entrusting the subgraph containing all these tasks to a single stakeholder.

A structured, analytical process is neither trivial nor insulting, even to the greatest of experts, especially if the parsing of the black boxes is based on their approach and facilitates their actions and interactions with the rest of the process in a transparent and operational framework. As for process managers, it is merely a matter of good housekeeping and discipline that amounts to feedforward (anticipating what might occur and establishing procedures for prevention, early detection and immediate action), as opposed to feedback (waiting until a problem emerges, deliberating about its significance and finding ways to resolve it). Feedback as a means of control seems inevitable in any process but feedforward greatly reduces the need for feedback and, above all, the pressures associated with it.

NARRATIVES AND COHERENCE

A realistic diagram makes the process inclusive, empowering each participant to track progress from their own perspective and identify interactions with others. Process management benefits from inclusiveness, too, because it becomes protected from the dangers of one-sided narratives and the frictions and imbalances they can cause. Instead of having a single narrative, from the perspective of a dominant participant and possibly accepted due to a halo effect, the various actors and stakeholders can project their own narratives on the process design and so escape inside views and planning fallacies. In this way, coherence is not apparent or imposed but real and constructed by all participants together, resulting in scenarios that are realistic (i.e. scenarios that may include conflicts and lacunae but also make them clear to all) and combat *probability neglect:* multiple perspectives help give each risk the right consideration, so that big risks are not ignored and small risks are not given too much weight (as is often the case with inside views).

This also puts performance before compliance: rather than trying to stay within the narrative, the process is driven towards the highest goals attainable. For example, the budget in Figure 2 is based on assumptions that may remain unchallenged if all that matters is that the design conforms to the budget. If, on the other hand, these assumptions are negotiable and adaptable to suggestions by project participants and outcomes, then the process can lead to a better relation between costs and performance.

To avoid straight-jacketing a process into a narrative, it is again advisable to avoid sequential process designs. Most narratives, certainly in AECO, tend to have a linear structure that imposes one narrow frame after the other on the interpretation of a problem, cutting it down into subproblems in a way that fits the coherence of the narrative but not necessarily the needs of the project. Combined tasks and parallel tracks can improve reliability, as well as effectivity, by allowing each participant adequate scope for their activities and priorities.

GRAPH MEASURES

As already mentioned, graph measures can be used to quantify indicators, checks and controls, making them easier to implement in a process diagram:

- Decisions nodes should have in- and out-degrees equal or higher than 2
- Linear, peripheral subgraphs with degree sequences of ones should have a length of 2
- Important tasks should be in the center
- Preparatory and external tasks should be in the periphery
- Actor and stakeholder nodes should have a distance of 2 from decision nodes

In addition to these:

- The degree of a node is a good indication of local complexity.
    - A high in-degree suggests complexity in information processing and decision making at the particular task, as well as dependence on multiple actors or previous tasks. If a high in-degree indicates a collection point, e.g. different specialists coming together to compile a brief, you should organize the resulting group processes with care without splitting the node into a sequence of tasks that gives the illusion of simplicity. On the other hand, if a node denotes an abstraction or agglomeration of too many tasks (e.g. a complete stage like concept design), its high degree should prompt a more analytical and explicit description of these tasks.

    - The out-degree indicates scope: how broad the effects of a task are or how widely a stakeholder is involved in the process. For example, it is expected that the products of a key task like briefing are used in many places in a process. But even if the significance of the task is low, a high out-degree means that many others may depend on its timely execution.
- Bridges indicate transitions from one part of the process to another (e.g. transition between stages), as well as connections that are sensitive to process delays or interruptions: if the transaction described by the arc does not take place, the whole process halts. A process diagram with many bridges usually describes a sequential or phased process. As processes with combined tasks and parallel tracks are preferable, a process diagram should contain as few bridges as possible. Those that remain should be strategically chosen: in the same way that a bridge in an access graph may disrupt pedestrian circulation but also presents opportunities for control, a bridge in a process diagram, even if unavoidable, should be coupled to actions that benefit the process and its management, e.g. synchronization of different aspects.

Key Takeaways

- *Processes can be described textually or diagrammatically; diagramatic descriptions are necessary because they afford overview*
- *Flowcharts are digraphs that can be used to describe a process as a sequence of interconnected tasks (process diagram)*
- *By making tasks and connections explicit, process diagrams are a useful basis for the social side of management*
- *In a process diagram, each thing should be represented by a single node (uniqueness rule)*
- *The in- and out-degrees of decision nodes should be at least 2 (decision degrees rule)*
- *Process diagrams are not abstract conceptual displays: every node and arc should represent a specific actor, task or relation, and no task or relation should be missing*
- *Process descriptions should stimulate reflective thinking, support cognitive simulation and provide instant feedback for learning*
- *Graph measures help with determining an appropriately broad frame, avoiding sequential designs and identifying potential interruptions (bridges)*
- *Actors and stakeholders connect to decisions indirectly, through the products of their tasks*

Exercises

1. Measure the degree and eccentricity of nodes, and the diameter and radius of the graph in the process diagram of Figure 6. What do these measures suggest, especially in comparison to Figure 2?

2. Expand the process diagram of Figure 6 with additional aspects, actors, tasks and feedback connections. What do the measures in the resulting graph suggest, especially in comparison to Figure 6?
3. Expand the process diagram of Figure 2 to cover all design stages, using increasingly more precise and informed cost estimates. What changes in the structure and measures of the graph? Do you observe patterns that are combined or repeated?

CHAPTER 10

Information diagrams

In this chapter we move from tasks to information by transforming the process diagram into an information diagram: a digraph of information instances and related actions and transactions. Information diagrams represent the information side of management, which both operationalizes and validates a process design. This chapter builds on the chapter on process diagrams and presupposes knowledge of graphs, in particular digraphs (see Appendix I).

PROCESS OPERATIONALIZATION

Process diagrams are essential for the social side of management: they tell us who is doing what and when, in an overview that supports both zooming in or out and tracking the contributions or interests of each stakeholder. What they do not do is specify tasks in terms of content and structure. For example, they tell us that we need a design to make a cost estimate but not exactly what the design should contain, which aspects of the design relate to costs, how these aspects are processed towards a cost estimate and what should be included in the cost estimate. Leaving this operationalization of the process design to the discretion of the actors inevitably causes uncertainties and conflicts that undermine the process and its management.

Translating the process diagram into information instances and actions makes the individual tasks operational and unambiguous at a practical level, so that every participant knows exactly what to expect and do. This guides implementation and allows for evaluation and control throughout the process. For example, a task like "calculate the net area of a room" becomes a matter of obtaining a complete and truthful description of the room, including all dimensions of the room as well as of any obstacles that should be subtracted from it, making the necessary calculations and producing either a total area measurement or an analytical list of measurements that includes obstacles. At this level, there is little if any room for omissions or misunderstandings and we can easily ascertain if things are done correctly. The actor who makes the calculation has clear expectations concerning the room description another actor delivers and equally clear instructions as to how the calculation results should be communicated. How the calculation is made (with a computer, a calculator, an abacus or mentally) is usually a matter for the actor, their capacities in relation to the demands of the task and applicable professional standards.

Such specificity is necessary for the information side of management: the guidance and control of a process on the basis of what actors produce and consume in it. It is also essential with respect to digitization: it ensures that the use of digital resources is meaningful and constructive. Quite often digitization is managed by imposing standards and restrictions on the means. For example, we can stipulate that building designs should be made in BIM but this does not help achieve the performance promised by BIM. We must also stipulate what constitutes proper and acceptable usage of BIM. In fact, it should not matter which software or approach is used if the requirements of the deliverables are met: design representations with the right content and a structure that facilitates retrieval and processing of this content. An information diagram that bypasses all assumptions concerning digitization means and approaches, and describes what should be done with precision and accuracy not only supports IM but also explains why e.g. BIM is required rather than CAD.

Finally, expressing a process in terms of specific information is helpful in avoiding "mental shotgun" situations: when confronted with unexpected problems, we tend to confound our Type 2 processes by mentally computing too much information, clearly more than we need or is relevant to the issues at hand. Panic is often the cause of the mental shotgun, as well as its effect. To countermand this, we must be clear not only concerning which data are relevant to each task but also how these derive from primary data and how primary and derivative data are structured in the representations we use. This facilitates identification of pertinent information and its provenance even under unforeseen circumstances, so that decisions can be taken and evaluated without confusion or uncertainty.

FROM PROCESS TO INFORMATION DIAGRAM: I-P-O

The transition from process to information diagram starts by superimposing the I-P-O scheme on each task, with the P on the task node (Figure 1). This expresses what takes place in the task in information-processing terms by adding an input node before and an output node after the task. Usually, the output of a task becomes direct input to the following task, so only a single node needs to be added between the two. Note that this is not always the case: the output of a task may connect to more tasks, in ways not anticipated in the process diagram. Similarly, the input of a task may merge the output of several other tasks.

The process diagram may also miss nodes that describe external sources, for example the published unit prices a cost specialist uses or reference projects for the brief or budget. The same applies to the outcomes of a process: design approval usually implies some information deliverables, such as a representation of the approved design. These nodes must be added to the information diagram, too.

In general, the transformation of a process diagram amounts to the following graph operations:

- Subdivision of arcs to introduce nodes for their input and output

- Splitting of process diagram sources to create nodes that represent the input to these tasks
- Splitting of process diagram terminals to create nodes that represent the output of these tasks

Alternatively, the first point can be expressed more precisely as:

- Splitting of each task node twice to create one node for its input and one for its output
- Contraction of edges between input and output nodes that respectively have an in- and out-degree of 1

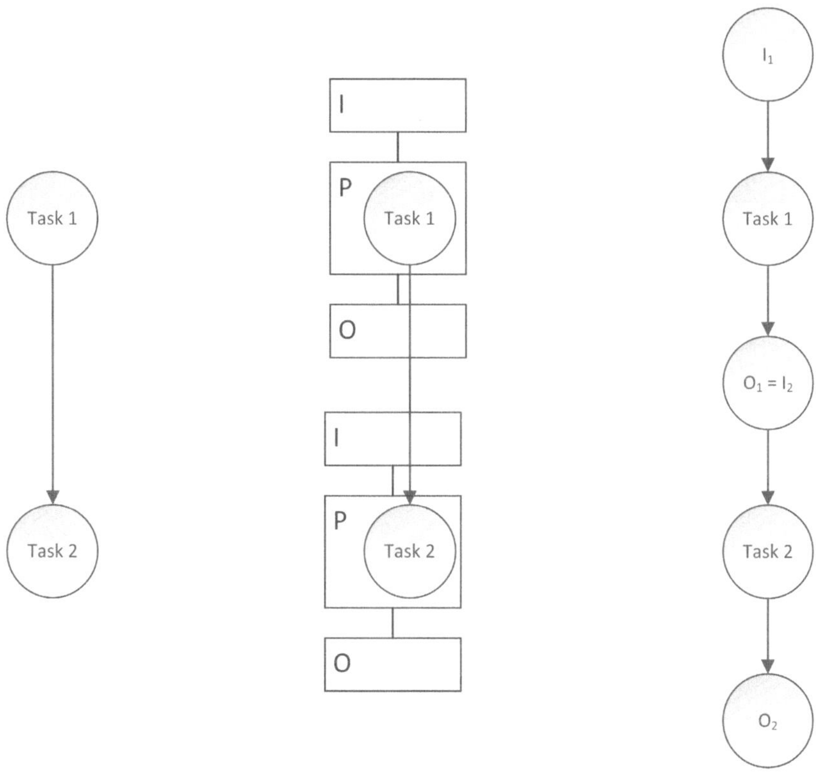

Figure 1. From process to information diagram: the I-P-O scheme is superimposed on each task in the process diagram (middle), resulting in an augmentation of the graph with a new source and terminal, and an input/output node between the two tasks (right)

The input and output nodes in an information diagram must be made as specific as possible. The design node in Figure 2 is expected to contribute to a cost estimation involving gross floor areas. This means that the design cannot exist solely in the architect's mind; we need some external representation as input, on the basis of which we can measure floor areas, moreover by use category (as these have different unit prices). The obvious candidate is a floor plan and, more precisely, one where all spaces are indicated and labelled by their use. This floor plan rather than some abstract notion of a design is the appropriate input for the processing we require (calculation of gross floor areas). In the same manner, one can establish that these areas are the output of a new task, as well as the input to the next processing step (cost estimation).

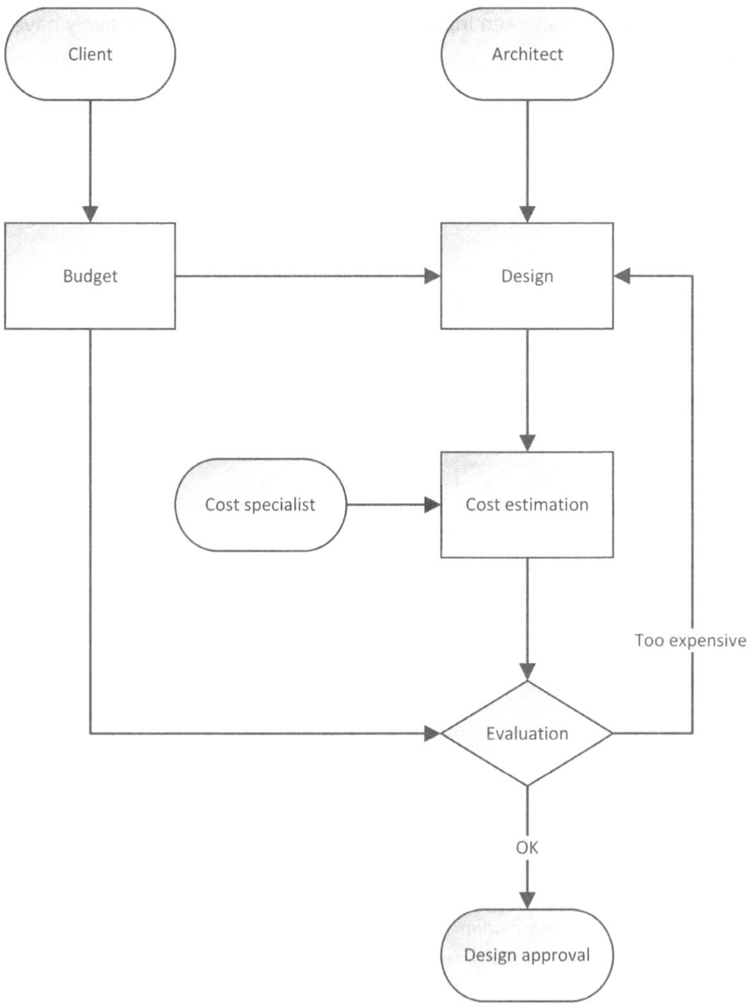

Figure 2. Cost estimation process diagram

Figure 3 illustrates the results of the transformation. Between design and cost estimation it was necessary to insert two nodes, so as to be quite specific concerning the input to the cost estimation calculations. Note that in this way some tasks are attached to the arcs: the information diagram does not specify how the floor plan is produced from the design or how the floor areas are calculated in the floor plan. This is because emphasis is now firmly on *what* (information); *how,* as the remit of the actors, is assumed to be known or standardized and, in any case, constrained by the specified output. Similarly, the actor / stakeholder nodes have been removed in order to put emphasis on task and information nodes, as well as save space. In this version, who determines the budget, who makes the design and who calculates the cost estimate is implicit in their tasks and products but, at the same time, unambiguous. If this is not the case and there are multiple actors or stakeholders involved in different tasks with varying capacities, it is advisable to keep them in the information diagram, too, so that there can be no misunderstanding as to e.g. which designer or engineer is responsible for each design aspect. Referring to the process diagram concerning such matters is less practical; the information diagram should be self-sufficient and self-explanatory.

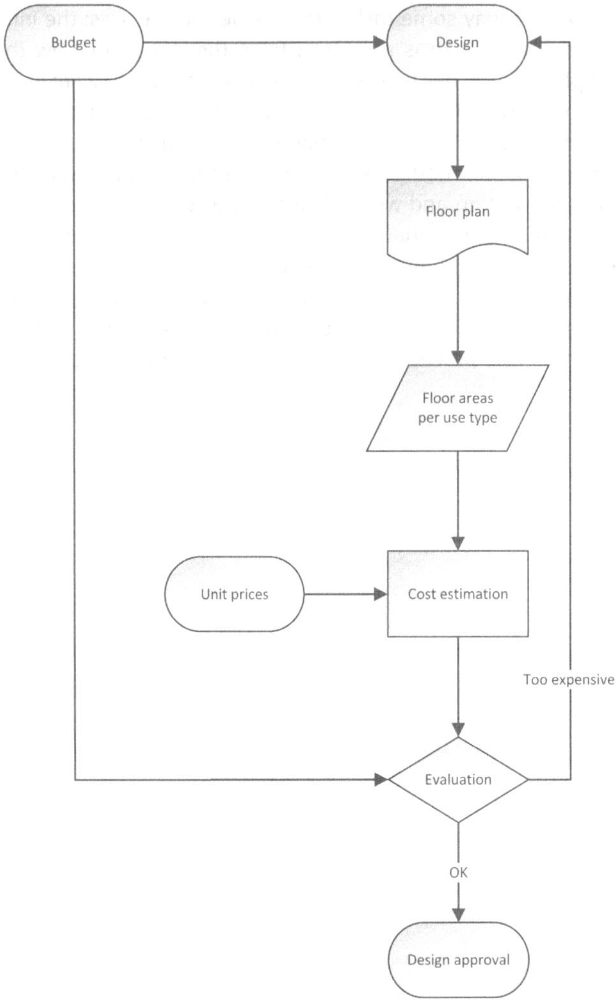

Figure 3. Cost estimation information diagram

The uniqueness rule applies to information diagrams, too: each object should appear only once, as a single node. So, if the design must be improved because the design is deemed too expensive, the diagram should contain a feedback arc to the design. On the other hand, if the cost evaluation leads to a radically new design, requiring a new node in the diagram, then this should be made clear by means of unambiguous node labelling (e.g. *Design 1* and *Design 2*). Such new versions of the same nodes should be used cautiously and sparingly, only when absolutely necessary, e.g. when a process involves design alternatives. Feedback to the floor plan is also possible but not if it is the design that must be improved: any feedback to an information node is normally due to quality issues, e.g. if the floor plan contains no indications of use type. Such feedback is not part of process diagrams but information diagrams must include controls of information quality, too.

The other two rules of process diagrams, the decision degrees and the specificity and comprehensiveness rules, also apply to information diagrams, even more strictly. What may be excused as pragmatic fuzziness and abstraction in a process diagram is unacceptable and undermining in an information diagram. For example, it is necessary in Figure 3 to indicate that what is measured in the floor plan are the floor areas of different uses because the cost estimation applies different unit prices to each type of building use. One m^2 of storage area costs significantly less than one m^2 of office space, which in turn costs less than one m^2 of an operating theatre in a hospital. This means that it is not enough to calculate the total gross floor area of a hospital design; one has to know the use of every space, so as to be able to calculate the subtotals for each type. The subtotals are then multiplied by the unit prices to arrive at a correct estimate and ascertain which category may be too big or too costly. In an evaluation, it is imperative that the things that are compared are similarly unambiguously specified. If, for example, the hospital budget has separate chapters for each use type, it should be clear how the comparison takes place (e.g. per use type or per building part, which may include various types).

The example illustrates the key differences between process and information diagrams: the former can be abstract about what each task entails and focus on process flow but the latter has to be specific regarding information sources (e.g. which drawings are used), the information instances these sources accommodate and the actions through which these instances are processed. The higher specificity of information diagrams leads to a finer grain in the analysis of the process, resulting in nodes and arcs that allow one to be even more precise and hence certain about information flow, as well as safeguard information quality. While in general the flow is the same in both diagrams, the higher specificity of the information diagram may lead to new insights and local elaborations or changes in the process design.

One such elaboration is the analysis of the design node in the process diagram into a sequence of nodes (design, floor plan, floor areas per use type) in the information diagram. Such expansion is generally necessary at critical points of a process. Similarly, in making an information diagram one should pay particular attention to nodes with a high in- or out-degree in the process diagram. These indicate tasks of high complexity and density, which should possibly be analysed into several tasks in the information diagram, provided that this does not undermine parallel or integrated decision processes. As a rule of thumb, the results of such an expansion in an information diagram should include a large number of arcs between the new nodes, expressing the complexity of the task represented by the original node.

INFORMATION DIAGRAMS FOR BIM

Until now, we have discussed information diagrams as if we were in the previous century, working with analogue representations and their digital facsimiles. This is a far cry from the symbolic representations that form the present and predictable future of digitization in AECO. Adapting our example of the cost estimation to BIM means first of all that the model (the central information system) should be explicitly present in the diagram. This information system contains the symbols and relations in which primary data are found. Derivative data like floor area calculations are produced from the model and presented in views like schedules. These schedules are typically predefined in various formats, including room schedules that list spaces and their properties, including floor area calculations (Figure 4).

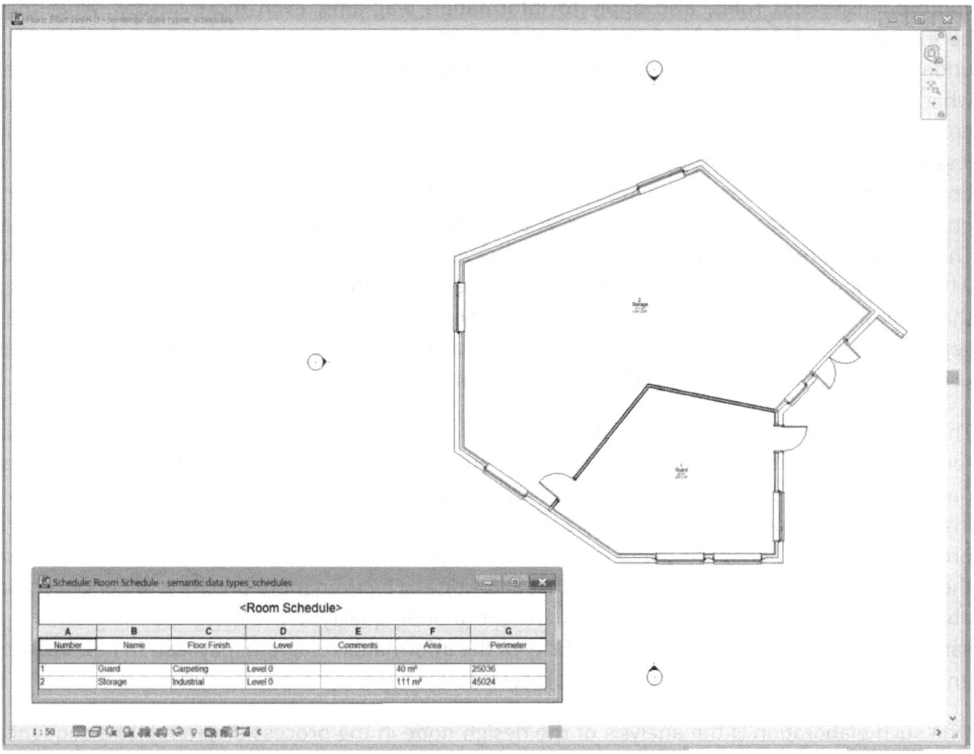

Figure 4. Room schedule in a BIM editor

Room schedules can be used to verify that the model contains all primary data needed for the cost estimation, i.e. the spaces, their dimensions and use types. They can also be expanded with unit prices and subsequent calculations, thus integrating cost estimation in BIM in a straightforward and transparent manner (Figure 5).

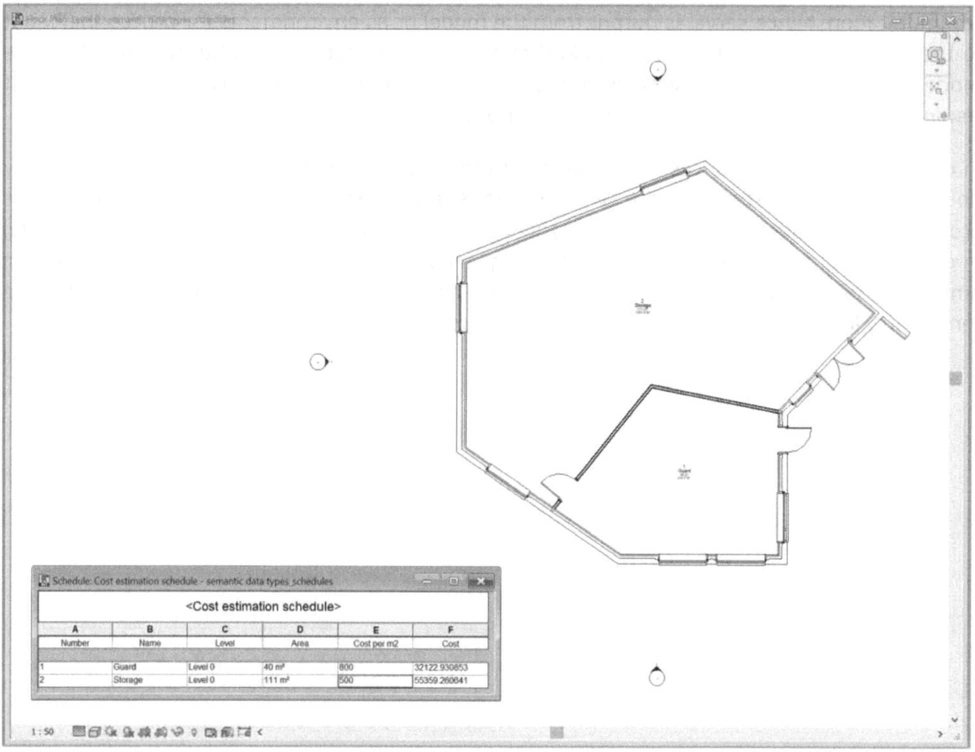

Figure 5. Room schedule with integrated cost estimation

Figure 6 is the information diagram for cost estimation in BIM. Interestingly, it is not significantly different from Figure 3, only feedback goes to the design representation rather than an abstract design node. Collaboration in BIM means that information processed by all actors resides permanently in a single, central representation. The properties and relations of symbols that accommodate this information cannot be detached from the representation, as was the custom with analogue information carriers, where each discipline had its own drawings of the same design. In BIM, any information action or transaction starts from the model and is usually followed by feedback to the model (with the exception of terminal nodes). This means that feedback should be specific, i.e. directed at the space symbols in the model, which could accommodate it as annotations or, preferably, constraints on properties and relations. By being specific about which symbols, properties and relations are affected, one can guide information actions with precision and certainty, avoiding the dangers of improvised interpretations by confused actors.

In general, any connection to a model in BIM, either output or input, should refer to specific symbols rather than the representation in general. For example, if an evaluation results in a decision to improve the thermal insulation of a building, the feedback from the evaluation should connect to the symbols of the particular building elements that must be improved, such as the windows or the roof. Views in BIM, such as schedules or floor plans, are for analysis and communication, hence serve as output from the model or as environments for processing. Input to the model (including feedback) should therefore not connect to views but to symbols in the model. In this respect, it is advisable to represent views in information diagrams in a way that reminds you that they do not normally accept input.

In our example, the unit prices are connected to the model through a schedule, i.e. a view: they do not become properties of space symbols. The reasoning behind this choice is that unit prices are values that relate to aggregates: sums that abstract the specific circumstances of each symbol in order to approximate averages. As such, they are derivative data that do not merit inclusion among the primary properties of a symbol. Their connection to a view indicates that they are temporarily linked to the model rather than integrated in it.

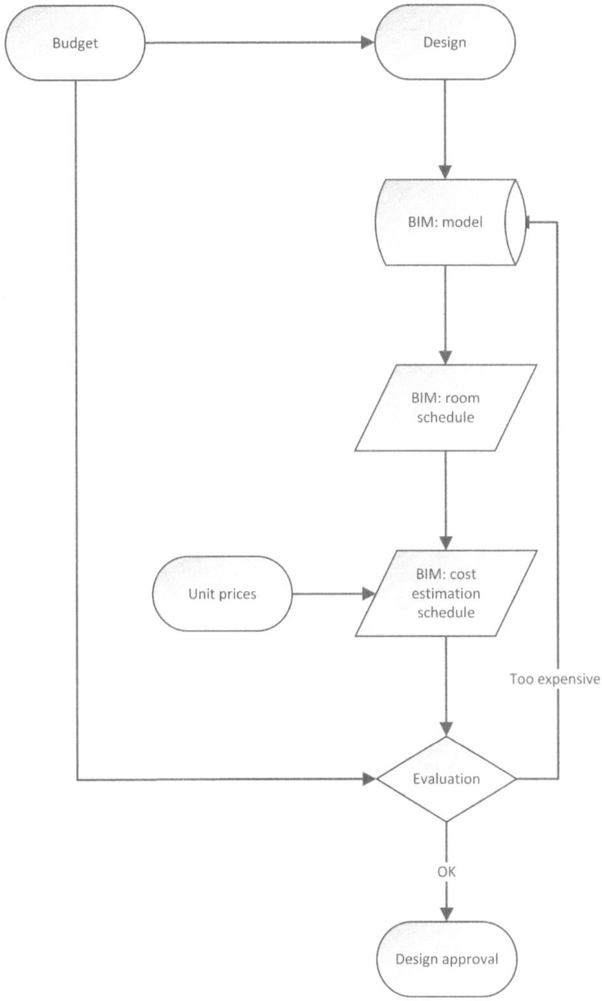

Figure 6. Information diagram for cost estimation in BIM

As an indication of the level of detail possible and frequently necessary in IM, Figure 7 is a variation of the same information diagram with a couple of information quality controls added. The controls concern the presence of essential information (the space symbols) and primary properties of these symbols (use type). Note that while the diagram is specific about which symbols and properties are concerned, it is elliptical about how the controls are implemented, leaving such matters to the technical BIM specialists. In fact, the diagram violates the decision degrees rule by missing one input in both control nodes.

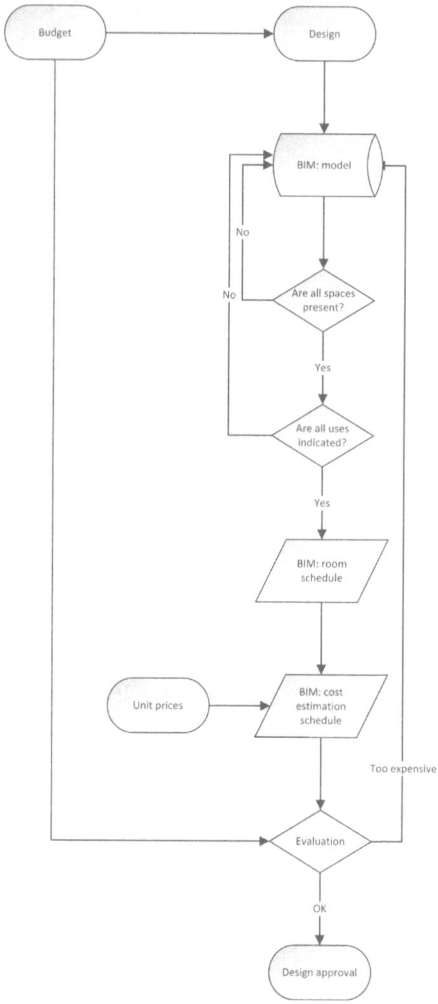

Figure 7. Information diagram for cost estimation in BIM including quality controls

TOLERANCES

When translating tasks into information, we must often consider the tolerances for each input or output. Care should be taken that these are kept as narrow as possible. Wide tolerances are unacceptable as an indication of either ignorance or unwarranted uncertainty. As a result, they offer no sound basis for decision making. For example, a tight time planning compels us to pay more attention to the requirements and feasibility of each step, as well as to how dependencies between tasks are ordered in time. Reversely, vagueness about deadlines and milestones promotes procrastination and deferment of decisions, especially concerning steps about which we are less clear.

TESTING INFORMATION DIAGRAMS

Information diagrams should be tested from the perspective of each actor and stakeholder, in the same way as process diagrams. The only difference is that the relation of an actor or stakeholder to each node should be specified in terms of input, output and processing: if the task (the processing) should be undertaken by the particular actor, for example the design by the architect, they should verify their capacity to undertake it and help with the specification of the necessary input, e.g. a budget, a brief and a site description (including applicable building codes and planning regulations). The same holds for the output: the content, structure and timing of information produced in the task should be agreed in unambiguous terms. Specifying where this information is used and by whom should be avoided in order to prevent deterministic, reductionist adaptations (e.g. "if they need it only for this cost estimation, I don't have to worry about aspects other than floor areas").

Tracking the involvement of each actor and stakeholder is done in the same way as in process diagrams, with subgraphs and directed walks, and afterwards a board-game-like simulation for the whole group of actors and stakeholders. In the group simulation, it is especially important to reach general agreement about the input and output of each task, as well as about the custodianship of information: it is not enough to know who is the author of some information; who takes care of it at different stages of the process is not necessarily the same, obvious to all or automatic. In the context of BIM, moreover, a distinction should be made concerning care for the technical aspects of a model (which can be delegated to digitization specialists) and the content of symbols and relations (which remains a responsibility of process stakeholders).

Finally, once an information diagram is finalized, one should consider the semantic type of information used as input in any task: if it is derivative, it should be possible to track it back to the primary data from which it is produced. Floor areas are derivative, so we must be able to identify the primary data from which they derive in the information diagram, as well as the representations that accommodate these primary data.

GRAPH MEASURES

The graph measures used to analyse process diagrams obviously also apply to information diagrams. The significance and meaning of degrees, bridges, distances, closeness, centers and peripheries are the same in both. Differences tend to be subtle and primarily reflect the shift of attention from tasks to information. For example, while a node denoting designing is central in a process diagram, it is the node of the design representation (e.g. the BIM model) that takes central position in the information diagram. Being more analytical and specific, information diagrams also have a larger size and order than their process counterparts. This makes graph drawing and legibility more difficult, and requires more careful analysis and measurement. A useful strategy is to consider each part of the process in its own subgraph, without neglecting arcs that connect nodes in different subgraphs. To make certain that no such connection is obscured, any analysis in subraphs should be followed by analysis of the whole graph. One should always keep in mind that any partial consideration of a process is simply for reasons of convenience and not subdivide the process in artificially distinct modules. If a process in truly modular, then each module should be treated as a separate process in order to verify its self-sufficiency.

PROCESS VALIDATION

Information diagrams are more than an operational version of process diagrams. Their utility extends to the validation of process designs: it establishes whether the processes can deliver what they are expected to. When we translate each task and relation into information-processing actions, operationalization predictably stumbles upon hidden problems, making lacunae and inconsistencies obvious by the inability to obtain or produce the necessary information. For example, the calculation of the net area of a room presupposes a detailed, accurate representation that includes obstacles. Therefore, it is not attainable if the available representation is a floor plan sketch with only a rough description of the shape of the room and its dimensions. By showing exactly how each task is performed, information diagrams validate individual tasks but also address consistency and coherence more accurately than process diagrams: they show if all tasks are organized in the same way, with workable connections between them and with the expected final deliverables. In the above example, the mismatch between the net area calculation and the floor plan can indicate a premature use of a precise technique, a delay in design or a haphazard management approach resulting in more incompatibilities and disharmonies.

Validation is not merely technical; it also targets many of the cognitive issues discussed in the previous chapter. Even the best process designs remain subject to the biases that characterize Type 1 processes. It is always possible that erroneous assumptions and vague specifications have slipped in and populate the process description, unnoticed by project participants who share the same biases. The specificity of information diagrams helps make the cautions about cognitive limitations and their possible effects on process diagrams stronger and easier to identify on the basis of clear cues.

Eradication of Type 1 biases and illusions that have escaped scrutiny is founded on the cognitive decoupling supported by information diagrams. Even though the process and the information diagram appear quite similar, they are quite different in contect and abstraction level. The process diagram represents tasks in a way that is more rigorous than conventional process descriptions but essentially in similar terms. The information diagram shifts attention to the input and output of these tasks, and so forms a departure from the descriptions we usually apply to a process. Moreover, it supports Type 2 algorithmic processes by making such input and output explicit, often quantitative and unambiguously linked to actions and transactions.

The most obvious cue about biases in the process design is inability to obtain or produce the necessary information, as in the above example of a net area calculations. If the process diagram has been carefully set up, this suggests more than a local problem and should make us critical about what we think we know: illusions of knowledge may have resulted in grey areas that make connections between tasks uncertain. This combats overconfidence in the beliefs behind the process design and reveals biases in our expectations from it, so that predictable mistakes (often caused by adherence to customary or conventional procedures) can be avoided. As for unpredictable mistakes, information diagrams help reduce their error margins and anchor decisions around realistic, transparently derived values.

Many problems are caused by the substitution of a demanding task by a simpler one that does not deliver the necessary performance or output. Any instances of inappropriate substitution in the process design can be identified and removed on the basis of the following criteria:

- *Precision and accuracy requirements:* rather than accepting existing practices, consider what each task actually needs in order to achieve the highest possible performance. Compromises that reduce this performance may be inevitable but try to make them only when necessary.
- *Information availability and processing capacity:* basing a cost estimate on the floor area of a design may be acceptable when little is yet known about the design but doing so with a full simulation of the construction process at your disposal makes no sense. So, when translating a task into information instances, always consider what is already available in the process (information and processing tools), in particular with respect to the precision requirements of each task.

Any illusions of cause that may have persisted in the process diagram are generally easy to detect, as precedence in time (as in e.g. a time schedule) does not translate into connections of information output and input in the information diagram. In particular, information diagrams help identify the true causes of problems by tracking the derivation of information. For example, a mismatch between the load-bearing structure and the required span widths for rooms is not necessarily due to poor decision making concerning the load-bearing structure. It might also derive from vagueness or inconsistencies in the brief or from inappropriate cost constraints on the structure (i.e. inconsistencies between brief and budget).

Focusing on information is a good antidote to change and inattentional blindness, too: it is hard to ignore what is available, expected or required at any step in a process. This also subverts any narrow focus by being inclusive and comprehensive by necessity, while removing opportunities to add fictitious information that does not come from a specific internal or external source. The coherence and consistency that can be achieved with information diagrams is important for avoiding planning and sunken-costs fallacies: being specific on information leaves even less room for illusions of knowledge and confidence. Finally, information diagrams help develop an outside view of the project by making clear the connections between internal information to external sources, including through *reference class forecasting*: references to relevant classes of projects, reliable statistics on these projects and baseline forecasts from these statistics that are adapted to the characteristics of the particular case.[1] The development of reference classes may initially seem daunting but it is something any enterprise or professional body can do if projects are properly documented.

Despite its rigour, validation at the information level is less confrontational than at the process level. Challenging suspect parts in a process description with general facts, principles and opinions leads to discussions that can be dismissed merely because they conflict with basic assumptions ("we've always made our budgets this way"). Expressing the process in terms of information actions and transactions returns more objective, comprehensive and practical arguments why a process may or may not deliver the expected results. The discussion consequently shifts from general principles to how and which information is processed with respect to stated goals, such as delivering a building with the required qualities and performance on time and within budget.

VERACITY

An important aspect of validation concerns the veracity of information. The problem is that, even without the halo effect, our natural tendency is to believe that others are telling the truth. Defaulting to truth makes sense for the economy and efficiency of communication, which would suffer if we were to test the veracity of all incoming information. We are suspicious of others only when we expect them to deceive us. Suspicion is often triggered by the demeanour of the information sender but unfortunately this is a very poor indicator. We become suspicious of nervous presenters who look away and mumble, paying too much attention to the delivery rather than the content. Suspicions about the intentions of others are much more reliable but they do not normally arise in reasonably harmonious projects. Given sufficient trust, which is reinforced by inside views, actors and stakeholders routinely default to truth, failing to detect inconsistencies that undermine the veracity of information they receive. We are alert to inconsistencies only in projects that have experienced adversities such that cast doubt on the integrity or intentions of others but by then the project may be beyond saving.

Relying on the actual content of communication is more reliable and quite accurate.[2] If information is self-contradictory or inconsistent with known facts, it is easier to evaluate it and develop controls that anticipate unexpected problems. Switching from task to information therefore facilitates the integration of veracity controls in a process, usually as preliminary evaluations of information before important decisions or actions. For example, prior to analysing construction costs we should check the veracity of information input in the estimation. This involves tracing the primary data from which this information derives, as well as checking how it is derived. If the information is derived from contradictory of irrelevant sources, e.g. from a different design or an earlier version, this can be both easily detected and directly corrected. If the derivation involves questionable procedures, e.g. measurements of a supposedly typical part of the design only, these too can be detected and adjusted.

INFORMATION DIAGRAMS IN INFORMATION MANAGEMENT

An information diagram that captures both the needs of a process and the capacities of BIM can make IM clear and unambiguous to both managers and actors in the process. Information flow is explicitly depicted in the diagram, especially concerning what, who and when. Managers can use the information diagram to guide and control the process at any moment, while actors have a clear picture of the scope and significance of their actions. Addressing *how* questions depends on the fineness of the grain in the description of information instances: the finer it is, the more specific answers one can draw from the diagram. As such specificity affects interpretation, care should be taken to balance the two: many actors in a building project are knowledgeable professionals who may not take kindly to IM approaches that overconstrain their actions.

On the other hand, IM has to be strict about matters of authorship and custodianship because not everybody is yet accustomed to the possibilities and responsibilities of digital information processing. By linking stakeholders to information with accordingly labelled arcs in the information diagram, one can indicate responsibilities and actions throughout a process. Note that roles can be variable: an actor who authors some information in one task may become custodian of other information in another task.

Concerning information quality, the information diagram forms a usable background for pragmatic value: applying the I-P-O scheme at any node is a critical part of measuring it, i.e. establishing what users need to process and must produce in a task. Similarly, the information diagram is essential for the evaluation of completeness, coherence and consistency in BIM: any output from the model and especially any feedback to it is an opportunity to identify violations and conflicts that affect these aspects.

Information diagrams are also essential for our parsimonious approach to information quality. The approach focuses on primary data and their propagation; both can be traced with accuracy in the diagram, including explicit, manageable connections to derivative data. This enables managers and other project participants to know what should be preserved or prioritized. Finally, in the same manner one can identify anti-data, on the basis of expectations (e.g. knowing when information from different disciplines comes together in a process) and interpretation (e.g. that a space without a door is a shaft). This leads to directed action (e.g. requiring that two disciplines work together to solve interfacing problems), which should be present in an information diagram of appropriate specificity.

Above all, information diagrams illustrate the importance of IM for managing processes and products: information flow and quality are not technical issues but essential parts of any process, with direct relevance for specific problems and related decisions. Requiring complete, coherent, consistent and true information for a task is purely for the successful completion of the task. Any requirements on information, including syntactic ones, draw from project needs, including the drive towards avoiding cognitive biases and illusions. This confirms IM as a core part of any management approach, especially with respect to digitization and its promise for decision support.

Key Takeaways

- *Information diagrams operationalize and validate process diagrams by translating them into information-processing actions and products*
- *The validation of process designs with information diagrams includes addressing cognitive biases and illusions*
- *The superimposition of the I-P-O scheme on process task nodes helps translate a process diagram into an information diagram*
- *Information diagrams should take into account the implementation environment of BIM: the symbols and relations that contain the primary data and the views that present derivative data, as well as the possibilities for quality control*

Exercises

1. Compare the graph measures of Figure 2 to those of Figure 3: which differences do you observe and what are their causes and significance for the process design?
2. Add symbols, properties and relations to the information diagram of Figure 6 (especially with respect to feedback). Does the increased specificity make IM easier or more reliable?
3. Add actors to the information diagram of Figure 6. How does the result compare to Figure 2 (also in terms of graph measures)?
4. Complete Figure 7 by specifying how quality controls are performed (correct the diagram with respect to the decision degrees rule).
5. Make an information diagram for Figure 6 in the previous chapter (the "more comprehensive process diagram").

Notes

1. Reference class forecasting is explained in: Flyvbjerg, B. (2011). Over Budget, Over Time, Over and Over Again: Managing Major Projects. In Morris, P.W. G; Pinto, JK; Söderlund, J. (eds.), *The Oxford Handbook of Project Management.* Oxford: Oxford University Press.
2. Levine, T. R. (2014). Truth-Default Theory (TDT): A Theory of Human Deception and Deception Detection. *Journal of Language and Social Psychology,* **33**(*4*), 378–392. https://doi.org/10.1177/0261927X14535916

PART V

EXERCISES

CHAPTER 11

Exercise I: Maintenance

THE BRIEF

Organize the process of repainting all walls in a large lecture hall at a university. The walls are in good condition, so a single coat of pain suffices. The process therefore can be reduced to the following tasks:

- Make a model of the lecture hall in BIM using direct measurements and photographs
- Classify wall surfaces and their parts with respect to:
    - Labour (e.g. painting parts narrower than 30 cm are more time consuming)
    - Equipment (e.g. parts higher than 220 cm require scaffolding)
    - Accessibility (e.g. parts behind radiators or other fixed obstacles are hard to reach and therefore also time consuming)
- Measure the wall surfaces
- Make cost estimates
- Make a time schedule in 4D BIM

DELIVERABLES

1. Process and information diagrams, accompanied by short explanatory comments
2. Basic model of the lecture hall in a BIM editor
3. Schedules for classification, measurement, estimates and scheduling in BIM

EVALUATION CRITERIA

1. The process diagrams should:
    1. Make all actors, stakeholders and tasks explicit
    2. Include feedback loops in decision making

    3. Have no unnecessary bridges
2. The information diagrams should:
    1. Indicate how symbols relate to the necessary measurements and estimates
    2. Allow to detect how information is derived from primary data
3. The model in BIM should contain:
    1. All relevant symbols
    2. All necessary equipment
    3. The necessary subdivisions of surfaces with respect to labour (tip: these are often determined by relations between symbols, e.g. wall to scaffold height)

ROLES

If the exercise is a group assignment, consider roles for the following aspects:

- Process management
- Information management
- BIM modelling (two or more people)
- Analyses in BIM (using schedules – two or more people)

CHAPTER 12

Exercise II: Change management

THE BRIEF

Organize how changes to a design in the development and realization stages can be registered and processed in BIM. These changes may refer to:

- Change to a property of a symbol (e.g. lengthening of a wall)
- Change of the type of a symbol (e.g. change of family for a door)
- Change in a relation between symbols (e.g. relocation of a door in a wall)
- Change in a time property of a symbol (e.g. as a result of a scheduling change)

Organize the process of change management in both stages as a series of tasks that reflect the above types of changes and take into account possible causes of change, such as:

- Changes in the brief (e.g. new activities added)
- Changes in the budget (e.g. increase of façade cost necessitating reduction of cost elsewhere)
- Changes in an aspect of the design (e.g. change in the heating solution or the fire rating of internal doors and ensuing interfacing issues – not just clash detection)
- Changes in the construction schedules (e.g. due to delays in the delivery of components or to bad weather)
- Errors in construction (e.g. wrong dimensioning or specifications of an element)

DELIVERABLES

1. Process and information diagrams, accompanied by short explanatory comments
2. Basic model in a BIM editor demonstrating the way changes can be implemented

EVALUATION CRITERIA

1. The process diagrams should:
    1. Make all actors, stakeholders, tasks and their relations explicit
    2. Include feedback loops for controlling the changes and their effects
2. The information diagrams should:
    1. Indicate which symbol properties and relations change, and how
    2. Allow to detect how changes are propagated from one symbol to another
3. The model in BIM should contain:
    1. Relevant examples for each kind of change
    2. Schedules that allow tracking of changes

ROLES

If the exercise is a group assignment, consider roles for the following aspects:

- Process management
- Information management
- BIM modelling
- Case analyses (for finding realistic examples)

CHAPTER 13

Exercise III: Circularity for existing buildings

THE BRIEF

The existing building stock in the Netherlands has to undergo extensive improvements, so as to meet new user or environmental requirements, from hybrid working and effective cooling to the energy transition. To reduce costs, one can adopt a circular approach to both components or materials released from existing buildings and the new components and subsystems that will be added to the buildings. Organize the following tasks for a typical Dutch single-family house:

- Document the existing situation in a model appropriate for renovation, i.e. including realization phases, distinction between existing and planned, what should remain and what should be removed
- Identify in the model components and materials that should be extracted (e.g. radiators: the house will switch to underfloor heating), explaining how identification takes place (preferably automatically) in the model
- Estimate the expected circularity form for these components and materials (recycle, remanufacture, repurpose, re-use etc.), explaining which factors play a role (weathering, wear, interfacing with other elements etc.) and how these factors can be detected in the model
- Identify which elements should be upgraded and specify what this entails in the model (paying attention to phasing and element type changes)
- Specify how new elements (for any renovation) should be added to the model to support the above in the remaining lifecycle of the house
- Make a time schedule for a renovation in 4D BIM

DELIVERABLES

1. Process and information diagrams, accompanied by short explanatory comments
2. Incomplete model in a BIM editor containing demonstrations of your solutions
3. Schedules for circularity analyses in BIM

EVALUATION CRITERIA

1. The process diagrams should:
    1. Make all actors, stakeholders and tasks explicit
    2. Include demolition as an option, with clear feasibility criteria
    3. Include feedback loops in decision making
    4. Have no unnecessary bridges
2. The information diagrams should:
    1. Indicate which classes of symbols and which types of properties and relations are relevant
    2. Allow to track how decisions are based to primary data
    3. Explain how circularity relates to information, e.g. which properties and relations are used to estimate it
3. The model in BIM should contain:
    1. A clear indication of how circularity (as derivative information) is described for each symbol
    2. A reliable solution for the time dimension, e.g. phases with clear connections, including precedence
    3. An efficient way of achieving overview, e.g. identifying all similar or interconnected components in an existing or projected situation

ROLES

If the exercise is a group assignment, consider roles for the following aspects:

- Process management
- Information management
- BIM modelling
- Analyses in BIM (using schedules – probably more than one group member)
- Legal and technical aspects of the energy transition
- Building documentation (emphasis on how to deal with incompleteness and uncertainty)
- Subsystem integration
- Circularity in design (technical aspects)

CHAPTER 14

Exercise IV: Energy transition

THE BRIEF

In the Netherlands, as in many other countries, there are far-reaching plans for reducing the energy consumption required by housing, such as the envisaged energy transition (https://www.government.nl/topics/renewable-energy/central-government-promotes-energy-savings, https://www.iea.org/reports/the-netherlands-2020). Despite the wide acceptance of the necessity of energy reduction and climate improvement, these plans meet with opposition, reluctance, operational complexity and failure. Particularly painful are cases where apparently straightforward improvements, such as the placing of solar panels on roofs, turn out to be a waste of public and private investment. Practically all websites on solar panels are clear about the required conditions, such as roof size and orientation. Still, as any walk through a Dutch town or suburb reveals, there are many, presumably subsidized, panel configurations that are too small or improperly oriented, delivering only around 25% of the expected performance. This even happens in new construction, which suggests that the reasons for failure are deep and significant.

A wise municipality acknowledges the immensity of the task and, rather than rushing into action and wasting time and money in questionable procedures and unproductive subsidies, wants to start from understanding the possibilities and limitations for the *existing* housing stock: how can they ascertain what can be done with each individual residential building, which retrofit packages apply to different categories in the municipality and what the costs and performance of energetic refurbishments can be.

To this effect, they hire you to manage the process of information collection, with the following brief:

1. Determine which information is necessary for each existing residential building: what we need to know to evaluate the existing situation, determine which improvements are required or possible and estimate the costs and effects of these improvements. The information should be explicitly linked to parts of the building, such as components in the building envelope and the building services. In addition to building information, also consider the usage of buildings (activities deployed in them, type of occupants, energy consumption).

2. Decide how this information should be organized in BIM, so that there is a complete and reliable model of each building in the municipality: which symbols, properties and relations accommodate the information in the model. Assume that there is affordable and reliable storage for the models.
3. Design a process for collecting data about each dwelling in a way that the information in BIM is permanently up to date. The municipality does not want to be burdened with the costs of periodical visits to every building, in which some expert inspects and documents what has changed since the last visit. They prefer to have an automatic system that connects to all relevant sources, stakeholders and actors, from the drawing in the archives of architectural offices to maintenance activities such as replacing a window pane. They want all involved parties to have access to the model of a building, be supported by the information it contains and, in return, update it with the results of their actions (e.g. change the type and construction year of the window panel).
4. Explain how the collection of models could help with the development of retrofit packages for the whole building stock in the municipality and how these packages could be matched to specific properties (e.g. how insulation needs in the building stock can be clustered into types and matched to solutions). This should be the foundation of municipal strategies for energetic improvement and is perhaps the most important product of the project (its culmination from the perspective of the client).

DELIVERABLES

1. Process and information diagrams, accompanied by short explanatory comments
2. A draft of a short policy document that summarizes the diagrams
3. Incomplete model in a BIM editor containing a typical case and demonstrations of your solutions

EVALUATION CRITERIA

1. The process diagrams should:
    1. Make all actors, stakeholders and tasks explicit
    2. Include feedback loops in decision making
    3. Have no unnecessary bridges
2. The information diagrams should:
    1. Indicate which symbols, properties and relations are essential for this project
    2. Allow to detect how information is derived from primary data
    3. Contain clear measures for safeguarding information quality (given the extent of the project)
    4. Explain the relations between individual buildings and the whole building sock (i.e. between private project management and municipal strategies or policies)

3. The model in BIM should contain:
    1. All relevant symbols of an indicative case
    2. Schedules for the necessary calculations

ROLES

If the exercise is a group assignment, consider roles for the following aspects:

- Process management
- Information management
- BIM modelling
- Analyses in BIM (using schedules)
- Policy development
- Building documentation (emphasis on efficient solutions for large-scale data collection)
- Energetic solutions and performance (technical aspects underlying the choice of building features and retrofit packages)

CHAPTER 15

Exercise V: Waste management

THE BRIEF

Buildings are often consider as a major secondary source of valuable materials, such as metals.[1] However, these materials are not easily or frequently released. In fact, buildings prolong the in-use life of many materials, primarily because of the longevity of buildings: rather than replace buildings in relatively short cycles, as we do with e.g. cars or computers, we tend to preserve them, often for longer than originally intended, mending and fixing what still functions, even if performance is low.

This suggests that renovation and refurbishment rather than demolition may be the main release of materials from buildings. Kitchen and bathroom renovations, for example, are quite popular and frequent in many countries. Unfortunately, they are less rigorously regulated than demolition, also concerning waste production and management. A local authority wants to change this in a manner that provides reliable insights into the quantities and quality of materials released. To this effect, they need an information strategy for:

- Making explicit the quantities and qualities of materials released by renovations and refurbishments, starting with kitchens and bathrooms.
- Making reliable estimates of the circularity level of released materials, from reuse to recycling.
- Stimulating efficient and effective waste management by both enabling secondary material makers and imposing different disposal rates for different kinds of building waste.

To help the local authority achieve these goals, you are asked to develop a BIM-based process that will be compulsory for all building renovations and refurbishments. This process should include:

1. A clear description of the existing situation (current phase)
2. A precise account of what is to be taken out of a kitchen or bathroom (extraction phase)
3. The exact process of extraction, from deconstruction to local demolition (important for the quality and reusability of components, as well as for the cost)
4. Guarantees that no hibernating materials or pollutants are left in the building

5. A precise specification of all new components to be added to the kitchen or bathroom (construction phase)
6. Expectations for waste management in future renovations and refurbishments (how the new components will help higher extraction rates or circularity levels)
7. Arguably the most important for your client: a way of connecting information on individual cases to strategic management and policy making for the whole municipal stock

Note that the overarching goal of the project is not to promote specific circularity approaches but to provide unambiguous and reliable information that helps understand the potential and feasibility of any approach to waste management, sustainability and circularity. To this end, your process design should include the ability to handle uncertainty and vagueness, as well as the ability to remove them.

DELIVERABLES

1. Process and information diagrams, accompanied by short explanatory comments
2. Model of an indicative case in a BIM editor
3. Schedules for quantitative and qualitative analyses in BIM

EVALUATION CRITERIA

1. The process diagrams should:
    1. Make all actors, stakeholders and tasks explicit
    2. Include feedback loops in decision making
    3. Have no unnecessary bridges
2. The information diagrams should:
    1. Indicate which symbols, properties and relations are relevant for this project
    2. Allow to detect how information is derived from primary data
    3. Contain clear measures for safeguarding information quality (especially with respect to circularity level)
    4. Illustrate how relevant quantities and qualities are estimated
    5. Explain the relations between individual buildings and the whole building sock (i.e. between private project management and municipal strategies or policies)
3. The model in BIM should contain:
    1. All relevant symbols of an indicative case
    2. Schedules for the necessary calculations

ROLES

If the exercise is a group assignment, consider roles for the following aspects:

- Process management
- Information management
- BIM modelling
- Analyses in BIM (using schedules)
- Building documentation (emphasis on efficient solutions for high specificity)
- Kitchen and bathroom design
- Waste management

Notes

1. For a critical account of this: Koutamanis, A., et al., 2018. Urban mining and buildings. *Resources, Conservation and Recycling,* **138**(November), 32-39 https://doi.org/10.1016/j.resconrec.2018.06.024

Epilogue

Every book deserves a concluding part. In some genres, like novels and thrillers, the whole book works towards a conclusion that terminates the readers' journey and brings all narrative strands neatly together. Others have more difficulty with the ending, for example textbooks that deal with a series of subjects, like this one. A common practice in such books is to write a conclusion in the style of scientific papers: essentially a copy of the introduction, only with answers instead of questions — essentially a summary of key points made in the intervening chapters. This works well in papers, even if the summary is a mere list of points, but books require more coherence: a story, not a list. Therefore, it often leads to selective narratives that discriminate against some aspects. It is perhaps not accidental that introductions and conclusions are the most read sections in scientific papers, while prologues and epilogues are the least read chapters in scientific books.

I shall keep my summary brief:

> *Thanks to digitization, we are producing and processing huge quantities of information for practically everything we do. This will become even more intensive in the foreseeable future, making information management (IM) a key concern in our personal and private lives. The significance of IM is acknowledged in AECO but AECO remains attached to outdated, analogue practices that are replicated in digital environments, distorting digitization and restricting its potential.*
>
> *To improve the situation, we need to understand that digital representations like BIM are symbolic and start thinking in terms of symbols, properties, relations and the graphs they form instead of views like drawings and implementation mechanisms like lines. We must also approach information from a semantic perspective and realize that our main focus should be the primary data that define symbols and relations in our representations, and from which other data derive. This makes the two priorities of IM, information flows and information quality, means for the preservation of primary data and the transparent definition of derivative data.*
>
> *To achieve these goals, we need to represent processes, too, as directed graphs of tasks and information processed around these tasks. The duality of process and information diagrams matches the social and information sides of management, and stimulates Type 2 thinking, through which we can prevent AECO failures and improve decision making.*

Is this summary sufficient? It certainly encapsulates the main message of the book and should be clear enough to its readers. The problem is that this message may fail to connect to other messages students and professionals receive in abundance with respect to information and digitization, for example the extensive push of BIM as a panacea, the apparently impending transition to the magic of digital twins, golden threads, AI, smart buildings and cities: a never-ending procession of easy, automatic solutions that seem to be directly available.

The sad truth is that there are no easy solutions in information or digitization. The promise of a solution may be simple to describe (narratives, again) but, as anyone who has attempted anything substantial in any digital environment can affirm, everything comes at considerable cost and effort. All those things we take for granted on the Internet or on our smartphones hide behind them expensive infrastructures, set up in longer periods and with more failures than we care to imagine. They are often still problematic, as we can see from e.g. the environmental impact of the colossal data centres that have become a necessity for maintaining our hybrid lives.

As for AECO, its existing digital technologies may be not good enough both for its needs and in comparison to what is generally available. More worryingly, our use of these tools may be even worse. This suggests that digitization in AECO, including BIM and other promising technologies, is in a crisis but the crisis is not evident to the world and perhaps not that important. After all, we still manage to produce large, complex buildings, as well as large volumes of buildings, which are snapped up by a willing market, at prices higher than ever. We can see that in the current housing situation in the Netherlands: both demand and prices are high, as is supply — only supply is not as high as demand. There are several ways to raise production volumes but, if demand keeps growing, it is questionable that supply will ever satisfy it. In fact, it may be rather undesirable.

Demand and cost are not limited to having a roof over one's head: we are spending more and more on our buildings, heating, cooling and refurbishing them with a regularity and to standards that would have astounded previous generations. This obviously improves living quality (although we have so far failed to address the environmental factors in the COVID-19 spread) but also generates a lot of economic activity around the built environment that keeps several industries in good health. Our ways may be wasteful but somehow we manage to pay for them, making everybody happy. Why then should digitization and IM matter and to whom?

The answer is that they should matter to AECO professionals because they have yet to enjoy the full potential of digitization either for easing their burdens of for improving their performance. And they are not bound to find enjoyment if all that happens is that new software and new technologies like blockchains and digital twins become available to them. What they need above all is rational approaches, founded on clear principles that explain problems in full and guide solutions. Once we have and understood them, finding the right implementation tools or even learning to live with less than optimal solutions becomes easy and productive. This is not insignificant for an industry widely accused of underperformance.

Beyond their general impact, these new, rational approaches are an opportunity for the new generations of professionals that enter the AECO ranks, yet unfettered by its conventions and accustomed to more advanced digitization in their private lives. These new professionals need to find their place in a competitive world, full of elders with more practical experience and wider networks. Meaningful, productive digitization can help them as a specialization that is relatively scarce, as well as a powerful means for achieving other, social or economic goals.

What this book tries to convey is the core of such an approach, which will not age as fast as the various kinds of software AECO has been using and will therefore serve its users for longer and better than the usual stuff that passes for computer literacy. Knowing how to use this or that program is of little significance in decision making. AECO professionals need to start from what they want to achieve with digitization, instead of what is possible or customary with existing software.

Appendix I: Graph theory

UNDIRECTED GRAPHS

Graphs are mathematical structures that describe relations between pairs of things. They can be represented by diagrams, where a *vertex* stands for a thing and an *edge* for a relation between two things. In the graph of a family tree, for example, the vertices represent the family members and the edges their relationships (Figure 1). Any part of the graph, for example, the nuclear family of father, mother, child and their relations to each other, is a *subgraph*. Two vertices are *adjacent* if they are joined by an edge. The two vertices are *incident* with this edge and the edge is incident with both vertices.

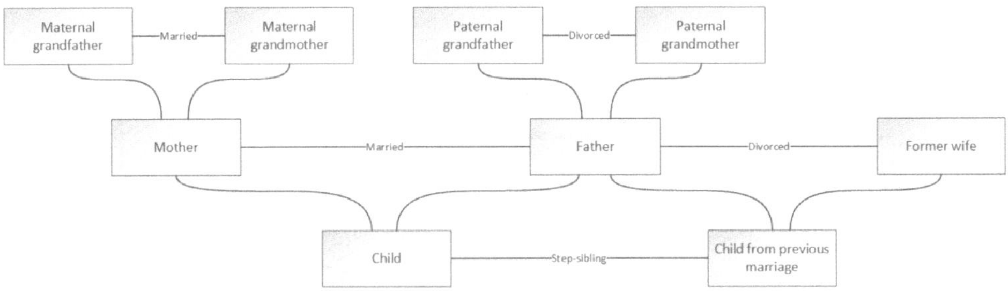

Figure 1. A family tree as a graph

Graph diagrams are dimensionless: the size of a vertex and the length of an edge do not matter either for the vertex and edge or for the whole graph. The *size* of a graph is measured by the number of edges in it, while the number of vertices is the *order* of the graph. This means that different arrangements of the vertices and edges in a graph drawing are equally acceptable, so long as they follow a logic that helps legibility (Figure 2). The graphs in Figure 1 and 2 are *isomorphic:* they have the same vertices and, whenever a pair of vertices in either graph is connected by an edge, the same also holds for the other graph.

The main concern with graph diagrams is that care should be taken that edges do not cross each other in the drawing because this indicates that the graph is *planar.* Planar graphs have mathematical advantages that relate to the subject of this book (representation of buildings and processes), so you must try and draw your graphs in a way that demonstrates this. Note that a graph may be planar even if you are unable to find an arrangement where no edges intersect. Graph drawing remains a hard task, even with computers. To ensure legibility, do the following in your graphs:

- Arrange the nodes in a logical manner (e.g. in columns, rows or other clusters), without worrying for the size of the drawing or the length of the edges
- Try to have no crossing or overlapping edges, again without worrying about the resulting length or shape of the edges

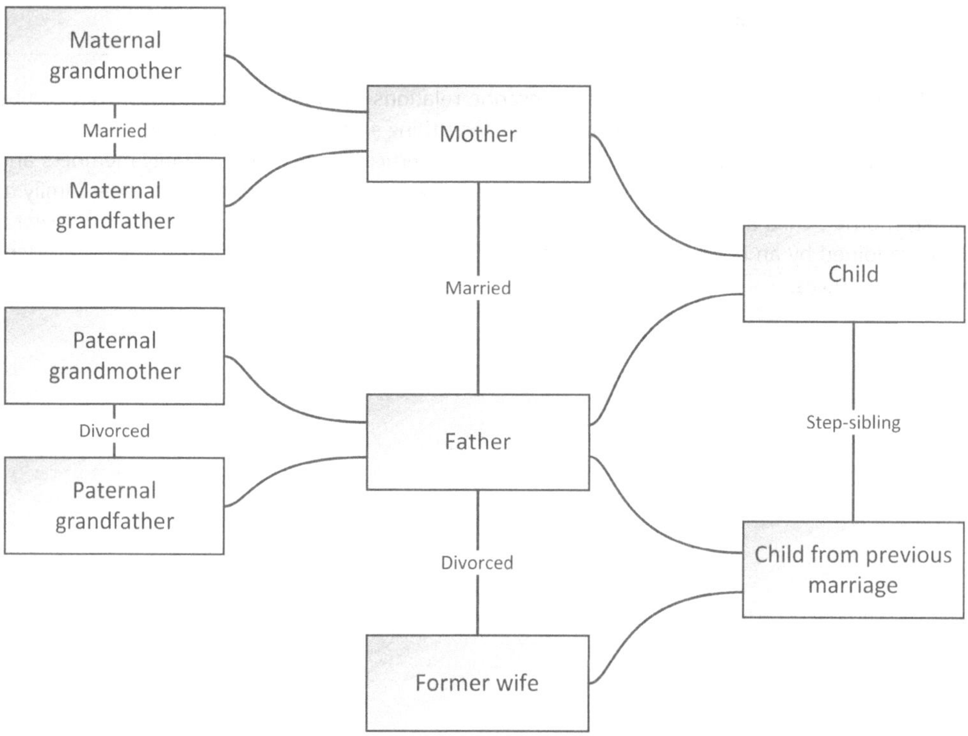

Figure 2. The same family tree and graph

Properties (including size) can be attached to vertices and edges as labels (textual or visual). The edges of the family tree are labelled with the relationship between the persons represented by the vertices they connect. The default relationship between parent and child is left unlabelled. In general, it is recommended that you use textual labelling rather than visual because it simplifies graph drawing and reading.

Graphs can also be described by adjacency matrices, in which each cell contains the connection between the vertex in the row and the vertex in the column. Table 1 shows if there is a direct connection between the two family members (usually a first-degree relationship). Table 2 shows the relationship as labelled in the graph. Table 2 therefore conveys exactly the same information as the graph drawing, only in a different form.

Table 1. Adjacency matrix of the family tree graph

	Maternal grandmother	Maternal grandfather	Paternal grandmother	Paternal grandfather	Mother	Father	Former wife	Child	Child from previous marriage
Maternal grandmother	×	1	0	0	1	0	0	0	0
Maternal grandfather	1	×	0	0	1	0	0	0	0
Paternal grandmother	0	0	×	1	0	1	0	0	0
Paternal grandfather	0	0	1	×	0	1	0	0	0
Mother	1	1	0	0	×	1	0	1	0
Father	0	0	1	1	1	×	1	1	1
Former wife	0	0	0	0	0	1	×	0	1
Child	0	0	0	0	1	1	0	×	1
Child from previous marriage	0	0	0	0	0	1	1	1	×

Table 2. Adjacency matrix of the family tree graph (labelled)

	Maternal grandmother	Maternal grandfather	Paternal grandmother	Paternal grandfather	Mother	Father	Former wife	Child	Child from previous marriage
Maternal grandmother	×	married	0	0	parent	0	0	0	0
Maternal grandfather	married	×	0	0	parent	0	0	0	0
Paternal grandmother	0	0	×	divorced	0	child	0	0	0
Paternal grandfather	0	0	divorced	×	0	child	0	0	0
Mother	child	child	0	0	×	married	0	parent	0
Father	0	0	child	child	married	×	divorced	parent	parent
Former wife	0	0	0	0	0	divorced	×	0	parent
Child	0	0	0	0	child	child	0	×	step-sibling
Child from previous marriage	0	0	0	0	0	child	child	step-sibling	×

Each vertex in a graph has a *degree*: the number of edges connected to it. In the family tree example, each grandparent and child vertex has a degree of 3, the mother vertex 4 and the father vertex 6. The former wife, whose parents do not appear in the graph, has a degree of only 2. The degree of a node is a good indication of its importance or complexity. In this case, it is logical that the father node has the highest degree because the family tree focuses on his former and current marital situation. An *odd* vertex is one with a degree that is an odd number, while the degree of an *even* vertex is even. A vertex with a degree equal to zero is called *isolated,* while a vertex with a degree of 1, as the end stations in the metro map from the chapter on symbolic representation (vertices A, H, G and N in Figure 3), is called a *leaf*.

The *degree sequence* of a graph is obtained by listing the degrees of vertices in a graph. This is particularly useful for identifying heavily connected subgraphs. In a metro map, for example, it shows not only which vertices are busy interchanges but also their proximity and distribution: which parts of a line present the most opportunities for changing to other lines.

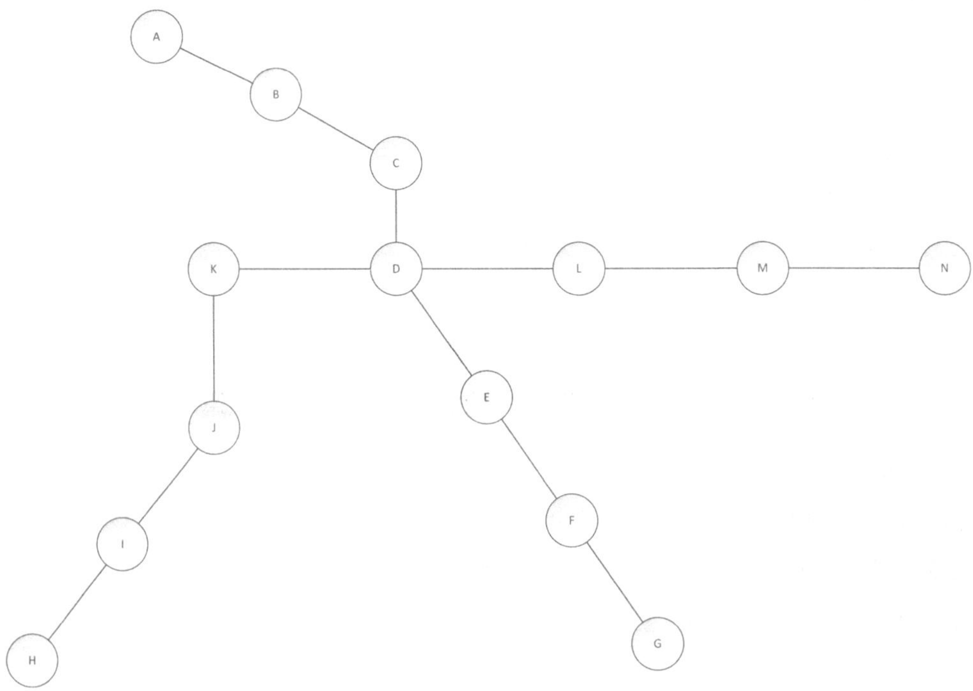

Figure 3. The graph of a metro map

A graph in *connected* if each of its vertices connects to every other vertex by some sequence of edges and vertices (a *walk*). The graphs in this book are by definition connected: in a building there is practically always a way to go from one place to another, while processes should be characterized by continuity from beginning to end. In fact, we pay particular attention to interruptions of connectedness, such as bridges and minimal cuts. A *bridge* is an edge that divides a graph into two separate parts, so its removal renders the graph *disconnected*. In the family tree, no edge is a bridge. If an edge is removed from it, there are always a connection between two family members it connected. For example, if the two children sever direct communication between them, there is always the possibility to communicate via the father or, more indirectly, through the rest of the family. Such *bridgeless graphs* hold advantages for communication and continuity: a metro map that is a bridgeless graph means that passengers can reach their destination, even when the connection between two stations is disrupted. In this respect, our metro example is poor: in Figure 3, all edges are bridges. The removal of any edge causes an interruption in one of the two metro lines (Figure 4) and makes the graph disconnected.

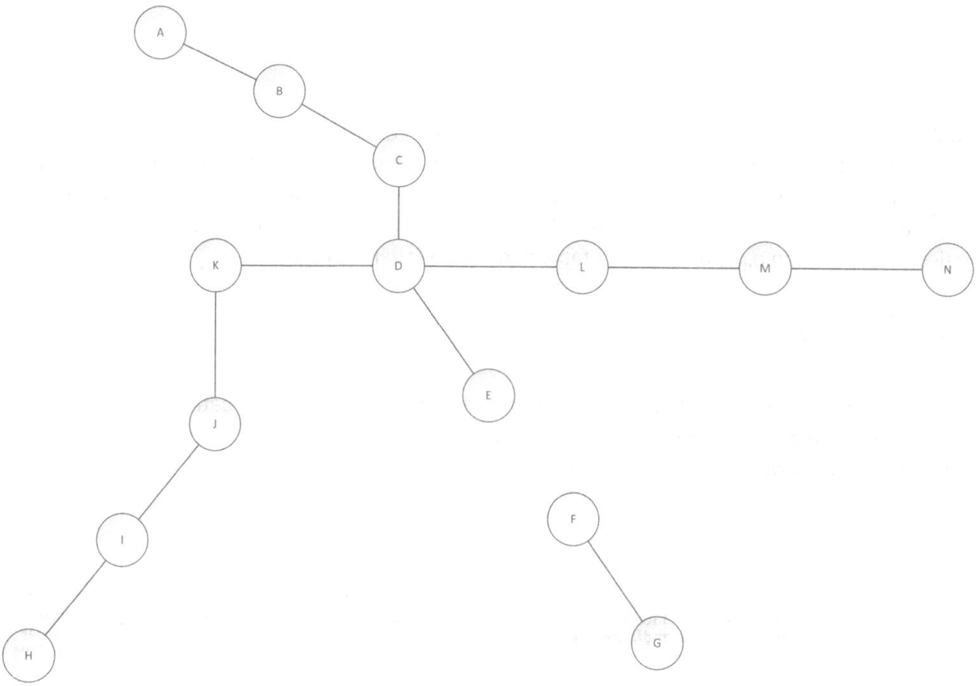

Figure 4. The removal of a bridge renders a graph disconnected: vertices F and G are now connected only to each other

To disconnect the family tree, you need to remove a number of edges: a *cut set*. The smallest such set is called the *minimum cut*. In our example, the minimum cut consists of the two edges incident to the former wife vertex (Figure 5). If these are removed, the vertex becomes isolated. The number of edges in the minimum cut is the *edge connectivity* of the graph.

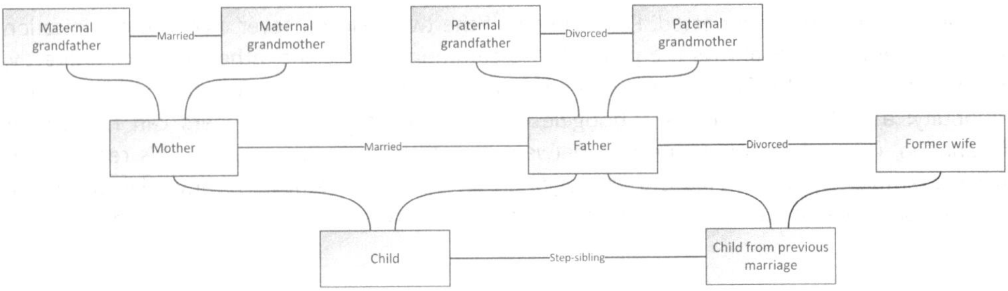

Figure 5. The minimum cut in the family tree graph

A walk that connects two vertices without any repetition in either the edges or the vertices is called a *path.* For example, in Figure 1, the maternal grandmother vertex connects to the child vertex through the path consisting of the parent-child edge to the mother vertex, the mother vertex and the parent-child edge from there to the child vertex. This is also the *shortest path* between the two vertices, shorter than e.g. paths via the father and former wife vertices.

GRAPH MEASURES

The *distance* between two vertices is the number of edges in the shortest path between them. In a family tree, the distance between parents and children is always 1 and the distance between grandparents and grandchildren is 2 (Table 3).

Table 3. Distances in the family tree graph

	Maternal grandmother	**Maternal grandfather**	**Paternal grandmother**	**Paternal grandfather**	**Mother**	**Father**	**Former wife**	**Child**	**Child from former marriage**
Maternal grandmother	×	1	3	3	1	2	3	2	3
Maternal grandfather	1	×	3	3	1	2	3	2	3
Paternal grandmother	3	3	×	1	2	1	2	2	2
Paternal grandfather	3	3	1	×	2	1	2	2	2
Mother	1	1	2	2	×	1	2	1	2
Father	2	2	1	1	1	×	1	1	1
Former wife	3	3	2	2	2	1	×	2	1
Child	2	2	2	2	1	1	2	×	1
Child from previous marriage	3	3	2	2	2	1	1	1	×

The distance is the basis for a range of measures, starting with *eccentricity:* the greatest distance between a vertex and any other vertex in a graph. Eccentricity is a good indication of the centrality of a vertex in a graph. It is also an indication of the size of the graph: the *radius* of a graph is the smallest eccentricity of any vertex in the graph and the *diameter* of a graph is the greatest eccentricity of any vertex in the graph. The vertices with an eccentricity equal to the radius form the *center* of the graph, while the vertices with an eccentricity equal to the diameter form the *periphery* (Table 4).

Table 4. Distances in the metro graph

	A	B	C	D	E	F	G	H	I	J	K	L	M	N	Eccentricity	Closeness
A	×	1	2	3	4	5	6	7	6	5	4	4	5	6	7	0,31
B	1	×	1	2	3	4	5	6	5	4	3	3	4	5	6	0,38
C	2	1	×	1	2	3	4	5	4	3	2	2	3	4	5	0,50
D	3	2	1	×	1	2	3	4	3	2	1	1	2	3	4	0,72
E	4	3	2	1	×	1	2	5	4	3	2	2	3	4	5	0,59
F	5	4	3	2	1	×	1	6	5	4	3	3	4	5	6	0,50
G	6	5	4	3	2	1	×	7	6	5	4	4	5	6	7	0,41
H	7	6	5	4	5	6	7	×	1	2	3	5	6	7	7	0,43
I	6	5	4	3	4	5	6	1	×	1	2	4	5	6	6	0,54
J	5	4	3	2	3	4	5	2	1	×	1	3	4	5	5	0,65
K	4	3	2	1	2	3	4	3	2	1	×	2	3	4	4	0,72
L	4	3	2	1	2	3	4	5	4	3	2	×	1	2	5	0,59
M	5	4	3	2	3	4	5	6	5	4	3	1	×	1	6	0,46
N	6	5	4	3	4	5	6	7	6	5	4	2	1	×	7	0,36

In the example of the metro map, these measures suggest that vertices D and K are the center, and vertices A, G, H and N the periphery (Figure 6). In between the two are vertices with eccentricities of 5 and 6. These groups agree with intuitive interpretations of the metro map. You may also choose to form the center out of vertices with an eccentricity of 4 and 5 or the periphery out of vertices with an eccentricity of 6 and 7. Using ranges of values also agrees with intuitive interpretations and can be useful with large graphs.

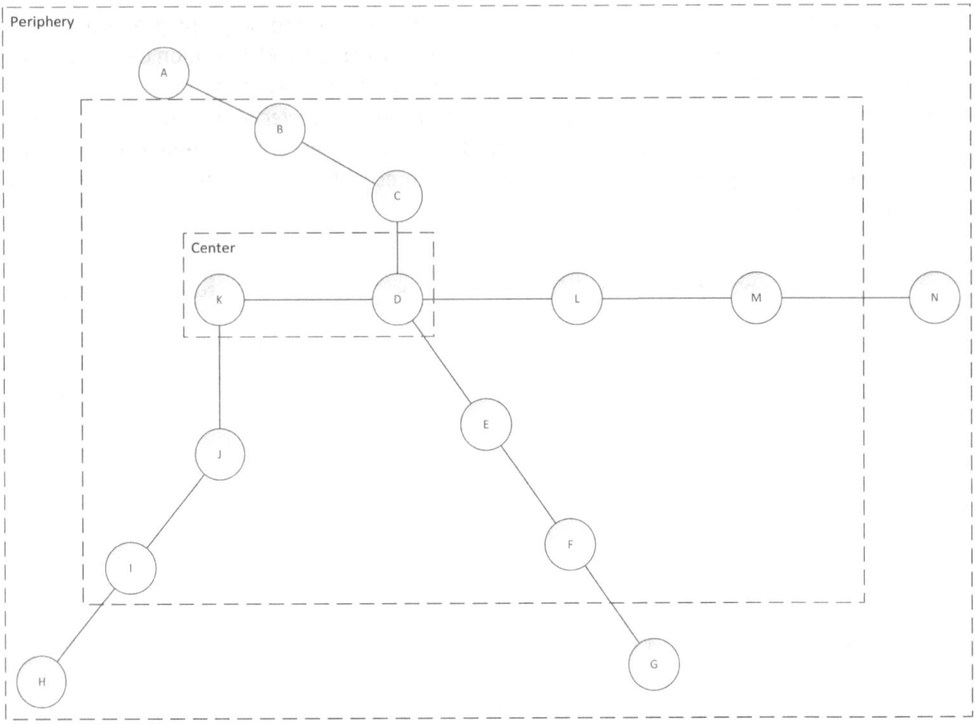

Figure 6. The center and the periphery of the metro graph

In addition to eccentricity, you can use the *closeness* of a vertex: its inverse mean distance to all other vertices in the graph, calculated by dividing the number of all other vertices (the order of the graph minus one) by the sum of distances to these vertices. The higher the value of closeness, the more central the position of a vertex (Table 4). In the example of the metro map, closeness and eccentricity agree that vertices D and K are the most central. As for the rest of the vertices, the closeness values offer more variation than eccentricity and thus a more refined basis for grouping them.

DIRECTED GRAPHS

Many relations are directed by their precedence in time, in relation to movement or through another dependence, as in the relation between parent and child. These can be represented in *directed graphs (digraphs)*, where things are represented by *nodes* (a synonym of vertex, which we will use to indicate that we are dealing with a digraph) and relations by *arcs* (i.e. directed edges). Due to directedness, some things are slightly different from undirected graphs:

- A node has an *in-* and an *out-degree,* measured respectively by the number of incoming and out outgoing arcs. A node with an in-degree of 0 is called a *source.* Source nodes are the starting points of processes. A node with an out-degree of 0 is called a *terminal* (or *sink*) and represents an endpoint in a process.

- A walk is directed: it consists of arcs with the same direction.
- A path is similarly directed (*dipath*): This obviously affects connectivity: a digraph is *strongly connected* if there is a dipath that connects every pair of nodes or *weakly connected* if the undirected underlying graph obtained by replacing all arcs with edges in connected.

Graphs that contain both edges and arcs are called *mixed* and are to be avoided in the context of this book. In the subjects discussed here, either the direction does not matter (as with most doors in a building) or is strictly defined by time or dependence (as in the transition from one task to another in a process). It may be tempting to add bidirectional arcs to process diagrams but these, too, should be avoided because they merely obfuscate the process, e.g. obscure feedback.

GRAPH OPERATIONS

The changes you apply to a graph include:

- *Edge contraction*: the replacement of an edge and two vertices incident to it with a single vertex
- *Edge subdivision:* the replacement of an edge with a vertex and connection of the new vertex with new edges to the ends of the original vertices
- *Vertex identification:* replacement of any two vertices with a single vertex incident to all edges previously incident to either of the original vertices
- *Vertex splitting:* the replacement of a vertex with two adjacent vertices and of each edge incident to the original vertex with an edge incident to either new vertex (but not to both)

In all transformations of a graph, it is advisable to think in terms of these operations to ensure consistency and avoid omissions, such as forgetting to connect a new node to the existing ones when refining a process diagram. They help connect the previous state of the graph to the new one and to meaning of the changes you want to implement. In particular, the transition from process to information diagram involves changes that benefit from considering them as graph operations.

Appendix II: Parameterization

WHAT IS PARAMETERIZATION

To understand what parameterization is and how it works, let us consider a simple, basic example: the equation that describes a straight line:

$$y = a \cdot x + b$$

In this equation, x and y are the coordinates of each point on the line, and a and b are parameters. The values of these parameters do not change the line type: the equation always describes a straight line. What a and b do is determine key properties of the line:

- a determines the slope of the line: if it is negative, the line goes down to the left; if it is positive, down to the right; if its is 1, the slope is 45 degrees; if it is zero, the line is horizontal
- b determines the y intercept: the point where the line crosses the y axis

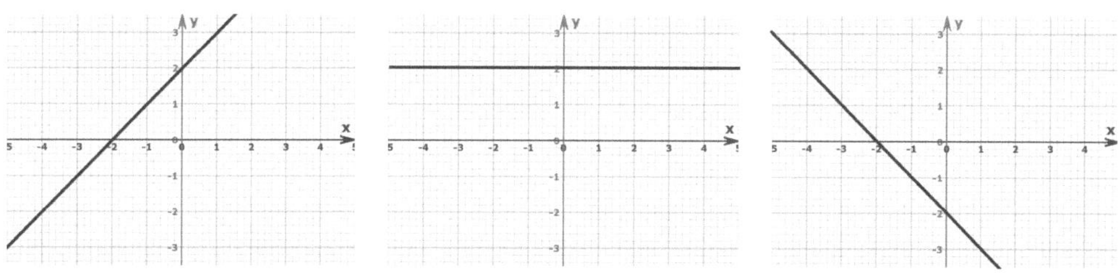

Figure 1. left to right: $y=x+2$; $y=0x+2$;$y=–x–2$

Instead of fixed values, the two parameters can be variable, so that we can control them in a transparent and precise manner. Moving a line to a new position without changing its slope, for instance, amounts to adding a number to b. Parameter values can be constrained to take specific values, e.g. if a can only be -1 or +1, the equation is allowed to produce only line slopes of 45 degrees. They can also be constrained relative to parameters of other lines. For example, this equation describes lines that are always parallel to our original example:

$$y_1 = a \cdot x_1 + (b + c)$$

The following equation describes lines that are always perpendicular to our example:

$$y_2 = (-1/a) \cdot x_2 + (b + d)$$

Any change to the parameters of the original line also triggers changes to the other two lines, so that they always remain respectively parallel and perpendicular to it. Constraining one thing relative to another in this way is the foundation of parameterization in design, for example, keeping walls parallel or perpendicular to each other, keeping their dimensions in the same proportions etc.

KINDS OF PARAMETERIZATION

There are three kinds of parameterization in design:

1. *Geometric:* affecting the geometric properties of a symbol, e.g. length or slope
2. *Topological:* concerning the number and configuration of symbols, e.g. the number and position of steps in a stair in relation to the height that has to be bridged
3. *Symbolic:* concerning non-geometric properties of a symbol, e.g. the type of a wall one may enter in a model can be constrained by applicable fire safety regulations or acoustic requirements

The above line example is of the geometric kind. Figure 2 is an example of the topological kind: a helical stair, consisting of geometrically identical steps. Each step is positioned with the bottom line of its riser fully aligned with the far end of the tread of the previous step. In this way, there are no gaps between them and they form a steady progression from a lower level to a higher.

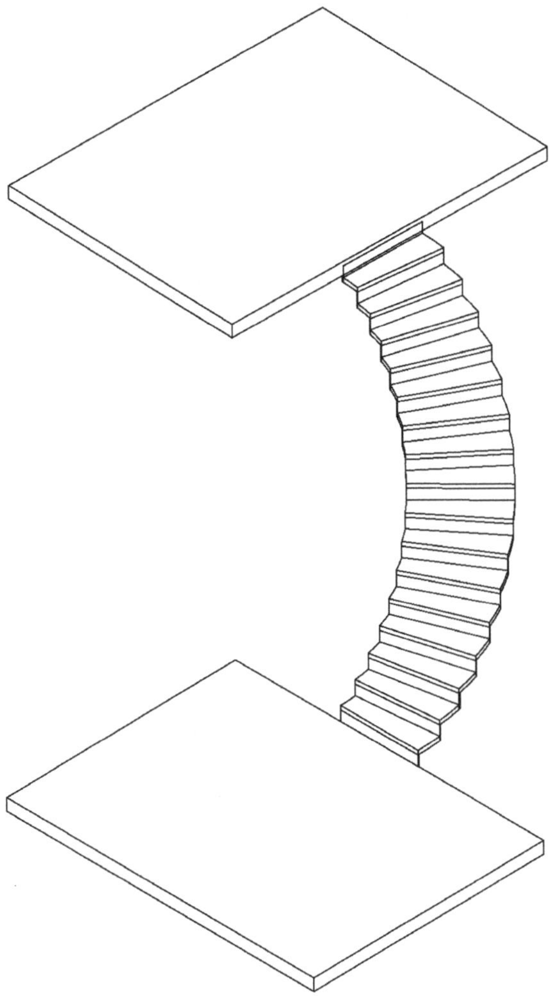

Figure 2. Helical stair

If the height difference between the two floors changes (Figure 3 and 4), more steps are added in the same fashion: topological parameterization affects the number of required steps. The geometry of the steps and their relation do not change, in contrast to the overall form of the stair.

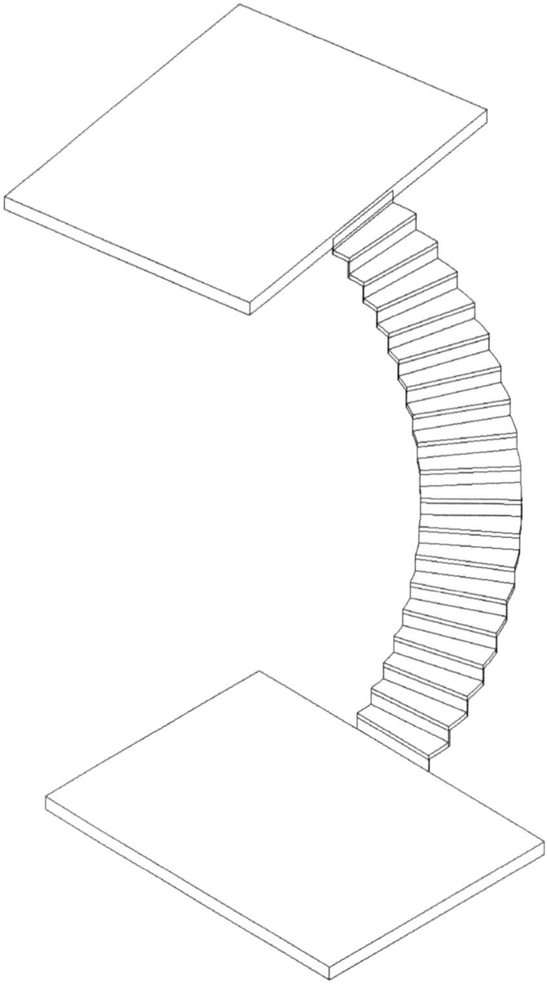

Figure 3. Helical stair lengthened

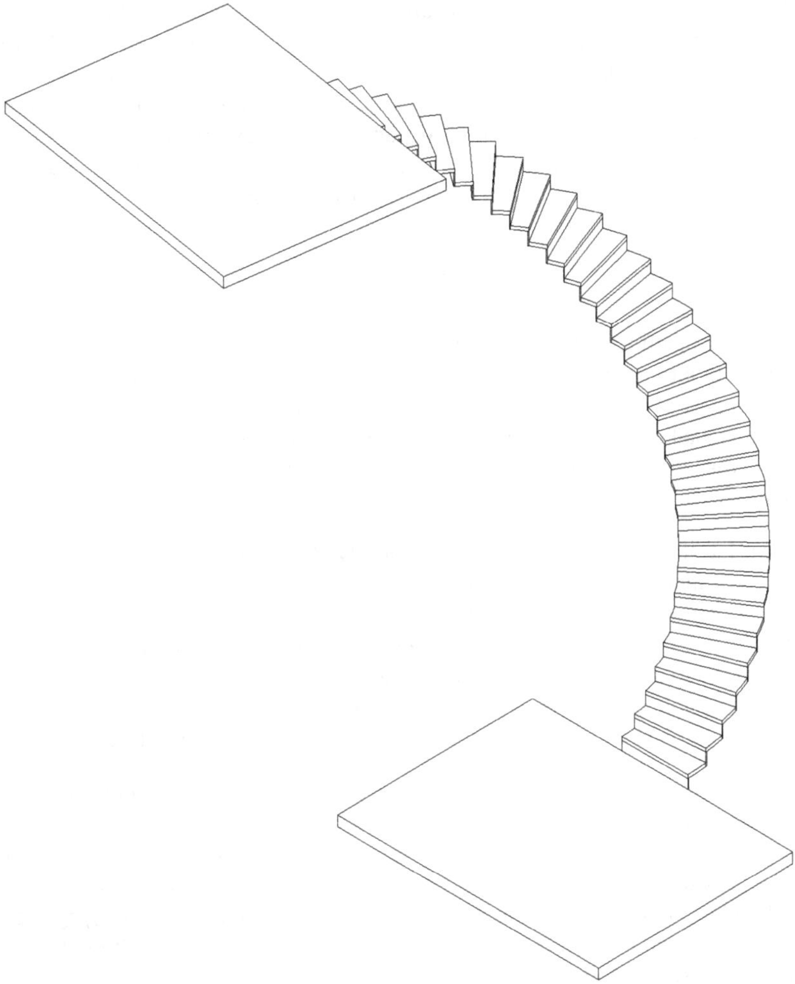

Figure 4. Helical stair further lengthened

One can also choose to modify the geometry of the steps when the height difference between floors changes: keep the number of steps the same and increase or decrease the rise of each step. In this case, which is possible only with small height differences that do not destroy the climbability of the stair, the parameterization is geometric.

Symbolic parameterization concerns non-geometric values, which can nevertheless be fundamentally quantitative. For example, around a music room in a school one needs to have walls and floors with a heavier acoustic insulation than in other parts of the building, while the walls and floors around a chemistry lab must have a higher fire resistance: the use of the space imposes a threshold of acceptable acoustic or fire-resistance performance. Each type of wall and floor in BIM can be automatically evaluated against this threshold, resulting in automatic warnings or even refusal when an inappropriate symbol is entered in the model. The values that are compared in this example are numerical (the threshold required by the space versus the relevant performance of the wall) but the parametric relation is between space use type and wall or floor type. Similarly, the colour design of a space can be based on a monochromatic scheme with variations in lightness and saturation. If the primary colour in the scheme changes, then all these variations are adapted, resulting in different RAL or Pantone codes.

PARAMETERIZATION AND SEMANTIC DATA TYPES

One of the interesting effects of parameterization is on the semantic type of symbol properties: it turns primary data into derivative. The length of a wall is normally primary information because it is an essential part of its identity. However, if a particular wall is constrained to have the same length as another wall, then the length of the former becomes derivative, as it follows any change to the length of the latter. Removing the constraint makes the two walls independent of each other and makes the length of both primary again.

This example illustrates the significance and complexity of parameterization in design: on one hand, parameterization makes the configuration and modification of a symbolic representation easier and safer. Rather than having to adjust the dimensions of every wall separately, we can relate them all to each other, establishing a parametric network that supports the propagation of changes to one wall to all others. Unfortunately, such a network is had to define because we have to anticipate all possible changes to every wall and their significance to others. Relating everything to a single wall and then manipulating only than one is practically never the answer.

Moreover, each symbol in the representation may belong to multiple networks. A wall, for example, can be related to geometric parametric networks that affect its dimensions; to acoustic parametric networks that constrain properties relevant to acoustics, such as mass and rigidity, relative to the activities taking place on either side of the wall; to fire safety parametric networks that constrain other material properties relative to the location of the wall along egress routes or fire compartment boundaries. Resolving conflicts between the effects of different networks is a major problem in design parameterization and information management.

References

Attneave, F., 1959. *Applications of information theory to psychology; a summary of basic concepts, methods, and results.* New York: Holt.

Blair, A. et al. (eds.), 2021, *Information: a historical companion.* Princeton: Princeton University Press.

Bytheway, A., 2014. *Investing in information*. New York: Springer.

Chabris, C. F., & Simons, D. J., 2010. *The invisible gorilla : and other ways our intuitions deceive us.* New York: Crown.

Cosgrove, D., 2003. Ptolemy and Vitruvius: spatial representation in the sixteenth-century texts and commentaries. A. Picon & A. Ponte (eds) *Architecture and the sciences: exchanging metaphors*. Princeton NJ: Princeton University Press.

Cover, T.M., & Thomas, J.A., 2006. *Elements of information theory* (2nd ed.). Hoboken NJ: Wiley-Interscience.

Dean, J., & Ghemawat, J., 2008. "MapReduce: simplified data processing on large clusters" *Commun. ACM* **51**, 1 (January 2008), 107–113, https://doi.org/10.1145/1327452.1327492

Detlor, B., 2010. Information management. *International Journal of Information Management, 30*(2), 103-108. doi:10.1016/j.ijinfomgt.2009.12.001

Eastman, C., Teicholz, P.M., Sacks, R., & Lee, G., 2018. *BIM handbook* (3rd ed.). Hoboken NJ: Wiley.

Emmitt, S., 2014. *Design management for architects* (2nd ed.). Hoboken NJ: Wiley.

English, L.P., 1999. *Improving data warehouse and business information quality: methods for reducing costs and increasing profits.* New York: Wiley.

Evans, J. S. B. T., & Frankish, K. (2009). *In two minds : dual processes and beyond.* Oxford: Oxford University Press.

Evans, R., 1995. *The Projective Cast: Architecture and Its Three Geometries.* Cambridge MA: MIT Press.

Eynon, J., 2013. *The design manager's handbook*. Southern Gate, Chichester, West Sussex, UK: CIOB, John Wiley & Sons.

Flett, A., 2011. Information management possible?:Why is information management so difficult? *Business Information Review, 28*(2), 92-100. doi:10.1177/0266382111411066

Floridi, L., 2008. Trends in the philosophy of information. P. Adriaans & J. v. Benthem (eds), *Philosophy of information*. Amsterdam: North-Holland.

Floridi, L., 2009. Philosophical conceptions of information. G. Sommaruga (ed), *Formal Theories of Information: From Shannon to semantic information theory and general concepts of information*. Berlin, Heidelberg: Springer.

Floridi, L., 2014. *The fourth revolution.* Oxford: Oxford University Press.

Floridi, L., 2016. Semantic conceptions of information. *The Stanford Encyclopedia of Philosophy*. https://plato.stanford.edu/entries/information-semantic/

Flyvbjerg, B., 2011. Over Budget, Over Time, Over and Over Again: Managing Major Projects. In Morris, P.W. G; Pinto, JK; Söderlund, J. (eds.), *The Oxford Handbook of Project Management.* Oxford: Oxford University Press.

Gantz, J. & Reinsel, D., 2011. "Extracting value from chaos." 2011, https://www.emc.com/collateral/analyst-reports/idc-extracting-value-from-chaos-ar.pdf

Gawande, A., 2010. *The checklist manifesto : how to get things right.* New York: Metropolitan Books.

Goodman, N., 1976. *Languages of art; an approach to a theory of symbols* (2nd ed.). Indianapolis IN: Hackett.

Graham, M., & Dutton, W.H. (eds.), 2019. *Society and the Internet.* Oxford: Oxford University Press.

Kahneman, D., 2013. *Thinking, fast and slow.* New York: Farrar, Straus and Giroux.

Kanizsa, G., 1979. *Organization in vision: essays on Gestalt perception.* New York: Praeger.

Klein, G. A., 1998. *Sources of power : how people make decisions.* Cambridge MA: MIT Press.

Koutamanis, A., 2020. Dimensionality in BIM: Why BIM cannot have more than four dimensions? *Automation in Construction*, **114**, 2020, 103153, https://doi.org/10.1016/j.autcon.2020.103153

Koutamanis, A., et al., 2018. Urban mining and buildings. *Resources, Conservation and Recycling,* **138**(November), 32-39 https://doi.org/10.1016/j.resconrec.2018.06.024

Levine, T. R., 2014. Truth-Default Theory (TDT): A Theory of Human Deception and Deception Detection. *Journal of Language and Social Psychology,* **33**(4), 378–392. https://doi.org/10.1177/0261927X14535916

Lyman, P. & Varian, H.P. 2003, "How much information." http://groups.ischool.berkeley.edu/archive/how-much-info/

Pierce, J.R., 1980. *An introduction to information theory : symbols, signals & noise* (2nd, rev. ed.). New York: Dover.

Rider, F., 1944, *The Scholar and the Future of the Research Library*. New York: Hadham Press.

Richards, M., 2010. *Building Information Management – a standard framework and guide to BS 1192*. London: BSI.

Rosenfeld, L., Morville, P., & Arango, J., 2015. *Information architecture: for the web and beyond* (4th ed.). Sebastopol CA: O'Reilly Media.

Shannon, C., 1948. A mathematical theory of communication. *Bell System Technical Journal, 27*(July, October), 379-423, 623-656.

Shannon, C.E., & Weaver, W., 1998. *The mathematical theory of communication*. Urbana IL: University of Illinois Press.

Simonite, T., 2016. "Moore's law Is dead. Now what?" Technology Review https://www.technologyreview.com/s/601441/moores-law-is-dead-now-what/

Sommaruga, G., 2009. Introduction. G. Sommaruga (ed.), *Formal Theories of Information: From Shannon to semantic information theory and general concepts of information*. Berlin, Heidelberg: Springer.

Stanovich, K. E., 2011. *Rationality and the reflective mind.* New York: Oxford University Press.

Steadman, P., 1983. *Architectural morphology: an introduction to the geometry of building plans.* London: Pion.

Thaler, R. H., & Sunstein, C. R., 2021. *Nudge: the final edition*. New Haven: Yale University Press.

Toffler, A., 1970. *Future shock*. New York: Random House.

Turner, V., Reinsel D., Gantz J. F., & Minton S., 2014. "The Digital Universe of Opportunities" https://www.emc.com/leadership/digital-universe/2014iview/digital-universe-of-opportunities-vernon-turner.htm

Van Sommers, P., 1984. *Drawing and cognition: descriptive and experimental studies of graphic production processes.* Cambridge: Cambridge University Press.

Wang, R.Y., & Strong, D.M., 1996. Beyond accuracy: what data quality means to data consumers. *Journal of Management Information Systems, 12*(4), 5-33. doi:10.1080/07421222.1996.11518099

Waltz, D., 1975. Understanding line drawings of scenes with shadows. P.H. Winston (ed) *The psychology of computer vision.* New York: McGraw-Hill.

Zins, C., 2007. Conceptual approaches for defining data, information, and knowledge. *Journal of the American Society for Information Science and Technology.* **58**(*4*) 479-493 DOI: 10.1002/asi.20508.

Index

N

O

P

R

S

T

V

U

Z